SACRED REVOLT

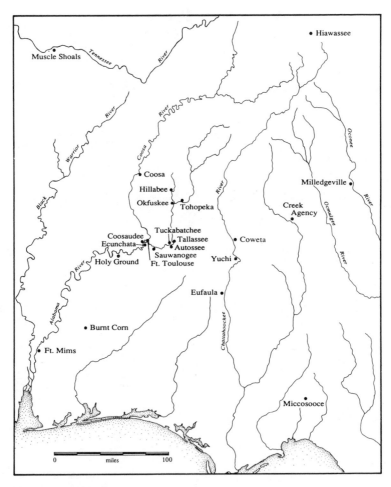

Towns in Muskogee

SACRED REVOLT

The Muskogees' Struggle
for a New World

JOEL W. MARTIN

Beacon Press · Boston

Beacon Press
25 Beacon Street
Boston, Massachusetts 02108

Beacon Press books
are published under the auspices of
the Unitarian Universalist Association
of Congregations.

98 97 96 95 94 93   8 7 6 5 4 3 2

Text design by Gwen Frankfeldt

Library of Congress Cataloging-in-Publication Data

Martin, Joel W., 1956–
Sacred revolt: The Muskogees' struggle for a new world /
Joel W. Martin.
     p.   cm.
  Includes bibliographical references and index.
  ISBN 0-8070-5402-X (cloth)
  ISBN 0-8070-5403-8 (paper)
  1. Creek Indians—Religion and mythology.   2. Creek Indians—Government
relations.   3. Creek Indians—History—19th century.   4. Horse Shoe, Battle of
the, 1814.   5. Indians of North America—Wars—1812–1815.   I. Title.
E99.C9M27   1991
973'.04973—dc20   90-24782
                                                                      CIP

*To my parents,
Bill and Patty Martin*

Contents

Car il faut tout à la fois guetter, un peu au-dessous de l'histoire ce qui la rompt et l'agite et veiller un peu en arrière de la politique sur ce qui doit incondition-nellement la limiter.

It is always necessary to watch out for something, a little beneath history, that breaks with it, that agitates it; it is necessary to look, a little behind politics, for that which ought to limit it, unconditionally.

Michel Foucault, "Is It Useless to Revolt?"

Preface

When people revolt against unjust systems of power, their struggles profoundly arrest our attention. It is often hard to com-prehend why and how people risk everything in struggles against seemingly insurmountable odds. That they do so, even against the awesome power of the modern state, suggests something very important. Their resistance suggests that human history is not finally predictable or controllable. In revolt, do we not glimpse something a little beneath history, a little behind politics?

Between 1813 and 1814, seven to nine thousand Muskogee (Creek) people revolted against the United States. Their revolt is the subject of this book. By studying it, we learn how these Na-tive Americans experienced colonialism and responded to colo-nial oppression not as victims but as people with religious vision and creativity. During the colonial period, the Muskogees con-fronted ever greater numbers of Anglo-American settlers invad-ing their lands, incurred mounting debts generated by a market system dominated by European nations and merchants, and faced aggressive Anglo-American governments and officials deter-mined to change fundamentally the way the Muskogees lived. Throughout the colonial period, the Muskogees employed reli-gious myths, symbols, and rituals to interpret their new experi-ences, and they found a particular spiritual vision compelling.

According to this vision, the world was about to be recreated by sacred cosmological forces. By identifying with these cosmic forces in their revolt, the Muskogees felt they could achieve a new collective identity and purge their land of colonizers; they could recreate their identity in the New World.

As Michel Foucault noted, human beings have often connected their ability to resist oppression with access to spiritual powers. Since people who revolt are " 'outside of history' as well as in it, and since life and death are at stake, we can understand why revolts have easily been able to find their expression and their mode of performance in religious themes: the promise of the beyond, the return of time, the waiting for the saviour or the empire of the last days, the indisputable reign of good. When the particular religion has permitted, these themes have furnished throughout the centuries not an ideological cloak but the very way to live revolts."[1] With myths of cosmological upheaval or judgment, religion mediates metaphors, symbols, and values that justify revolt. Through rituals of purification and world renewal, religion shows people how to destroy an old order. With its orientation to spiritual power, religion instills within them the courage to fight against seemingly invincible enemies. Because religion has so often provided the very way to live revolts, the history of religion is inextricably connected to the history of resistance to oppression. In encountering the story of the Muskogees' sacred revolt, we are asked to consider afresh the vital relation between religion and the invincible human desire for freedom.

Telling this story was a work of passion. I was concerned about hidden and repressed dimensions of American history, and subjugated populations and knowledges. More than anything, I was disturbed at the way historians left those people dead on the battlefield without ever bothering to ask who they were and why they fought? It was as if scholars were killing them over and over again by failing to imagine their lives, symbols, desires, and perspectives.

I determined to write a different kind of history. The history of religions provided the method to channel the passion and produce the precision. Working with the categories and constructs of this approach, details that other historians had not noticed started to carry significance. Homologies between ritual and revolutionary acts appeared. The meaning of numbers became apparent. Insights followed. Alternative narratives were generated.

Through writing about the Muskogees, I now recognize that I have also been working out my relationship to my own painful, violent, and complex cultural heritage. Not the first Southerner who had to write about the South, I wanted to imagine it differently and inclusively. I wanted to face and to go beyond the violence and terror. The entire process has been personally liberating. I can only hope that the book itself will in some way contribute to collective liberation.

In researching, writing, and revising this work, I have benefited from contact and conversations with many gifted individuals. It would be impossible to name all the scholars, librarians, archivists, and students who have helped this work emerge. Scholars who have read and commented on the work include Sandra Robinson, Michael D. Green, Mary E. Young, William G. McLoughlin, Charles H. Hudson, Gregory A. Waselkov, Peter H. Wood, Catherine L. Albanese, William Poteat, Stephen J. Stein, Charles H. Long, James H. Merrell, Joel Williamson, Jay Geller, Annette Aronowicz, Craig Livermore, Thomas Watson, and David Eliades. By generously sharing their immense knowledge, incisive questions, and critical insights, they have consistently made this a much better book.

Every author should enjoy the ministrations of an editor as gifted as Deborah Chasman. She read the entire work with great care, made significant critical contributions, and arranged for its timely publication. Julie Barnes Smith drafted three original maps. The expense of the maps was covered by a grant from

Franklin and Marshall College. Research was supported by a Kearns Fellowship from Duke University, a Jacob Javits National Fellowship, a Graduate Fellowship from the Smithsonian Institution, and a National Endowment for the Humanities Summer Institute Fellowship on "Spanish Explorers and Indian Chiefdoms" at the University of Georgia.

In the half dozen years I have worked on this project, I have enjoyed the company and counsel of friends Jim Stewart, Steve Bridges, Fran Ruthven, Conrad E. Ostwalt, Julia Hardy, and Alton Pollard III. Muskogee artist Joy Harjo shared her poetic vision. Charles Tignor, Joseph Peddy, and Thomas Pinzino gave me a much better understanding of the landscape in which this history occurred.

My parents, Bill and Patty Martin, instilled in me a love of learning and have always helped me fulfill it. By raising my brother Stan and me in the town of Opelika, Alabama, they sparked my interest in the history of the Muskogee people. This book is dedicated to my parents with loving appreciation.

Finally, Jane Marie Pinzino provided a close critical reading of the entire work. A true friend, she has stood with me through good and bad times. The inauguration, execution, and completion of this book would not have happened without her.

SACRED REVOLT

INTRODUCTION

"Like the Fall of Leaves"

At Tohopeka on 27 March 1814, an army of fifteen hundred Anglo-Americans, five hundred Cherokees, and one hundred Muskogees surrounded one thousand rebel Muskogee warriors. The warriors were located behind fortifications they had constructed across the neck of a peninsula formed by a horseshoe-shaped bend in the Tallapoosa River in what is now Alabama. Many of the rebels, known by Anglo-Americans as "Redsticks," were armed only with red war clubs, bows and arrows, knives, and spears.[1] Although less than one-third held firearms, many of the Redsticks felt invincible. Following shamanistic leaders and acting in accord with their religious visions, they claimed access to sacred power and believed enemy fire could not harm them. Six months before the battle of Tohopeka, a rebel had warned the U.S. Agent, "If whites came among them, the prophets [shamans] would draw circles around their abode, and render the earth quaggy and impassable. [White soldiers] would be sunk with earthquakes, or hills turned over them."[2]

At Tohopeka, however, these particular hopes were not realized. Fighting against militiamen armed with rifles and cannon, the Redsticks suffered staggering losses; eight in ten died in the battle or in the river attempting to escape. A Redstick survivor said his fellow warriors dropped "like the fall of leaves."[3] In the history of warfare between the United States and Native Americans, no other battle cost more native lives. After this crushing defeat, the final in a series of defeats suffered by the Redsticks in the fall and winter of 1813 and spring of 1814, the rebels had to flee. The revolt against the United States was over in this region.

The Battle of Tohopeka and the Treaty of Fort Jackson signed soon afterward provided key lines that shaped the history of U.S.–Native American relations. First, the treaty provided a new boundary between the United States and the Muskogee Nation, a political line that enlarged Georgia and created the territory of Alabama. The defeat at Tohopeka forced the Muskogees to cede the largest amount of land ever surrendered by southeastern Native Americans to the United States, some fourteen million acres. This land, which included much of the Black Belt, was rapidly settled by thousands of Anglo-Americans and African American slaves and transformed into the productive heart of the Cotton Kingdom.

Second, Tohopeka and the treaty helped American propagandists and politicians in incarnating and strengthening the ideology of Manifest Destiny. According to this ideology's major narrative, the United States, moving from east to west, would inevitably assimilate all Native American lands across North America. It is no accident that the war with the Muskogees produced several of the young republic's greatest expansionist leaders and heroes: Davy Crockett, Sam Houston, and Andrew Jackson.

Third, Tohopeka and the treaty have long provided a decisive chronological line, a historiographic fault line that historians of the Deep South rarely cross. Because of this fault line, the Deep South's native peoples appear in southern and American history only at that moment when Anglo-American armies and settlers arrive to kill, tame, and remove them. Just as scholars studying early America have for the most part ignored Native Americans, most southern historians, in describing the South before Tohopeka, have neglected Native American peoples, their leaders, and their movements, in spite of the fact that rich documentation exists to reconstruct their stories, biographies, and trajectories.[4]

Because these three lines—territorial, narrative, and historiographic—drew firm boundaries between the original inhabitants of the land and the African and European newcomers, they have obscured an important history of multicultural contact. They have obscured the complex range of intercultural linkages, overlaps, conflicts, and fusions that constituted southeastern life before Tohopeka. As a consequence, a rich history of indigenous cultural expressions and celebrations goes unappreciated. Instead of inquiring how various interior peoples experienced, interpreted, and created history, historians write as if nobody important lived between the Oconee and the Tombigbee rivers in the seventeenth, eighteenth, and early nineteenth centuries. The impact of southeastern Native Americans on the course and shape of American history remains unarticulated, and southeastern Native Americans' innovative and critical responses to contact remain largely unnarrated.[5]

The present study recovers a neglected and very important part of the history of southeastern Native Americans. A central goal of this study is to appreciate the Muskogees as subjects of their own history and ultimately to grasp how and why a great number of them came to rebel against the United States and fight at Tohopeka.[6] The aim is not just to evaluate the Redstick revolt of 1813–14 from without but also to understand it as much as possible from within, from the perspective of the Redsticks themselves. This aim necessarily involves a serious study of Muskogee religion, for religion was a crucial force in the revolt against the United States. Visions of cosmological renewal or millenarian upheaval motivated and prophetic shamans led the rebels. Ritual patterns, drawn from traditional religious ceremonies, provided a dramatic form that helped organize and give meaning to significant acts of rebellion.

Much of this book concerns Muskogee religion, but the approach is not theological. The approach does not presuppose that

Muskogee religion must be measured in the light of the putative truth of any revealed religion. Nor does the text assume that Muskogee religion is epiphenomenal, a superstructural reflex of an underlying social structure or a symbolic eruption of the human unconscious. Rather, the approach is that of the contemporary scholarly field known as the comparative study of religion. The "comparative study of religion" refers to the systematic cross-cultural study of basic religious forms such as myth, ritual, gods, and systems of purity.[7]

Using this approach, the historian of Muskogee society can articulate how religion shaped Muskogee history and empowered their will to resist colonialism. Prophetic talk about spiritual beings and ritual practices of shamans are treated as real and important historical forces, as real as the price of bullets in Pensacola in 1813, as important as the profits from cotton in Tennessee or Black Codes in Georgia. Comparative religion can contribute something very significant to the general project of bringing Native Americans back into southern and American history. Using the concepts and methods of comparative religion, revisionist historians will write histories that give to rituals, myths, and shamanistic practices something closer to the weight they had in Muskogee society.

Because I am interested in the comparative study of religion, it was initially this radically transformative movement that drew me to study Muskogee history. While exploring the history of the revolt of 1813, I noticed a discrepancy between the contemporary documents (government reports, travel accounts, narratives) and the history books. The primary documents written by U.S. agents in the field brimmed over with references to the Muskogees' creator god, talk of prophets and magic, and charges of "Fanaticism." The secondary documents barely mentioned these things. Conventional historians have been more interested in talking about generals and battles, and revisionist historians have preferred to dwell on the specific complex of economic forces that shaped southeastern development.[8] There remains, however, a real surplus of meaning and spiritual power with which these prevailing approaches do not deal, a substantive matter with which any postcolonial true story must come to terms: the sacred power that the Muskogees referred to as the Maker of Breath. Thus, in this study, I use a variety of approaches, including comparative religion, to reconstruct and interpret the Muskogees' experiences from the seventeenth to early nineteenth centuries, concentrating on the period from approximately 1700 to 1814.

Part I consists of chapters 1, 2, and 3, which provide, respectively, the spiritual, economic, and social background of the revolt. Chapter 1 discusses the sacred life of the Muskogees, relating the important religious rituals, myths, and values that shaped the Muskogees' social order. This culture of the sacred directly inspired the Redstick revolt, providing ritual structures and mythic meanings that the prophets employed in organizing and disseminating the movement. Chapter 2 traces the Muskogees' involvement in the eighteenth-century deerskin trade. It details their production of skins, discusses their various trading partners, and establishes some basic chronological watersheds for the colonial era of the southeastern frontier. After 1763, and especially after 1783, the trade emerged as a tool of land speculators, a debt-producing practice linked to forced land cessions. The loss of land and erosion of culture caused by the trade were two of the prophets' chief concerns. Chapter 3 places the trade in its social matrix. It describes how Anglo-American traders, African American interpreters, runaways, and slaves mingled with the Muskogees to produce individuals of multicultural background.

Part II consists of four chapters (chaps. 4–7) that unfold the religious meaning of this entire history. Chapter 4 analyzes Anglo-American views of Native American land. In the conflict between Anglo-Americans and Native Americans over land, it is possible to detect a profound conflict in cosmologies. By studying this conflict, we can learn much about the underlying religious apperceptions of Anglo-American invaders and the original inhabitants of the land.

Chapters 5 and 6 seriously examine the Redstick revolt as a religious phenomenon. Without denying any of the cultural, economic, and political dimensions of the revolt, these chapters treat the shamans' revolt qua religion. These chapters detail and interpret hidden mythic dynamics, ritual patterns, and symbolic valences that inspired and shaped Muskogee rhetoric and action. As these chapters demonstrate, the rebel Muskogee revolt of 1813–14 was a spiritual movement of profound significance to its participants. It was an anticolonial movement empowered by contact with spirits of earth, water, and sky, led chiefly by shamans, patterned according to mythic narrative patterns, and enacted in the form of a grand collective initiation process.

As an anticolonial movement, the Redstick revolt evoked a violent response from Anglo-Americans. Chapter 7 relates how Anglo-American armies from Georgia, Mississippi, and Tennessee invaded and defeated the Redsticks, and absorbed millions of acres of Muskogee land for cotton culture. Finally, chapter 8 offers some concluding observations on the character and career of the Muskogees' sacred revolt, linking it with the creative struggles of other Native American peoples.

A Note on Nomenclature

In the seventeenth and eighteenth centuries, no Native Americans of the Southeast identified themselves as "Creeks." Rather, the name "Creeks" was originally applied by English traders to a certain group of native people living near an English post on a large creek. These people had moved eastward from the Chattahoochee River towns of Coweta and Kashita for the purpose of trading with Carolinians. They called themselves "Ochese" (ò ci sì), and the English knew them as the people living on Ochese Creek. With time, the traders started calling them the Ochese "creek" or, more simply, the "creeks."[9] In 1715, these "creeks" returned to their former homelands on the Chattahoochee River.

English traders began applying the name "Creeks" generically to the whole montage of peoples living along the Chattahoochee.

Throughout the eighteenth century, the name was applied to more and more native groups. As historian J. Leitch Wright, Jr., noted, "eventually all Indians on the Chattahoochee and Flint rivers, whatever their language and ethnic background, became known as Lower Creeks, and all Indians on the Alabama and its tributaries the Coosa and Tallapoosa as Upper Creeks."[10] By the mid-eighteenth century, "Creeks" had become the name the English applied to most native peoples living in what is now central Georgia and Alabama, an area of roughly ten thousand square miles. Thus, "Creeks" is not simply a name of English origin but an English synecdoche, a figure of speech in which a part stands for the whole. The recourse to synecdochical figures of speech commonly occurs in cultural contact situations and sometimes leads to pernicious results.[11] In a colonial situation, it is precisely the power to name that the colonizing group attempts to monopolize for itself and deny the colonized. In the Southeast, Anglo-Americans insisted on renaming native peoples even though they already had names. The English forced the name "Creeks" to stick even though the various peoples to whom it was applied resisted it.

After the American Revolution, longstanding tensions between Georgians and the "Creeks" threatened to produce large-scale open warfare. When some "Upper Creeks," perhaps Tallapoosas or Abekas, killed a couple of Georgia frontier settlers in 1787, Georgians quickly exacted vengeance, killing some nearby "Creek Indian" hunters. It turned out that the Georgians had killed "Lower Creeks," probably Cussetas or Cowetas. The "Lower Creek" chiefs protested that a serious mistake had been made:

> You always promised that the innocent should not suffer for the guilty. You certainly knew us, we were always among the houses, we did not know of the Upper Towns doing any mischief nor did we think that our own friends would kill us for what the bad people

did. . . . We don't think but You must have known that we were your friends or we would not have been among you and hunting. We look upon all white people as one, and suppose you look upon all Indians as one is the reason you have killed your friends.

By alerting the Georgians of this synecdochical error, the "Lower Creeks" hoped to "keep the path White," so that the two could "love like brothers . . . for peace is better than War." [12]

The Georgians' response was chilling. They suspected the "Lower Creeks" of "deceit," asserting that the latter were "secretly our enemies." Most important, they claimed that the "Lower Creeks" were responsible for any acts committed by warriors of their "nation." The Georgians announced a policy of unlimited indiscriminate terror:

> *Now* open your ears *Wide,* and hear what we tell you. Should any act of hostility, or depredations be committed on our people by your nation be perfectly assured we will not hesitate to do our selves ample justice by carrying War into your Country burning your Towns and staining your land with blood. you will then be compeled to flee for refuge to some other Country. [13]

As this threat made clear, the Georgians took their synecdoche very seriously; in their usage, "Creeks" was no longer a generic name loosely applied but a unified "nation." On the basis of their common membership in this "nation," any group of native peoples was subject to reprisals for the acts of any other group. The synecdoche provided Georgia with a rationalization for terrorism. At any time, the Anglo-Americans, invoking their power to name, might strike an innocent individual or town. [14]

In a colonial context, the colonizer's power to make names stick is often linked to the practice of terror and violence. The name "Creeks" was not a neutral term but a colonial signification that concealed and rendered invisible a tremendous diversity of peoples and enabled Georgians to rationalize violence. For these reasons, using the term "Creeks" to denominate southeastern native peoples of the colonial period is problematic, especially in a history aiming to recover their sense of their own history.

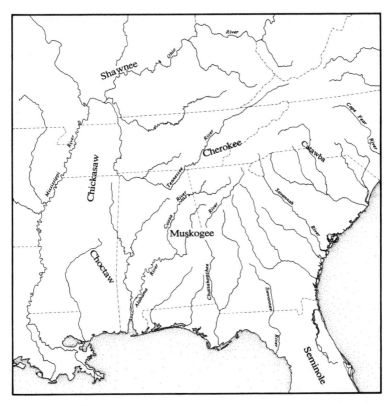

Figure 1. Location of Native Americans in the Southeast. Adapted from John R. Swanson, *The Indians of the Southeastern United States* (Washington, D.C.: Smithsonian Institution, 1979).

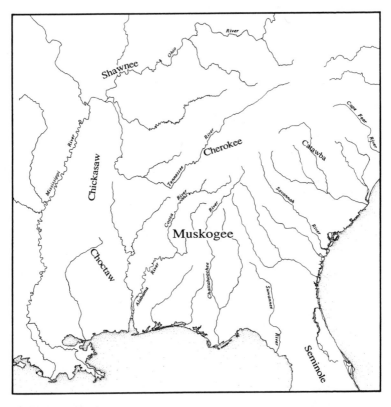

Figure 2. Muskogee

One alternative would be to use only the plurality of names associated with their ceremonial centers or *i:tálwa*. An *i:tálwa* was a town with a square ground (a special set of open buildings framing a sacred precinct and fire). Square ground towns included Kialigee, Tuckabatchee, Hillabee, Autossee, Woccoccoie, Wewokee, Foushatchee, Columee, Hoithlewaulee, Ecunhutke, Muclassee, Coosaudee, Aubecooche, Coosa, Eufaula, Tallassee, Hookchoi, Hookchoioochee, Ocheobofau, Okfuskee, Tuskeegee, Coweta, Cussetuh, Chehaws, and Hitchiti. Several of these square ground towns had outlying villages (*talofa*) affiliated with them. Individuals, when identifying themselves, would give their individual names and titles and the name of their square ground polity. Whenever it is possible to designate the *i:tálwa* of persons mentioned in this text, I will attempt to do so.

A problem yet remains. Despite diversity, these Native American groups did share similar histories and interacted closely with one another. In the late eighteenth century, they linked their towns in a political confederation designed to transcend local autonomy.[15] Consequently, we do need a term to refer to the whole ensemble. Rather than use the term "Creeks," there are good reasons to employ instead a name that has enjoyed currency among the people themselves for a much longer time: "Muskogees."[16]

From before European contact to today, native peoples have used the name *mosko:kalki* (Muskogee or Muscogee) to designate their cultural identity or tribal affiliation. Great linguistic diversity characterized the region, but the majority of the Southeastern Native Americans treated in this work spoke a language in the Muskogean linguistic family.[17] Indeed, Muskogean languages were spoken by three of the four major ethnic groups in the region. Abekas, Tallapooses, and Cowetas spoke Muskogean tongues; the Alabamas did not. Among those Native Americans known as "Creeks," a late eighteenth century author noted, "The Muskogees are the prevailing nation, amounting to more than seven-eights of the whole." Even earlier, a Carolina governor had commented that the Creeks were "called sometimes Muskogee." [18] Because the Muskogees historically constituted a substantial part of the entire native population treated in this study, "Muskogee" provides the best single name to use when a single name must be used. In this text, it is the preferred synecdoche. For instance, to designate those peoples living near the Chattahoochee and Flint rivers, I use the name "Lower Muskogees." Again, to designate those peoples living near the Tallapoosa, Coosa, and Alabama rivers, I use the name "Upper Muskogees."

In addition to calling the people "Muskogees," we can also give a vernacular name to their land. The name is already present in figure 1. On the basis of a map drafted by ethnohistorian John R. Swanton in the first half of the twentieth century, figure 1 features the word "Muskogee" near its center. On his map, Swanton intended this name to signify the linguistic stock of the people living in the region of central Georgia and Alabama. However, let us read the name on figure 1 literally, as if it referred not to the language or the people but to the land itself. Let us call the region where the Muskogees lived "Muskogee."

The name "Muskogee" frees us from the anachronistic practice of referring to the states of Georgia and Alabama when describing the homeland of the Muskogees. More important, by speaking of Muskogee, we acknowledge that this land has had a life apart from those political boundaries that Anglo-Americans and nation-states have imposed on it. There was already something rich, complex, and delicate here before the Spanish, French, and English arrived. The land, streams, forests, swamps, flora, and fauna of the region had already been known, named, and narrated by the Muskogee people. By representing Muskogee without the lines that obtained after Tohopeka, figure 2 imaginatively moves us a step away from the mighty epic of Anglo-American conquest of the "frontier" and one step closer to contact with the ongoing history of the land itself and all the peoples who have been born within it. By leaning in this direction, we incline toward a richer rendering of contact in the New World, a sketch that details the colonial invasion of Muskogee but also acknowledges the profound spiritual powers that shaped Muskogean cultural practices, renewed Muskogean religion, and inspired radical resistance in 1813–14.

PART I

The Context

O N E

Encountering the Sacred

"As moral men they certainly stand in no need of European civilization. They are just, honest, liberal, and hospitable to strangers."[1] So William Bartram, an English traveler, naturalist, and writer, described the Muskogees in a book published in 1791. Although he was a careful observer of the Southeast's peoples, Bartram romanticized them in order to criticize European culture. Believing that Muskogee society demonstrated the rational order of nature and humankind uncorrupted by the vices of civilization, he depicted the Muskogees as natural creatures. Bartram failed to appreciate the beauty and fragility of their social order or to acknowledge its dependence on culture.[2]

The social order that Bartram esteemed was to a great extent a product of the Muskogees' culture and, more specifically, an expression of their culture of the sacred. This culture of the sacred—a culture embodied in ritual, expressed in words and stories, and symbolized in space—oriented the Muskogee people so that they expressed a preferred range of behaviors, articulated a distinctive worldview, and organized a social order concerned with fostering reciprocity among themselves, with other peoples, and with nature. Their culture of the sacred habituated the Muskogees to exchange gifts and perform mediations in almost every important contact among themselves and in every critical exchange with other peoples and natural and spiritual powers. Sacred rituals, narratives, and spaces instilled in the Muskogees a deep concern for reciprocity and authorized violent and nonviolent practices dedicated to its restoration. One of the more dramatic attempts to restore reciprocity and balance to their world was the Redstick prophetic movement of 1812–14. In order to understand the cultural origins and religious motivations of this sacred revolt, we must first become familiar with the sacred rituals, myths, and spaces central to the religious tradition on which the Redsticks drew.[3]

Southeastern Native Americans did not experience time as homogeneous, words as totally mundane, or space as uniform. Rather, some times, some words and narratives, and some spaces stood out as special, incongruous, outstanding, or symbolically charged. These times, narratives, and spaces were carefully marked and anticipated. In approaching or telling them, villagers altered their behaviors, thoughts, and practices, intentionally preparing themselves for a qualitatively different kind of experience, perception, and expression. Once the time arrived or the storyteller began or the space was entered, villagers abandoned key aspects of ordinary life and thought. Depending on the occasion, they might alter their vocabulary or temporarily cease consuming salt, eating food, or relating to the opposite sex. They might wear special clothing, use esoteric speech, seek visions, and perform holy dances. In these and many other ways, southeastern Native Americans symbolized that ordinary time, speech, and space had been transcended and something extraordinary encountered.

The awareness of sacred times was especially keen and gave rise to a considerable richness of symbolic action and display. For instance, whenever they involved themselves in warfare, whether against other native groups or against Europeans, southeastern Native Americans took great pains to mark the time as special, nonordinary. Though its nature was short lived and small scale, warfare generated intense cultural meanings and elaborate ritual behaviors. Muskogees prepared for war by holding special council meetings, drinking purifying tea, and consulting diviners. If the latter discerned favorable signs, a war party, rarely more than a few dozen men, was organized. While on an excursion, warriors sang special songs in camp, adorned themselves with paints, talismans, and accoutrements, and fed themselves by hunting their enemies' game or slaughtering their livestock.[4]

After a swift raid on the enemy, the band of warriors returned home and underwent a period of purification. Because they were still considered ritually charged and dangerous, their movements and activities in the village space were carefully regulated: "It was their Custom when they returned from War to relate all their Transactions to the Head Men and other Ceremonies of Physicking, &c. to be undergone."[5] Warriors detailed and exaggerated their bravery in long discourses directed at other men in the town square.[6] Those who had distinguished themselves in battle might gain a new name and another tattoo; adult male captives were brutally tortured, women and children more frequently adopted and treated with sympathy.[7]

Just as the hunting of human enemies elicited the performance of richly symbolic acts, so did the hunting of animals. Because the hunt involved humans in direct and dramatic contact with animals, the forest, and blood, the hunt plunged humans into dangerous physical, psychological, and moral contact with wild and natural animated powers. For this reason, the Muskogees used a refined system of ritual that enabled them to show respect for boundaries between humans and animals and make amends for necessary transgressions.

Native hunters did not kill game animals, consume the meat, or take the skin without carefully considering their actions. Rather, before the hunt, Muskogee hunters prepared themselves for the coming contact with the wild. With prayers, they beckoned the support of the spirits of the hunt. With red ocher, they painted their cheeks in order to sharpen their eyesight. With songs, they drew the deer closer and rendered them easy to kill.[8] Before consuming game, hunters offered a piece of meat to the fire, to assuage its hunger and promote future success.[9] Fire was the hunters' benefactor, the spirit that transformed raw meat into the socialized entity of food. By acknowledging the needs of fire, hunters once again expressed the idea that their praxis involved humans in vital and unavoidable relationships with dangerous nonhuman powers. These relationships required respectful attention, or danger and evil would surely follow.[10]

The Muskogees said that, if one failed to acknowledge the relationships on which the people's existence depended, disease would strike. Not surprisingly, many diseases sprang from disrespectfully treating game animals, such as bears, squirrel, rabbit, raccoon, and especially deer. During the eighteenth century, deer were hunted extensively by Muskogees so that they could trade the skins to Europeans for manufactured goods. The Muskogees related a panoply of ailments to the deer. They named various maladies "deer eyes" disease, "tongue of deer" disease, and "deer chief" disease (rheumatism).[11] As a Cherokee myth put it, "No hunter who has regard for his health ever fails to ask pardon of the Deer for killing it."[12]

Rites associated with war and the hunt were performed primarily by men, but women's activities and experiences were also symbolized as sacred through ritual events. Among the Muskogees, a woman's first menses signaled that she was moving from childhood to adulthood. This passage evoked an initiation ceremony.[13] Thought to be in profound contact with the power of wildness and fertility, the initiate was treated as a powerful person. From elder women in her clan, she learned about her new powers and identity and the appropriate way to symbolize and respect them. Through dreams, she acquired a guardian spirit. Henceforth, she would experience her menses as a sacred time that came with lunar periodicity. Because her association with power to bring forth life was so potent during this sacred time, she would sequester herself for five, six, or seven days in a special hut on the periphery of the village, removed from ordinary life. She especially had to avoid contact with men, lest her power cause them pain and completely cancel their power to take life in the hunt.[14]

Pregnancy was a season also regulated by taboos, especially concerning food. In this matrilineal, matrilocal society, the woman's responsibility for her children was very great. She needed to prepare for her parenting duties well before giving birth. By focusing attention on food, ritual proscriptions heightened the woman's awareness of her power to shape the character of her offspring. Rabbit could not be eaten, lest the child's eyes be grotesquely large. Squirrel produced a nervous child, and bear meat would make the offspring ill tempered, but venison would make her child strong. To ease delivery, the woman drank tea brewed with slippery elm bark. The actual delivery took place in the menstrual hut with midwives or herbalists attending. For weeks and even months after giving birth, a woman's life-giving power remained strong, and contacts with her husband or lover were carefully restricted.

Warfare, hunting, menstruation, and childbirth were but a few of the sacred times, seasons, events, and relationships that Muskogees marked with ritual, signified through altered behaviors, and sacralized through symbolic performances, exchanges, and punishments. The list could be extended indefinitely and would include sacred times that involved different subsets of Muskogee society—individuals, clans, men, women, villages, clusters of villages. It would include sacred times related to subsistence activities, others related to the human life cycle, and still others that were gender coded. Some ritual times corresponded to natural cycles, others responded to accidents, and still others occurred because of human initiative or historical events. Some rituals marked crises in social relations or responses to natural emergencies (famine, disease, drought). Some depended to a great extent on ritual specialists who possessed esoteric knowledge and practiced arcane magic, but many could be performed entirely without their participation. A survey of Muskogee rituals would show decisively that time for the Muskogees was anything but homogeneous. The passage of time was punctuated with sacred times that were out of the ordinary, qualitatively different kinds of time when things were not as they seemed and humans were in touch with sacred powers. During such times, ordinary rules might be intensified or abandoned, everyday actions infused with extraordinary meaning, and identities transformed. The Redstick revolt was one such time. During its extraordinary time, people felt physically, morally, and spiritually invincible and could imagine that they would defeat Anglo-American invaders.

As the study of comparative religion teaches, sacred times do not occur in nature but are products of special systems of knowledge. Among the nonliterate Muskogees, the system of knowledge concerning sacred times was carried and communicated from one generation to the next in the oral tradition. These stories taught the Muskogees to perceive the extraordinary in the ordinary, to spot the uncanny in the routine. They described the primordial formation of the world, the characteristics of animals, the discovery of agriculture, the activities of sacred beings and monsters, and the origins of human races (Native Americans, Europeans, and Africans). Perhaps the most important of these stories were the creation stories or cosmologies.

Earth-diver myths began with a description of space/time where chaos, symbolized by water, held sway over creation: "In the beginning the waters covered everything." In a version of this myth told by the Yuchi residents of Muskogee, the state of chaos is overcome partly through the agency of Sock-chew, the Crawfish. Sock-chew dives deep and succeeds in retrieving mud from "the bottom of the water." Next, Ah-yok, the Hawk, fans his wings over the mud to dry it. Yah-tee, the Buzzard, uses his larger wings to make the land hard. The new land gains illumination thanks to Yo-h-ah, the Star, but the Star's light is dim. Brighter light is donated by Shar-pah, the Moon. Finally, T-cho, the Sun, gives full light and life to the land: "As she passed over the Earth a drop of blood fell from her to the ground, and from this blood and earth sprang the first people."[15]

Other types of creation stories focused less on the origins of the earth and more on the journeys, travails, and discoveries of the original human beings. A story told by Kasihta residents of Muskogee and recorded in 1735 describes the emergence of the people from the earth and their subsequent migrations through a dangerous landscape.[16] Though real places and peoples are named—Chickasaws, Colooshe hutches, Coosas—the narrative should be read not as history but as myth. It helped connect living people to sacred symbols. According to the narrative, the first Muskogees encountered mythic realities and performed timeless heroic feats. They crossed a red, bloody river and climbed a singing mountain. They made war on a gigantic man-eating eagle and killed an equally dangerous lion. They defeated a people whose heads were shaped in a distinctive manner. Just as important, during their migrations, the primordial Muskogees learned the meaning of sacred symbols and actions and obtained sacred things for themselves and their posterity. They learned that red and white symbolized war and peace. They collected sacred fire from a thundering mountain. They discovered four sacred herbs or roots. They learned why warriors should fast before battle and women sequester themselves during their menses.

Cherished as sacred and retold with reverence, stories such as the Yuchi creation myth and the Kasihta migration legend could not help but structure the way that villagers perceived their existence and the world around them. As the Earth-diver story revealed, theirs was a world that had been barely extracted from chaos through the agency of powerful spirits. These spirits had used their power to found order and give life to humans, and, because they were represented in the form of animals and celestial beings, their power was still radically accessible. Similarly, the Kasihta story reminded listeners of the primordial origins and timeless sacrality of their basic forms of religious life. By embracing these symbols and actions, contemporary villagers could access primordial sacred power in their daily life. Because they heard and respected these and other stories, hunters said sacred prayers to the deer, warriors fasted for six days before battle, shamans recited esoteric narratives to young initiates, and women taught their daughters the right songs to sing when seeking medicinal roots and rhizomes. Symbols such as a moon disk earring, a tattoo depicting the sun, and a staff adorned with buzzard feathers were empowering, material means of symbolizing villagers' connections to the sacred. In these and other ways, the Muskogees related ritual to myth, particular event to timeless charter, the everyday to the sacred.

Because many of their sacred stories, prayers, and songs were eventually written down, it is possible not only to elucidate how eighteenth-century Muskogees articulated the sacred in words but also to reconstruct at least partially their worldview. From their creation stories and other sacred tales, it appears that the Muskogees imagined the cosmos divided into three primordial worlds: the Upper World, This World, and the Lower World. This tripartite division was immensely important for it delineated three classes of sacred beings, three basic kinds of sacred power, and three modes of symbolizing the sacred. Even more important, the division encouraged Muskogees to see reality as fundamentally dynamic. Reality was always being pulled simultaneously in opposite directions by contrary powers. If reality held together, it was only because it was held together by the creator, the god that the Muskogees called Hesákádum Eseé, "the Holder of Breath," the Breathmaker, the Maker of Breath, the Giver and Taker of All Life.[17] The Maker of Breath was the good spirit that "extends above all things and . . . hath created them."[18] The Maker of Breath inspired all the good things of life, making spring waters pure, corn abundant, and the hunt productive. The Maker of Breath made it possible for a delicate life-giving equilibrium to be maintained or, if upset, restored. In "old" or mythic times, the Maker of Breath had communicated customs, medicines, and principles to the people that enabled them to order their lives in the best possible manner. Holding the Maker of Breath's activity most sacred, contemporary Muskogees sought to balance contraries and restore equilibrium, and would pay any price to do so.

Because of the Breathmaker's essential role in preserving reality, this god was esteemed by the Muskogees beyond any other god, spirit, or being. The Breathmaker's power was invoked most commonly in times of crisis or ritual celebration. In everyday life, however, the Muskogees freely acknowledged that other gods, spirits, and beings also wielded significant kinds of sacred power. Some lived in the Upper World. Others were associated with the Lower World. Still others lived in between. The Upper World was dominated by the Sun and the Moon, Thunder, and other gigantic beings. Just as the Sun and the Moon illuminated the earth, manifested order in their movements, and helped demarcate temporal boundaries, the Upper World released the powers of perfection, order, permanence, clarity, and periodicity. Individuals tapped these powers by wearing jewelry and gorgets etched with moon signs or emblazoned with solar motifs. During the eighteenth century, this highly symbolic jewelry became very popular because trade with Europeans vastly increased the Muskogees' access to metals such as copper, iron, and silver.

Pitted against the Upper World and releasing exactly contrary powers was the Lower World, the realm of reversals, madness, creativity, fertility, chaos. In the Lower World, there lived a second major class of sacred beings, one not taken lightly for it included the most dangerous spirit beings. Foremost among these was the Tie-Snake, a primeval dragon-like antlered monster snake. Although most Europeans denied the existence of Tie-Snakes, a few traders claimed to have seen these denizens of rivers. Muskogees strongly affirmed their reality. According to Muskogees, these great snakes could stretch themselves across the channel and practically dam the stream. During the early nineteenth century in Muskogee, the Tie-Snake was closely associated with a particularly dangerous rocky stretch of the Chattahoochee River and could often be seen there. "It had the appearance, when floating on the water, of a large number of barrels strung together, end to end, and could, almost at any time, be seen catching its prey by folding its helpless victims in the coils or 'tie' of its tail and instantly destroying life by a deadly hug."[19] In addition to making water travel dangerous, these snakes brought numerous sicknesses to humans. Merely looking at the creature could cause insanity or death. Yet it was very difficult for a human not to look for the Tie-Snake was strangely beautiful. Dreadfully alluring, its body was armored with crystalline scales that shined iridescently, its forehead crowned with an extraordinarily bright crystal. Highly prized as aids in divination, these dazzling scales and crystals could be obtained only by a shaman purified for contact with the dangerous powers of the Lower World.

Also resident in the Lower World were unhappy ghosts. Condemned to wander at old village sites or other specific places, these ghosts were identified as the shades of suicides or unavenged dead warriors. The restless dead could bring illness or trouble to a clan or village. They showed no mercy to their kin, but haunted the clan home until their death was avenged. When their presence became oppressive, villages might relocate to find peace. Henceforth, hunters knew to avoid these old haunted places and never felt comfortable camping too close to these sites.

Perhaps the most feared Lower World beings were malignant supernatural beings that could appear in any form, including that of a man or woman. When one of these beings assumed the form of an owl, it was named *stí: kinni*. This chameleon-like power made this class of Lower World beings especially treacherous. Muskogee myths held that they were extremely long lived because of their practice of consuming human souls, absorbing to themselves the lives of their victims. *Stí: kinni* preyed on vulnerable individuals, commonly the newborn or very old but also the isolated man hunting deer or woman searching for an herb. Unless a shaman could retrieve the stolen soul, the victim's body would sicken, wither, and die. A final category of Lower World beings was the aquatic cannibal, a human-killer monster that resided beneath bodies of water, particularly rivers. These beings afflicted their victims with stomach pains, retching, and vomiting.

Between the Upper and Lower worlds, This World existed precariously between those powers that structure nature and human life and those that rupture order and empower freedom. In This World, human beings lived (along with four-footed animals and plants) and thrived by tapping the powers of both the Upper and the Lower worlds without allowing the two worlds to come into direct contact. Thus, fire, which was associated with the Sun and the purifying spirit of the Upper World, was never mixed with water, which was the very essence of Under World chaos. The Muskogees doused fire, not with water, but with a safe intermediary, sand.

A Muskogee myth taught the importance of preserving proper relations between the three worlds. The myth related how a hungry hunter found a fish in the hollow of an uprooted tree. His friend warned him that this seemed very unnatural, that the fish surely belonged to the Lower World. Unable to resist his appetite, the man ate the fish. Of course, he soon became sick. His stomach was filled with pain. Finally, he transmuted into a snake. Having failed to pay adequate respect to the cosmic order of things, he had lost his humanity. When the balance between worlds was disrupted, horrible outcomes resulted in This World.[20]

By emphasizing the need for balance and reciprocity in all affairs of life, sacred stories and cosmological theory taught the Muskogees to weigh carefully their acts, to treat each other and nonhuman life forms with respect, and to redress imbalances caused by human maleficence of carelessness. At times, this latter imperative resulted in very harsh and cruel forms of counterviolence. Willful children were scratched with sharpened sticks to lessen the "heat" of their blood. Clan elders killed murderers and mutilated adulterers. Communities mercilessly tortured male war captives to death. Yet these modes of redress were carefully circumscribed; they held sway only until the outstanding blood debt had been paid.[21]

The concern for social equilibrium and reciprocity was also expressed in nonviolent ways. For instance, the Muskogees, like other southeastern Native Americans, considered it very important to symbolize, secure, and balance human relationships through the exchange of gifts. They exchanged the widest possible variety of gifts, some material, others symbolic. Before contact with European Americans, southeastern peoples exchanged stones, metals, shells, animals, paints, and skins. They probably exchanged other objects as well that have not survived over time.[22] These artifacts include basketry, textiles, wooden objects, leather, bark, and food. Finally, native cultures valued and exchanged immaterial gifts: songs, a shaman's knowledge, herbal lore, and ritual procedures. The extraordinary variety of gifts exchanged suggests that more important than the gift itself were the social relationships that the gift articulated.[23] Every gift implicated and altered an ongoing relationship. Depending on the receiver's desire for or repulsion toward the giver, the gift may have been esteemed or reviled. For example, in 1737, the Alabamas were loathe to accept gifts from the Cherokees because the latter had violated a peace twenty years earlier and sided with the English. Though four Cherokee chiefs brought the Alabamas bead necklaces, calumets, and tobacco, this present was found inadequate and rejected. To make things right, the Cherokee would have to bring "a magnificent present the next year."[24] Gifts, as this example demonstrates, were signs whose fluctuating values depended on a complex relational economy, an ongoing historical praxis of cultural contact.

Because gifts interpreted and incarnated cultural contact, they were crucial in establishing a group's identity and alliances and maintaining peaceful relations among different peoples. As understood by southeastern Native Americans, the reciprocal exchange of valued gifts brought two peoples together by providing a "true footing" of "mutual Friendship."[25] The social result was a delicate balance between intimacy and difference, solidarity and enmity.

Although Europeans did not share the southeastern Native Americans' perspective on gift giving, they found it politically prudent to provide the Muskogees with ample gifts. At annual conferences in Mobile and through the officers at Fort Toulouse, the French provided the chiefs of the Alabamas with clothing, knives, pipes, and a wide variety of manufactured goods. Competing for the favor of the Muskogees, the English had no choice but to give generous goods and hospitality. It was not until 1763, when the French departed the region, that the English could afford to ignore the Muskogee norms concerning diplomatic relations. After 1763, English gift giving declined sharply.

The logic of gift exchange helped the Muskogees create a social order with a remarkably egalitarian character. Exchange in Muskogee society did not typically lead to the accumulation of property or the evolution of class divisions. Instead of producing individuals or institutions that desired to aggrandize their material holdings, Muskogee cultural practices instilled and routinized within Muskogee men and women a sociality concerned with perpetuating reciprocity. Gift exchange promoted an economic order predicated on the redistribution of food and other goods. Land was owned communally, and its produce belonged to all. Villagers filled a common granary against famine times. In times of need, the food would be shared without discrimination until the supply was exhausted. While Europeans did not share this ethic, they could not help but be struck by its results. Describing the ordinary Yamacraw hunter of the 1730s, the German artist Philip Georg Friedrick Von Reck wrote, "If he has two of anything, he gladly gives one to him who needs it more."[26]

If the Muskogees' exchanging of gifts, telling of sacred narratives, and conceiving of a dynamic cosmology placed a premium on restoring and maintaining balance and order, their sacred spaces physically symbolized and reinforced their concern for equilibrium. In the Oconee Valley, the sixteenth-century ancestors of Muskogees commonly built homes that were circular in shape with walls supported by saplings sunk in a foundation trench. Significantly, the number of sapling posts was usually a multiple of four (e.g., twelve, sixteen). This was not coincidental but carried symbolic significance, for four was a sacred number throughout the Southeast. Representing the four cardinal directions, this number evoked the totality of creation. By incorporating this symbolism in the very frame of their homes, Oconee people ensured that their dwellings were not only materially sound but also spiritually well founded and secure, symbolically anchored in that which was primordial and sacred.

Eighteenth-century Muskogees carried the tradition forward. They built a variety of domestic structures using different materials and designs, but the most common plan manifested a concern for symmetry and embodied the symbolism of the four cardinal directions. An eighteenth-century visitor to a Muskogee town on the Tallapoosa River observed the following domestic architecture: "Their houses are neat commodious buildings, a wooden frame with plaistered walls, and roofed with Cypress bark or shingles; every habitation consists of four oblong square houses, of one story, of the same form and dimensions, and so situated as to form an exact square, encompassing an area or court yard of about a quarter of an acre of ground, leaving an entrance into it at each corner."[27] It was in just such a complex that many of the activities of everyday life were performed. Here men, women, and children slept, shared stories, cultivated a small garden, and processed and prepared food. Yet, as important as this space was to all members of Muskogee society, this space ultimately belonged to women; in this matrilineal, matrilocal society, the home complexes belonged to women and were clustered according to clan. When a woman married, she remained close to her clan, and her husband came to live with her, to supply meat for her fire.

Although the domestic complex was ultimately the property of women, men were not without a space that they controlled. Men dominated the communal plaza and its complex of buildings. The plaza contained the communal building known as the hothouse or rotunda and the complex known as the square ground or square yard.[28]

The public square's plan was basically the domestic complex writ large: "A quadrangular space, enclosed by four open buildings, with rows of benches rising above one another." Muskogee civic and ceremonial life centered on the square ground, and almost every village was affiliated with a square ground town or *i:tálwa*. Here important visitors were received, rituals performed, and communal decisions formulated. One of these buildings served as the council house, where *mikkaki* (chiefs) and warriors assembled every day in council "to hear, decide and rectify all grievances, complaints and contentions, arising betwixt the citizens; give audience to ambassadors, and strangers; hear news and talks from confederate towns, allies or distant nations; consult about the particular affairs of the town, as erecting habitations for new citizens, or establishing young families, concerning agriculture, &c."[29] Dominated by men, the square ground was also the Muskogees' most important symbolic space.

Every space within the bounds of the square ground signified something vital. In some towns, those men who were not yet warriors sat in the south building, and warriors sat in the north. The specific seating arrangement varied from square ground to square ground, but, despite the variability, in every yard each cardinal direction evoked certain symbolic values and meanings. If old honorable men were to sit in the east building, it was so they could look toward the west, the direction of the setting sun, and contemplate the waning of their own lives. If the *miko* was located in the west building, it was so that he, his assistants, and the chief shaman could look toward the east, the direction of the rising sun, and thus be oriented toward peace and purity and concerned for the welfare of future generations.

Each building was further subdivided into three cabins. For instance, in the warriors' cabin, the head warrior (*Tustunnuggee thlucco*) would sit at the west end of the cabin. "The next in rank sits in the center division and the young warriors in the third." [30] Where a man sat signified not only his vocation but also his status based on merit. A successful warrior would move from the third to the second cabin to sit with other leaders (*Istepuccauchau*). From there he might move to the first cabin and join the ranks of the Great Leaders (*Istepuccauchau thlucco*), one of whom would be picked by the chiefs as the head warrior. If he proved wise or otherwise distinguished himself in the service of his people, he might leave the warriors' building and join the great men and chiefs in their building. Because the individual man's status was based almost solely on his merits and was so clearly a matter of public record, young men passionately concerned themselves with their reputations; they zealously sought the approbation of their elders and the envy of their peers. If the chiefs determined it was necessary, young men were most willing to fight and die for their people.

In addition to providing an architecture articulated in a way that allowed males to display a status hierarchy, the square ground provided a secluded place to protect things "dedicated to religion or rather priestly craft" and a public place to exhibit religious art and the paraphernalia of war and peace. In the square ground of Autossee, a room built onto the back of the *miko's* building harbored "all the sacred things, the physic pot, rattles, chaplets of deer's hoof and other apparatus of conjuration; and likewise the calumet or great pipe of peace, the imperial standard, or eagle's tail curiously formed and displayed like an open fan on a sceptre or staff, as white and clean as possible when displayed for peace, but when for war, the feathers are painted or tinged with vermillion." [31] Although these things were carefully guarded by shamans and revealed only at special times, other forms of the sacred, paintings of Muskogee symbols and figures, were constantly visible in the square ground. Muskogees painted the clay-plastered surfaces of buildings with brightly colored clan totems—"men . . . having the head of some kind of animal as those of a duck, turkey, bear, fox, wolf, buck, &c, and again those kinds of creatures are represented having the human head."[32] Thus, the square ground served not just as a place for social ranking, not just as sanctorium, but also as art gallery, armory, and trophy room.

Richly imbued with social and symbolic meaning, the square ground inevitably served as the ceremonial center within which were performed many of the Muskogees' most important rituals. During the warm season, the square ground provided the place where men gathered to drink and then disgorge or spout *acee*, "a strong decoction of the shrub well known in the Carolinas by the name of Cassina." Called the "black-drink" by European visitors because the liquid was dark as molasses, the beverage, rich in caffeine, was brewed daily by ritual specialists (shaman priests) in a small shed near the square ground. Shortly after dawn, young warriors warned "the people to assemble by beating a drum." All adult men within earshot were obligated to come and drink the decoction, for the beverage had a salutary social effect. A late eighteenth-century Anglo-American visitor reported that *acee* "purifies" the Muskogees "from all sin, and leaves them in a state of perfect innocence;. . .it inspires them with an invincible prowess in war;. . .it is the only solid cement of friendship, benevolence, and hospitality." Since the Muskogees associated purity with the color white, they called the beverage the "white-drink," despite its dark color.[33] By consuming the beverage regularly in the square ground during the warm season or the rotunda during the cold season, Muskogee men repeatedly reaffirmed their connection to the Maker of Breath.[34]

As important and ennobling as it was, the *acee* ceremony had to be canceled if the world became spiritually imbalanced. This occurred when death stripped the square ground of one of its members. "If a man [or woman] dies in the town, the square is hung full of green boughs as tokens of mourning; and no blackdrink is taken inside of it for four days." This interval provided sufficient time for the spirit of the dead person to depart the village. Unfortunately, no interval of time was sufficient if the person had been murdered. "If a warrior or other Indian is killed from any town having a square, black-drink must be taken on the outside of the square; and every ceremony in its usual form is laid aside until satisfaction is had for the outrage."[35] Until the dead person was avenged, the spirit of the deceased polluted the square ground and frustrated normal religious life.

Whether it was a single murder or a large-scale war, bloodshed and conflict polluted and therefore canceled ceremonies devoted to peace and order. Just as the wrongful death of a single man prevented them from performing their ordinary ceremonies, so war prevented the Muskogees from performing their most important and serious communal rite, the *póskita* or Busk. Red, the color symbolizing war, temporarily supplanted white, the color symbolizing peace. Ceremonies of war supplanted the Busk. War chiefs sent messages to allied towns. Warriors sequestered themselves in the hothouse for four days and drank the purifying *miko hoyanidja* (willow bark tea). Shamans consulted auguries and prepared special protective medicines and talismans.[36]

In times of peace, however, the Busk could be performed. A ceremony requiring considerable preparation, involving the entire community, and carrying tremendous social and spiritual significance, the Busk was the Muskogees' greatest rite. To match its meaning, one scholar has stated that Europeans or Anglo-Americans would have had to combine Thanksgiving, New Year's festivities, Yom Kippur, Lent, and Mardi Gras.[37] In many ways, the Busk provided a kind of template that shaped the Redstick prophetic movement. The Busk emphasized collective renewal. Its intent was to rekindle a sense of the sacrality of life. Its effect was to strengthen Muskogee cultural traditions during a period of intensive cultural contact. All these concerns would become central to the Redstick movement. Moreover, in forming their movement, the prophets borrowed several key symbolic acts and meanings directly from the Busk. These included rites of purification such as fasting, the destruction of old things in order to make way for collective renewal, the significance attached to sacred numbers, the performance of esoteric speech acts by shamans, the prominence given to male ritual specialists, and the invocation of the Muskogees' highest god, the Maker of Breath.

An annual ceremony, the Busk lasted four days in smaller towns and eight days in important ones such as Cussetuh or Tuckabatchee. It almost always occurred in July or August.[38] Linked to the ripening of the second or late crop of corn, the ceremony was the most important of twelve monthly feasts dedicated to the first fruits of horticulture and hunting. Other feasts celebrated the gathering of chestnuts, mulberries, and blackberries. In the Muskogees' lunar calendar, the Busk took place at the time of "the big ripening moon," and its celebration marked the turning of the seasons from summer (primarily devoted to horticulture and harvest) to winter (primarily devoted to gathering and hunting). The Busk was the time that the Muskogees set aside to appreciate the plant on which they depended to satisfy more than 50 percent of their caloric needs. Despite their sophisticated knowledge of cultivating maize, the Muskogees did not consider themselves masters of the plant.[39] In celebrating the primordial origins of maize, the Busk challenged the Muskogees to remember that maize was rooted not just in little hills of earth but in a mystery.[40]

The plant, as sacred myths related, was originally given to the Muskogees by a woman. More precisely, corn came from the body of a primordial woman, an earth goddess. In one myth, "she washed her feet in water and rubbed them, whereupon what came from her feet was corn." In another, she scratched "the front of one of her thighs, whereupon corn poured down into the riddle."[41] In both these stories, ungrateful males would rather not consume food thus produced. Always giving, the goddess ultimately sacrificed herself by telling these men to burn her body or drag her bloody corpse across the ground so that they might have future crops of corn. Thus, the story symbolized the way life came from death, the unlimited power of female fertility, and the important but circumscribed power of males to impose order on that fertility. The myth reminded listeners that, no matter how successfully they controlled the production of corn, maize was ultimately a gift given to the Muskogees by a primordial mother.

The myth may not have been formally recited during the Busk, but its profound message was communicated. Just as the myth of the Corn Mother used words, symbols, and narratives to remind listeners of the sacred origins of corn, the Busk ritual resacralized corn by carefully orchestrating human energy and action in time and space.

Before the ritual began, the square ground was cleansed and refurbished; fresh white sand was spread in the plaza to sanctify the area. "No stranger's foot [was] allowed to press the new earth until the consecration [was] complete."[42] New pottery vessels were crafted to be employed in the ceremony. Warriors painted the posts and beams of their cabin with red clay, shamans coated the white-drink shed with white clay, and men refurbished all cabins with new cane seating mats. But the cleansing was not restricted to the square ground. While the adult men renovated the public space, fasted, and drank an emetic beverage (button snakeroot), women swept the domestic structures, extinguished the individual clan fires burning on domestic hearths, repaired those hearths, decorated their houses with green boughs, and cared for the children. In some towns, the effort to cleanse the community was radical and involved the wholesale destruction of old things. "Having previously provided themselves with new cloaths, new pots, pans, and other household utensils and furniture," the people of Autossee collected "all their worn-out cloaths and other despicable things, [swept and cleansed] their houses, squares, and the whole of the towns, of their filth, which with all the remaining grain and other old provisions, they cast together into one common heap, and consume[d] it with fire."[43] In Autossee, as in all Muskogee towns, fire purified and was sacred.

Each town square had a hearth with a fire burning that represented the entire community and the people's connection to their ancestors and the Maker of Breath. This particular fire was most sacred, but it could become polluted. Acts of violence, the misuse of spiritual power, the mistreatment of game, violations of taboos concerning sex, and the unsanctioned consumption of the newly ripened or "green" corn symbolically polluted fire. A pure fire enabled the people to communicate their wants to the Maker of Breath, the purifying power that rebalanced the cosmos. In contrast, a polluted fire could not connect the people to the Maker of Breath. Over the course of a year, as the people's fire became tainted, its power eroded and needed renewal. The proper context for this vital renewal was provided by the Busk.

One of the crucial ritual acts of the Busk was the kindling of a new, pure fire. In the Busk ceremony of Autossee, the making of new fire occurred on the fourth morning. In some square grounds, it was on the third morning. In Little Tallassie, the fire was ignited on the first day. "On the morning of the first day, the priest, dressed in white leather moccasins and stockings, with a white dressed deer-skin over his shoulders, repairs at break of day, unattended to the square. His first business is to create the new fire, which he accomplishes with much labor by the friction of two sticks. After the fire is produced, four young men enter at the openings of the four corners of the square, each having a stick of wood for the new fire; they approach the fire with much reverence, and place the ends of the wood they carry, in a very formal manner, to it." Specifically, the logs were placed so that they pointed "to the four cardinal points," invoking the symbolism of the entire world.[44]

Once ignited and sufficiently kindled, the new fire, understood to be most pure, was an extraordinarily powerful embodiment of the sacred. It was used for cooking meat or warming hominy, but it also possessed the power to resanctify things, relationships, and the entire community. During the Busk, the Muskogees tapped this power in a series of carefully performed rites, the first and perhaps most important being the sacrifice of corn. "After the fire is sufficiently kindled, four other young men come forward in the same [formal] manner, each having a fair ear of new corn, which the priest takes from them, and places with great solemnity in the fire, where it is consumed."[45] By allowing the holy fire to burn and destroy the first ears of the new corn, the Muskogees expressed their profound awareness that the corn had once belonged entirely to the sacred realm. Although their ancestors had subjugated and domesticated this plant and living men and women now cleared fields and cultivated it, the Muskogees knew that the plant must periodically be returned to the sacred. By ritually removing corn from ordinary patterns of human consumption and giving it instead to the new and powerful sacred fire, this rite of sacrifice resanctified corn.[46]

Similar sacrifices often followed. White-drink tea leaves were "given to the new fire." Also consumed by the fire were portions of bear oil, freshly killed deer meat, and button snakeroot medicine.[47] The most important medicines and foods known to the Muskogees were temporarily removed from ordinary life and once again immersed in the sacred.

Broken human relationships were also healed. Because the Busk marked a critical threshold in time, the end of the last year and the beginning of the new, it enabled Muskogees to put personal grievances and animosities behind them and grant amnesty to all criminals, except murderers.[48] But if the major social import of the ceremony was to bring people back together and strengthen their ties to each other and to the square ground, one very important effect of the Busk was to reinforce differences based on gender. During most of the ceremony, the sexes were not only segregated but were also required to perform gender-coded activities. It was common for townsmen to perform war dances and engage in a mock battle and a ritual hunt. Meanwhile, women were expected to cleanse the domestic space, harvest and prepare food, and care for children. During the Busk, both men and women sought purity, but they achieved it through different means and by respecting different taboos. While men were "physicking," women were "constantly bathing." Men in the square ground could not directly refer to or even touch women, "even with the tip of the finger." For their part, women were ritually excluded from the square ground for most of the Busk ceremony. Such physical restriction had profound symbolic and social meaning.

Because men fasted and slept in the square ground during the Busk, they enjoyed a closer, much more intimate relationship to the sacred fire. The men kindled the new fire and made the key sacrifices to it. They were its first beneficiaries. Only after the men had witnessed its flame were the women allowed to enjoy its purifying power: "Some of the new fire [was] next carried and left on the outside of the square, for public use; and the women allowed to come and take it to their several houses."[49] This symbolism was powerful and clearly patriarchal. Placing males first and at the center and females second and on the periphery, the ritual claimed for and provided males superior access to the sacred. Thus, during the ritual, men were aligned with the sacred, women with the profane.

This carefully framed elevation of men and subordination of women stands out when it is contrasted with the spiritual statuses of men and women in everyday life in which the relationship between the genders was modeled not on dominance but on complementarity. Moreover, in everyday life, women could hardly be considered "profane." Women had access to sacred powers that men poorly understood. Because they knew the secrets of plants and fertility, women made better herbalists or medicine people and monopolized midwifery. To explain why women were spiritually subordinated during the Busk ritual, interpretative energy should focus not just on the relationship between genders but also on the relationship between two kinds of space. When the new fire was carried out of the square ground to supply every habitation in the town, it was not just moving from men to women, but it was moving from communal space to clan space. This movement from square ground to periphery and from men to women symbolized the tension between the common collective identity and the multiplicity of clan identities. The tension was ritually resolved in favor of the collective identity.

In any town, several clans were present, and conflicts were endemic among them. If a woman discovered that her husband had committed adultery, her clan pursued and beat the man, even at the risk of offending his clan. If a man from the Bear clan killed a Fox, the latter's clan felt justified in killing a member of the Bear clan. In turn, if the members of the Bear clan felt the retaliation unwarranted, they might seek vengeance, and a spiral of violence ensued. Such conflicts and some less dramatic ones seriously threatened to tear the town apart and make impossible the communal efforts of clearing fields and defending territory. In sum, clan loyalties pulled villagers centrifugally away from a common identity.

Opposing this fragmentation were those rites, spaces, and symbols that transcended clan diversity. Public ceremonies, particularly the white-drink ceremony and the Busk, assembled and unified men from all clans. Public spaces—the rotunda and the square ground—provided a space for a common discourse and set of communal symbols to emerge and for men to define and display achieved status. Public symbols such as the sacred fire gave men, women, and children a common orientation point beyond the clan. Together, these communal rites, spaces, and symbols forged diverse clans into a unified *i:tálwa*. Thus, when the new sacred fire was transmitted from center to periphery, its movement symbolized the supremacy not just of men over women but of the public over the domestic, of "fire" over "blood," and of the power of male order over the power of female fertility. The symbolism was powerful, but it would require repetition. The ritual could never finally banish or resolve the fundamental oppositions and tensions that constituted and energized Muskogee society. Nor could its patriarchal construction of gender relations establish in any final way the sacrality of men or the profanity of women. Because clan identities and women's access to the sacred always remained strong in everyday life, the symbolism and rites would have to be repeated. In another year, a new fire would be needed.

With the conclusion of the Busk, the ritual restrictions and symbolic boundaries that had been so carefully constructed and enforced were decisively abandoned. Symbolic boundaries that had kept men and women separate (and unequal), taboos that had imposed a fast on men, and rules that had prevented the access of women and children to the square ground no longer held force. On the last day of the ceremony, the whole town assembled in the square; women cooked new corn over the new fire; men, women, and children mixed freely and devoted themselves to feasting, dancing, and other amusements.[50] Before this moment of collective celebration, the Busk, with its extraordinarily strict boundaries, taboos, and restrictions, had forced villagers to inhabit an uncanny and oddly imbalanced world. The ritual had constructed an impossible world of maximum difference between men and women, town council and clan, public and domestic, center and periphery, sacred and profane. The Busk had placed villagers in a world of stark polarities. Feasting together, villagers returned to ordinary life with new zeal, new appreciation of their complex community and its sacred foundations. By generating a tremendous desire for renewal of purity, balance, and wholeness and placing the Muskogees in vigorous contact with what was most sacred to their collective identity, the Busk gave villagers the energy to resume social life as if the world were once again fresh and balanced.

Because the ceremony enabled Muskogees to deal with some of the fundamental tensions inherent to their social order, to celebrate the harvest of corn, and to renew their collective life and public spaces, its performance remained very important throughout the period of colonial contact. The ceremony changed in only minor ways. For instance, new rules had to be created governing the consumption of alcohol and the use of manufactured goods during the Busk. In some towns, both were banned. At least in one square ground, it was "considered as a desecration for an Indian to allow himself to be touched by even the dress of a white man, until the ceremony of purification is complete."[51] This was the case in 1835, but it could have been true much earlier as well. Since rituals are dynamic expressions of a people's evolving relation to the sacred, rituals can and must change to fit new contexts. In the history of religions in North America, there are probably few examples of rituals that have succeeded so well in surviving through change and crisis as the Busk. In Oklahoma, the Busk or Green Corn Ceremony remains to this day a vital ceremony performed by the Muskogee people. The symbolism of the square ground, the sacred fire, and fasting remains powerful despite five centuries of intense contact with other peoples.

During the colonial period, Muskogee tradition proved itself to be very resilient, capable of linking an ancestral past to ever-changing contexts. As they passed this tradition down through the generations, Muskogee elders communicated to their children some important symbols and values that were hundreds and even thousands of years old.[52] Nevertheless, even as they carefully communicated this and other traditions, the Muskogees actively modified their culture of the sacred in three key ways. First, eighteenth- and nineteenth-century Muskogees supplemented and reworked their lore by importing fresh ideas, materials, and techniques from other peoples. Significant "imports," which demonstrated an unconscious pan-Native Americanism, included songs from the Choctaws, a dance from the Shawnees, and a sacred stone from the Yamasees. Muskogees also borrowed from non-Native Americans, taking among other things folktales from Africans and the symbolically powerful idea of the Book from Europeans.[53]

Second, a small number of specialists—medicine men and women, knowers, and shamans—were specially charged with preserving, disseminating, and applying the most important inherited traditions. These specialists modified sacred tradition to respond to specific needs and events.[54] They applied myth to history. Distinguished by an unusual birth (twins), extraordinary experience (visions), unique clothing, the gift of divination, and mastery of an esoteric or archaic-sounding speech, these specialists exercised key roles in the society. They dramatically affected the way people interpreted and applied cultural and religious traditions in ordinary times, but even more so in times of crisis. Ultimately, however, the influence of these specialists would be rejected if it did not lead to the desired results. If a medicine did not work or a prophecy failed to materialize or a battle led to disastrous defeat, the medicine person/prophet/knower was held responsible and punished.[55] This introduces the role of human praxis, the third and most important factor affecting the reception and application of lore.

Human praxis enabled the Muskogees to test and reform their culture in history. Without concrete praxis, the Muskogees' received lore and culture of the sacred would have remained static and abstract. Through praxis, Muskogee myth and history met and powerfully altered one another. Thought and action fused in ever-new syntheses. Through this flexible and finely modulated performance of culture in ever-changing situations, living praxis enabled the Muskogees to cross the manifold crises, passages, and events that history introduced and to do so without jettisoning their culture or religion. Praxis dynamically rewove the traditional web of reciprocities that defined and disclosed the world to the Muskogees.[56] This continually improvised web was fine and supple enough to give support to the specific events, passages, crises, and "contacts" that dramatized an individual's unique life, yet resilient and broad enough to ensure the survival of the entire society in very difficult times and historical crises (warfare, famine, disease, economic dependency).

This resiliency was to be sorely tested during the eighteenth and early nineteenth centuries. It was during this period that the Muskogees experienced extensive contact with Africans, the French, the English, and Anglo-Americans. Sustained contact with these peoples brought many changes and challenges to every area of Muskogee life. Novel diseases, new forms of trade and technology, and an unprecedented influx of settlers dramatically restructured the demographic, economic, social, and geographic world of the Muskogees and other southeastern Native Americans. These changes, because they gravely upset the ecological, social, and political balances of the Muskogees' world, would eventually precipitate a religious crisis. However, it would be a profound mistake to assume that the Muskogees were simply swept away by the changes produced by contact. When compared to the disastrous experiences of many if not most other southeastern Native Americans, it is clear that the Muskogees fared relatively well in the eighteenth century. Thanks in part to their relatively remote location, they were able to avoid utter devastation. While many other groups were almost completely destroyed by European diseases and slave raids (Apalachees, Guales, Timucuas, Sewees) or decisively subordinated by English armies and settlers (Yamasees, Catawbas, Cherokees), the Muskogees managed to survive and retain their land and a remarkable degree of political autonomy throughout the eighteenth century. During the same period, their cherished ritual acts, mythological stories, and special places continued to orient them toward the sacred.

It would not be until the first decade of the nineteenth century that the Muskogees would face the kind of crisis that had already shaken or destroyed other southeastern Native Americans a century earlier. When the crisis finally came, it came hard. As the nineteenth century dawned, the Muskogees faced a depleted supply of game and hunting grounds occupied by settlers. European Americans no longer gave generous gifts, and the rum trade brought debt and misery to villages throughout Muskogee. Millions of acres of Muskogee land had already been ceded to European Americans, and the U.S. government systematically absorbed much of the land that remained in Muskogee hands. Government agents and Christian missionaries attempted to destroy Muskogee culture by teaching the virtues of commercial agriculture, a market economy, private property, and the patrilineal family. Simultaneously, wealthy cotton planters dwelling in Georgia, Tennessee, and Mississippi were calling for the extermination of the Muskogees and organizing militias to carry out this objective. This multidimensional crisis was deep, tore the people apart, and threatened their religious tradition to the core. To weather this crisis and preserve their sense of the sacred, the Muskogees would have to rely on extensive cultural borrowing, intense shamanistic creativity, and significant practical and political innovations. The result would be a radical prophetic movement, a religious revolution unlike anything the people had ever experienced.

T W O

Muskogee and the English Trade in Slaves and Skins

The colonial encounter of the native peoples of eastern North America with the English has an extraordinarily complex and regionally varied history. For important historical reasons, the southeastern Native Americans' experiences of contact with the English were much different from the experiences of native peoples in the Northeast. In the Southeast itself, the contact and trade experiences of the Muskogees varied greatly from those of other groups in the Southeast. For nearly a full century, the Muskogees traded vigorously with the English without losing cultural integrity, land, or political autonomy. It was not until the end of the eighteenth century that the Muskogees' experience of contact and trade came to resemble the experience of those northeastern and southeastern peoples who had been exploited by the English trade in skins and slaves.[1]

Perhaps the most important force that makes the southeastern experience different from other regions in eastern North America was the early, powerful, and persistent presence of the Spanish. The Spanish brought old world diseases to the Southeast a full century before the English settled permanently in the region. Generations before the inauguration of English trade, native peoples experienced unprecedented epidemics. The native groups that survived the plagues of the late sixteenth century and early seventeenth century, however, had several generations to recover, reorganize, and reorient themselves before they had to deal with English traders. The Muskogees and other interior southeastern groups had time to adjust to diminished populations, to create appropriate kinds of polities, to rebalance subsistence strategies, to alter and make innovations in ceremonial life, to expand and amend mythologies and symbology, and to adjust to the presence of Europeans living in their midst or as neighbors. In sum, the Muskogees and other groups had time to learn how to live their lives in a new way. In contrast, New England Native Americans enjoyed no such respite, facing English traders even as their societies continued to reel under demographic devastation. Virginia Native Americans likewise faced a compressed contact history in which disease, trade, and settlers came almost all at once, an overwhelming experience that almost immediately prompted a great revolt, the Powhatan rebellion of 1622.[2]

When English traders eventually did arrive in the Southeast in 1670, after the founding of Charleston, not only had the native peoples recovered somewhat from the horrors of disease-spawned holocausts, but they had also gained some experience with Europeans or European goods. Their ancestors had faced Spanish conquistadors. Timucuas, Apalachees, and Guales living in Florida and Georgia had intimate knowledge of the Spanish way of life. Those beyond Florida had less direct knowledge of Spanish culture and its material forms, but they were not altogether cut off. Well before the English arrived, Spanish and Native American traders from Apalachee penetrated the interior, bringing iron manufactures, brass ornaments, glass beads, a few guns, and other goods to the Muskogees to exchange for deerskins, furs, and food. Spanish missionaries also made sporadic but unsuccessful ventures into the interior.[3]

Because the Muskogees first encountered Spanish and later English goods from Native American traders, an extra layer of mediation separated the Muskogees from Europeans. This buffer enabled the Muskogees to assimilate more fully the novel goods within traditional patterns and expectations. During the seventeenth century, they carefully turned new materials and technologies to time-honored purposes. European glass aided divination, and jagged shards could be used for arrow heads; imported beads provided additional bright colors to traditional dress motifs; iron celts displaced stone tools; lead balls were flattened into medallions.[4] Throughout the Southeast, the match between the trade and the indigenous cultures initially made the early deerskin trade appear quite benign to its Native American participants. Ironically, southeastern Native Americans would later find it difficult to prevent the trade from expanding and involving them more deeply in a market system that they could not control. Years later, the European trade would shift from a useful form of intercultural interaction that benefited both sides into a form of colonial exploitation that increasingly worked against the Muskogees, the Choctaws, the Cherokees, and other southeastern peoples. Yet such a shift would not fully take place for several generations, not until the latter part of the eighteenth century.

Given the long duration of Spanish occupation in Florida, the impact of diseases spread in the Southeast as a result of the Spanish presence, and the early forms of trade promoted by the Spanish, it makes little sense to describe the Muskogees that English traders encountered in the late seventeenth century as "aboriginal." They were not. Rather, these peoples consisted of communities that had already weathered demographic crises, re-created themselves politically, innovated culturally, and gained varying degrees of knowledge of Europeans and some of their goods. They were New World peoples who had already changed in response to contact. This certainly did not mean that they would avoid the perils involved in trading with the French and English, but it did mean that they faced these perils from a different and stronger position than did peoples in regions where contact history was more compressed.

Because they lived in the interior, the Muskogees survived the post-Columbian transatlantic exchange of pathogens somewhat better than coastal groups, and that fact worked to their advantage. Because the Muskogees possessed ample lands, they could successfully incorporate weaker groups and bolster their own strength. During the seventeenth and eighteenth centuries, this practice waxed in importance as chiefdoms throughout the Southeast collapsed and English slavers began raiding the outskirts of the region. Tuasis, Taskigis, Napochies, and Yuchis came from the north to live in Muskogee. From the northwest came the Alabamas. From the south and east came victims of epidemics and refugees from European coastal invasions and wars. These reduced, broken peoples included Shawnees, Tamas, Guales, Apalachees, Timucuas, Stonos, and Natchez, "the shattered remains of the various nations who inhabited the lower or maritime parts of Carolina and Florida, from Cape Fear to the Mississippi."[5] In a remarkable coalescence, these groups joined Muskogees living along the fall line in the lower Tallapoosa and Chattahoochee river valleys. Although obligated to observe the laws and customs of the Muskogees, these immigrants flourished. The Shawnee population increased and eventually constituted several thriving towns along the Tallapoosa River; the Yuchi town on the Chattahoochee became one of the largest native towns in the entire Southeast.[6]

To facilitate this unprecedented melding in an age before pan-Native Americanism was fully developed, there emerged a complex clan system involving several dozen clans. Prominent clans included the Deer, Wind, Beaver, Turkey, Wildcat, Tiger (Panther), and Wolf clans. Clan identity, which was inherited from one's mother, became tremendously important to each individual. Besides defining one's "family," clan identity influenced where one lived (clan members' houses were generally located together in a section of the village), entailed legal and political responsibilities (each clan exacted justice for crimes committed against its members; the elder male of each clan sat in council and helped govern the village), and, finally, determined whom one could and could not marry. A member of the clan Wind could not marry another Wind, but he or she could marry a person from any other clan. Because the clan system required exogamy, it encouraged the assimilation of strangers. Such a process explains why a town like Tuckabatchee, one of Muskogee's largest and most important, cannot be easily classified ethnically. Rather than representing any single group, it consisted of many peoples involved in a dynamic process of coalescence.[7]

In the new order emerging, the village, not the chiefdom, represented the main political unit and the square ground, not the mound center, the new sacred space; by the end of the eighteenth century, the diverse peoples in Muskogee had also forged a novel form of political integration, the confederacy. The confederacy united diverse *i:tálwa* (polities) for larger objectives, including wars with other polities over contested territories and hunting grounds. Rather than coercing loyalty and tribute to a common center or preeminent lineage in the manner of the defunct chiefdoms, the confederacy mode of organization respected the autonomy of villages and relied on consensus within and among them to form policy and guide common action. Confederacy was a weaker or looser form of political order, but, in this case, its very weakness was the thing that allowed proud, culturally diverse, and sometimes ethnocentric people to cooperate and occasionally to disagree without violence.[8]

With the immigration of these diverse newcomers and through natural increase, Muskogee's native population rose throughout the eighteenth century. The increase was sometimes interrupted and even reversed, as fresh outbreaks of smallpox, wars, and emigration removed population. Yet the prevailing tendency was for Muskogee to rebound from the demographic collapse of the seventeenth century.[9] By the time the English traders arrived in 1670, the Muskogees had restructured their political and social life.

Although the English had no sustained forms of contact with most inhabitants of the interior regions of the Southeast before 1670, some English goods reached the peoples of the interior. In the period before European colonization, an indigenous exchange network had moved exotic materials over considerable distances, linking regional centers and enabling their elites to signify and convey status.[10] Materials exchanged included marine shell and copper, unusual lithic materials such as quartz, mica, pyrite, and galena, and other distinctive or symbolically valuable substances. During the period after the founding of Virginia (1607) but before the founding of Carolina, these well-established paths and exchange practices enabled piedmont peoples such as the Tutelos, Occaneechis, Tuscaroras, and Catawbas to bring English goods to interior groups, including Cherokees, Muskogees, Alabamas, and Choctaws. By 1673, even Chickasaws along the Mississippi possessed "guns, axes, hoes, knives, beads, and double glass bottles," manufactures that may have been of English or Spanish provenance and were probably brought to the region by native middlemen.[11]

As native middlemen disseminated goods to interior peoples, they achieved a powerful but very precarious and short-lived position in the English trade network. Realizing that their power was based on nothing more than an accident of geography, the Occaneechees, Tuscaroras, and Catawbas tried to prevent direct contacts between Virginia's traders and more distant groups. Their efforts ultimately failed, for English traders were loathe to share their profits, and they were willing and able to travel hundreds of miles to reach new consumers. In 1676, Virginians led by Nathaniel Bacon attacked and defeated the Occaneechees, opening up the trade route for English packhorsemen. In 1711, the Tuscaroras were devastated in a war with the English. Although the Catawbas also fought the English, attacking, along with other southeastern groups, the colony of Carolina in 1715, the Catawbas fared a bit better and tenaciously survived.[12]

Though Virginia's commerce to the interior never directly involved the majority of southeastern Native Americans, it did demonstrate what successful commerce entailed, and it anticipated the particular features and perils that would characterize the English trading regime wherever it would later take hold. First, a successful trade venture relied on a critical number of Anglo-Americans who possessed frontier experience and knowledge of native inhabitants and the land. Because military men had personally experienced and surveyed the land and encountered, made treaties with, and formed allies among southeastern Native American groups, they figured prominently in all frontier trade ventures.[13]

Second, the Virginian experience showed that frontier knowledge had to be articulated with capital. Trade required extensive investments in goods, labor, and means of transport. Further, commerce relied heavily on obtaining, circulating, and floating credit. Traders obtained goods from London merchants and distributed goods to factors, hirelings, and clerks, who in turn gave the goods to southeastern Native American hunters. Thus, the line of credit extended from the warehouses of London to the woods of the American interior. To get the business off the ground in the first place required someone in the middle with enough wealth to inspire the confidence of London houses and suppliers. The only colonists able to do this were the substantial planters and merchants who already possessed land, mercantile businesses, and slaves. Thus, the early deerskin commerce depended on and helped enlarge the fortunes of many of Virginia's and Carolina's "first families."[14]

Third, a successful trade obviously required the services of a good number of native hunters. The enterprise presupposed the existence of a native group that had not been destroyed by the diseases of early contact or dispossessed of their hunting grounds. Because local or coastal populations were almost always terribly reduced in numbers and power by the spread of diseases and the massive intercultural violence that accompanied colonization, traders invariably had to travel beyond the limits of the colony to interior regions to find strong trading partners.[15] Virginia traders diligently sought trade with the Cherokees. Later, after Carolina was founded, English traders would cultivate trade with other strong interior groups and try to fend off the commercial advances of the Spanish and French.

A fourth feature of the deerskin commerce was its connection with regional politics and imperial contests. Exchange followed and cemented the forming of alliances, "bonds of peace" between the colony and its native trading partners.[16] In the 1630s, when Virginians Henry Fleet and William Claiborne bartered furs with Chesapeake peoples, they traded with those groups—Patawomekes, Accomacs, and Accohannocs—who had served as Virginia's allies in the Second Powhatan War (1622–32).[17] The connection between commerce and politics remained strong throughout the history of the deerskin trade.[18]

As exchange and imperial contests involved southeastern Native Americans in new kinds of power struggles, it also involved them in new forms of slavery, both as suppliers of slaves and as slaves themselves. Well before Europeans arrived, native peoples had held captives of war as servants. The vanquished survivors lived as marginal members of the victor's society. Some were abused, some adopted, some killed. After the English arrived, native people found a new use for the subjugated, and the subjugated found themselves facing an unprecedented destiny. War captives were sold for great profit to English tobacco planters. Raiding enemy villages to obtain captives appeared a quicker and more profitable way to obtain manufactured goods than hunting deer. On the Virginia market, a child was worth more than his or her weight in deerskins; a single adult slave was equal in value to the leather produced in two years of hunting. Armed by traders, native allies of Virginia did not hesitate to raid the villages of their enemies, kill the men, and capture the women and children. By the latter half of the seventeenth century, if not before, slavery was big business in Virginia, an important part of the English trading regime.[19]

By the middle of the seventeenth century, the Virginia trade was thriving and possessed a form that would characterize subsequent trading experiences. Trains of packhorses regularly journeyed from Virginia deep into the backcountry, carrying cloth and other manufactured goods into the southeastern interior and conveying leather and slaves out. By 1670, the network extended even farther away to the Savannah River, where traders from Virginia had located and armed a group of native people known as the Westoes. Employing the latter as slave catchers, the Virginians sent waves of terror far into the interior of the Southeast among peoples that the English had yet to meet face to face. Among peoples such as the Yamasees and the Muskogees, rumors spread that cannibals were about in the land. As they listened to and spread these stories, southeastern Native Americans were evidently bracing themselves for encounters with new kinds of people, unnatural powers, and novel dangers.

If distance cushioned contact, this fact was probably unappreciated by southeastern Native Americans in the interior, particularly by those who found themselves attacked by Virginia's slave-catching allies. It is much more likely that the Yamasees, Chickasaws, Choctaws, Muskogees, and Cherokees were painfully vulnerable to what they experienced: they must have heard stories about the "blond men," the "Virginians," but they could not establish direct contact with them. The Westoes seriously threatened southeastern peoples, including Yamasees and eastern Muskogee towns, and there was no available counterforce for the latter to tap. Although southeastern Native Americans found themselves in a situation of considerable terror, the Spanish officials of La Florida made it illegal to sell guns to non-Spanish subjects.[20]

The founding of South Carolina, an Atlantic coast colony located hundreds of miles to the south of Virginia, gave southeastern Native Americans a highly valued and extremely timely opportunity to trade for the arms they desperately needed to protect themselves from and empower themselves against other groups. From the very beginning of Carolina, there was never any question that Carolinians and southeastern Native Americans would engage in a vigorous deerskin trade. Before the colony itself was established, seafaring scouting expeditions out of Barbados, such as the one led by Robert Sandford in 1666, had contacted coastal communities, exchanged interpreters, and initiated a small trade. By March 1670, when a longboat landed near a village of Sewees, both Sewees and English knew what goods the other had to offer. An English captain described the first encounter in this way: "As we drew up to ye shore A good number of Indians . . . ran up to ye middle in mire and watter to carry us a shoare where when we came they gaue us ye stroaking Complimt of ye country and brought deare skins some raw some drest to trade with us for which we gaue them kniues beads and tobacco and glad they were of ye Market."[21]

Carolina's English founders quickly and aggressively expanded their influence in the Southeast. Charleston planters armed the Savannahs and waged war against the Westoes, virtually annihilating them in 1680 and thus removing the chief obstacle to trade with the great interior peoples, the Muskogees, the Cherokees, the Choctaws, and the Chickasaws. With similar independence, planters of the Goose Creek area boldly ignored proprietary rules limiting the extent of trade to the vicinity of the settlement. Not content with planting and raising cattle, they sent their agents hundreds of miles inland to establish contact with Cherokees, Muskogees, and Chickasaws.[22]

The Goose Creek planters forged a strong and direct trade with the interior groups. They directed a large caravan of goods to Coweta as early as 1685 and guided native burdeners carrying hundreds of pounds of deerskins back to Charleston. By 1690, Carolina planters virtually monopolized the southeastern deerskin trade. In a few more years, Charleston merchants used their command of the credit system to gain control over the trade, transforming it into one of the young colony's great mercantile interests. In 1693, an official remarked on its rising importance, noting that the interior southeastern Native Americans "are great hunters and warriours and consume great quantity of English goods."[23] Except for brief war-related interruptions, Carolina would remain overwhelmingly the most important player in southeastern commerce until the American Revolution.

The deerskin trade provided Carolina with a badly needed export commodity. In the reports of colonial officials, "buck and doe skins" were considered as important as the colony's other products: rice, beef, pitch, and tar. By involving thousands of native consumers in Carolina's commerce, the trade enabled Charleston merchants to import far more goods than English subjects alone could have consumed, thus strengthening mercantile and shipping interests. Finally, using the profits gained in trade, many colonists invested heavily in plantation slavery and increased the production of staple crops such as rice.[24]

Within the realm of imperial politics, the trade provided colonists with a means to spread English culture and combat the influence of European rivals, beginning with Spanish Florida. While the English relied on trade to mold and transform native cultures, the Spanish deployed the mission system. The mission system was initially most successful with the Guales of the Georgia coast and the inhabitants of the provinces of Apalachee and Timucua, places where missions were supported or accompanied by other colonial institutions such as the army, the crown, and the regular church. During the seventeenth century, the mission system extended its reach westward and southward to incorporate Apalachees and Calusas, respectively. Franciscan friars built an impressive network of churches, chapels, and mission stations to serve thousands of southeastern Native American converts. Nevertheless, as successful as the mission system was as a frontier institution of the Spanish empire, it was unable to extend its direct influence into interior piedmont regions of the Southeast. In a sense, the mission system was too organized, required too much state support, and intended to institute too many fundamental changes in native life to be spread easily and securely to regions beyond Spanish control.[25]

By contrast, the English trading regime expanded most successfully when it was least regulated. The trade seemingly required no fundamental changes in life, and traders could thrive in places far removed from colonial control and population centers.[26] The English trading regime was able to penetrate the interior Southeast with incredible rapidity and comprehensiveness. Unlike Spanish missionaries, traders did not directly oppose southeastern Native American religions, dances, or games. Nor did traders force southeastern Native Americans to provide labor for building, ranching, and mission projects. Nor did they interfere with native cultures' basic seasonal rhythms and subsistence strategies. Quite to the contrary, traders encouraged the traditional and very important indigenous practice of hunting deer. English or Scottish resident traders, most of them with Native American wives and offspring, connected themselves to the existing culture instead of proscribing or attacking it.

Throughout the last decades of the seventeenth and the first several decades of the eighteenth centuries, the trade seemed safe, and it made good sense to southeastern hunters. Thanks to the favorable deer-to-hunter ratio, interior hunters had little reason to worry about depleting the deer population. The supply of deer seemed inexhaustible. As European newcomers placed a premium on deerskins, southeastern Native Americans readily and successfully intensified their deer hunting. In exchange for skins, furs, tallow, oils, honey, horses, and slaves, southeastern Native Americans obtained a wide variety of goods, some necessities, some near necessities, and some outright luxuries. Among the most important necessities were the "powder, bullets and shot" that southeastern Native American men used to hunt deer and defend themselves. Interior groups appreciated the English willingness to sell munitions. Trade with the English seemed the best way to gain an advantage over or at least maintain parity with their traditional enemies. As important as munitions were, by far the most important trade items consumed by southeastern Native Americans were cloth and clothing. A comfortable and colorful substitute for leatherware, cloth was acquired in great quantity, diverse fabrics, and manifold styles. As Carolina's governor Nathaniel Johnson reported, southeastern Native Americans purchased noteworthy quantities of "English cottons, broad cloths of several colours, blue and redd beads of several collours, sorts and sizes, axes, hoes, faulchions."[27] Bright red or blue woolen leggings and skirts were extremely popular trade goods, but southeastern Native Americans also bought blankets, shirts, belts, hats, overcoats, ear bobs, bells, ostrich feathers, ribbons, combs, and mirrors.

By trading with the English, southeastern Native American peoples gained access to a world of novel, practical, beautiful, and destructive goods, goods and materials produced or gathered in every corner of the globe. Southeastern Native Americans enjoyed this access. Nevertheless, their reliance on it left them open to the colonists' influence and coercion. Because the English dominated manufacture and the market, the English could manipulate the trade to advance their own political purposes. Trade, like war, provided the English of Carolina with the means to secure and increase the fruits of colonial conquest. Indeed, in the colonial setting, trade went hand in hand with war.

The English constantly pursued profits and greater control over Carolina's territory and the entire Southeast. In pursuing these goals, Carolinians did not hesitate to encourage rivalries and conflicts between native peoples. The Goose Creek men sowed war, arming Savannahs against Westoes (1680), Yamasees against the peoples of Spanish Guale and Timucua (1680–90), Yamasees and Muskogees against Apalachees (1702–4), Muskogees against Chatot (1706), Yamasees, Chickasaws, and Muskogees against Choctaws (1690–1710), and Yamasees and Muskogees against Tuscaroras (1711–12). Through these and subsequent wars, South Carolina wrecked Spain's mission system in Florida, deepened divisions between native groups, squelched anticolonial revolts, and gained for itself thousands of Native American slaves.[28]

The Apalachees paid the heaviest price. Firmly allied with and successfully missionized by the Spanish, the Apalachees did not have access to English goods or firearms. They became prime targets of Carolina officials eager to extinguish Spanish influence in the Southeast and obtain native slaves for English plantations. In 1704, Colonel James Moore led a force of fifty English soldiers and one thousand warriors drawn from the Yamasees, Apalachicolas, and Muskogees on a ruthless slave raid. The invaders leveled fourteen mission villages, killed hundreds of Apalachees, and brought a thousand men, women, and children into captivity.[29]

As it had served Virginia, slavery provided early Carolina with cheap labor and marketable exports that were eagerly sought by planters in Barbados and as far away as New England. But Native American slavery was not destined for a lasting career in Carolina. Native Americans were still terribly vulnerable to European and African diseases, inexperienced in plantation agriculture, and prone to run away to their kinsmen and kinswomen in the interior. The supply of captives was finite and the costs of perpetual war too great, even for the English. In 1708, Governor Nathaniel Johnson informed the Board of Trade, "That which has been a considerable (though unavoidable hindrance) to the greater encrease of our trade is the great duty on goods both imported and exported occasioned by the debts of the country is involved in by the late expedition in the time of Governor Moore against St. Augustine."[30] Carolina's economy was still trying to recover from the tremendous debts incurred during prior military campaigns.

Additionally, colonial officials also began to fear that their policy of promoting conflicts among southeastern Native Americans might backfire and evoke a widespread rebellion. As early as 1705, Governor Moore was warned by the Cherokees to desist from the "trade of Indians or slave making" and to return to "the trade for skins and furs."[31] However, Moore and Carolina did not heed the warning, and, in 1715, the Muskogees and Yamasees grew so "Dissatisfied with the Traders" that they determined to "fall on the Settlement." They almost destroyed Carolina.[32] After this nearly fatal rebellion, which historians have named "the

Yamasee War," English planters considered it far wiser to meet the colony's labor needs by importing African slaves from the Caribbean and West Africa. In doing so, Carolina planters obtained laborers who were aliens to the land and hence less able to run away. Moreover, African laborers were experienced in plantation agriculture and less vulnerable than southeastern Native Americans to malaria, dengue fever, and yellow fever.[33]

As Native American slavery declined, the stronger groups of southeastern Native Americans steadily shifted their energies from hunting for human captives to hunting for deerskins, producing ever more skins for trade. Between 1699 and 1715, an average of 54,000 deerskins were sent annually to England from Charleston. In 1707, the total numbered more than 120,000; in 1748, the number was 160,000.[34]

After its founding in 1733, Georgia successfully diverted a substantial portion of the deerskin trade away from its elder sister colony. In 1735, Georgia governor general James Oglethorpe built "a handsome fort" that "drew the traders to settle the town of Augusta." By 1740, Augusta encompassed "several warehouses, thoroughly well furnished with goods for the Indian trade, and five large boats . . . which can carry nine or ten thousand weight of deerskins each, making four or five voyages at least in a year. . . . The traders, packhorsemen, servants, townsmen, and others . . . are moderately computed to be six hundred white men, who live by their trade, carrying upon packhorses all kinds of proper English goods; for which the Indians pay in deerskins, beaver, and other furs; each Indian hunter is reckoned to get three hundred weight of deerskins in a year."[35] At first, these deerskins were transshipped to London via Charleston. However, with the rapid development of Savannah and Sunbury, Georgia established direct links to London and by the 1760s exported almost as many deerskins as Carolina.[36]

Although the English in Carolina and Georgia dominated the deerskin trade for much of the eighteenth century, during the first half of the century they faced important and annoying competition from the French of Louisiana. From 1699 to 1763, the French offered a significant outlet for the deerskins of interior peoples. The French presence especially benefited the Choctaws and Muskogees. Enjoying access to both the English and the French, Choctaws and Muskogees were somewhat immunized from the pernicious control of either. Unlike the Catawbas and Cherokees, the Choctaws and Muskogees could continue to obtain large supplies of manufactured goods but simultaneously postpone the practice of overhunting deer and delay the moment when they would have to cede land to pay debts. Rather than having to rely too heavily on the hunt to provide materials to exchange with the English or French, Choctaws and Muskogees could rely on diplomacy and play-off politics to gain goods that came in the form of gifts. As long as the French were a viable presence in the Southeast, interior peoples could avoid economic dependency and the dispossession that inevitably followed.

The French provided the Choctaws, their main allies in the region, with gifts that annually equaled the value of thousands of deerskins, and it was these gifts more than anything else that kept the French-Choctaw alliance alive. The French also gave sizable gifts to the Alabamas. At annual conferences in Mobile, and through the officers at Fort Toulouse, the French provided the chiefs of the Alabamas with "knives, hatchets, swords, pipes, kettles, looking-glasses, needles, scissors, beads, vermillion, blue paint, red caps, white blankets, Limbourg and Alaigne cloths, trade shirts and stockings."[37] If the gifts stopped, the French knew the Alabamas would abandon them. As the French commissary general in Mobile wrote in 1717, "All the chiefs of the Indians, even those remote from these posts, ordinarily go to [the forts] to see the commandants, with the expectation of receiving some presents from these officers. That is what keeps these nations on our side. Deprived of these little attentions, they are less disposed in our favor. That makes them think that the French are beggars and slaves, just as the English, who heap presents upon them, have insinuated to them."[38] This remained true a dozen years later, as the governor of Louisiana recognized in 1730: "One is certain to be loved by them as long as one gives them what they wish, and in proportion as they feel that we need them they increase and multiply their needs so that the English, and we, are the dupes of these Indians who are less dupes than we are." Two dozen years later, the French were still giving generous gifts to keep the Alabamas loyal, but now, ironically, the French themselves "were under the necessity of purchasing from [English] Traders the very presents" they gave away. In 1733, Jean Baptiste Le Moyne (Sieur de Bienville) bitterly described "the insolence with which [southeastern Native Americans] pretended to consider as tribute the presents which the King is so kind to grant them." The French never successfully extricated themselves from the expense of giving gifts, and, indeed, it seems that, the more they gave, the larger became their partners' expectations.[39]

Fearing French influence, English colonists in Carolina and Georgia had no choice but also to give generous gifts to interior peoples. This practice first became significant after 1715. After the Yamasee War, Carolina colonists soon renewed trade with interior peoples. They invited the latter to visit Charleston and receive gifts. In May 1718, several head men of the Muskogees traveled to Charleston, where they met with the governor. In a careful negotiation, they determined the exchange rate of skins for English goods and reestablished a full trade (including guns, powder, pistols, flints, and bullets). While in Charleston, the head men enjoyed the hospitality of the government. On their departure, the board in charge of the Indian trade gave each of "the Headmen . . . a Bottle Wine and three dozen pipes." The board also ordered that "the Guns of the Head Men . . . now in Charles Town . . . be mended at the Charge of the Trade, according to the Desire of the Head Men."[40] Thus began a practice of officially sponsored gift exchange that would grow far larger than any English official ever anticipated.

In subsequent years, it became an annual practice for the head men of the Muskogees to travel to Charleston to discuss trade and politics, and to receive gifts. These annual "talks" grew into a major event, with ever-larger numbers of chiefs participating, expecting finer and more diverse gifts. By 1732, it was common for "all the Talapoosa chiefs and other neighboring round about" to leave every fall "with the English traders in order to go and get some presents in Carolina." In 1749, the English trader James Adair encountered "a considerable body of Muskohge head-men, returning home with presents from Charles Town." By 1753, the Muskogees considered it "a Practice of an old Standing to come hither [to Charleston] to see our Friends the English, and to re-new our Treaties with them." The mounting expense of these reg-ular visits prompted Carolina to petition the crown for help, ar-guing "that in order to keep up a good Understanding with several Nations of Indians, and to prevent the influence of the French and Spaniards, that Province has been at a charge in Trea-ties and presents amounting generally to about Fifteen hundred Pounds Sterling Pr. Annum."[41] The king agreed to provide three thousand pound sterling for presents to be obtained in England and distributed from Carolina and Georgia.

During the 1750s, as competition and conflict between the En-glish and the French increased, so did Carolina's and Louisiana's "Indian Expenses." From the simple bestowal of a bottle of wine and some dozen pipes to a few head men, English gift giving had evolved into a very large, expensive, and unwieldy annual distri-bution of goods and hospitality.[42]

During the 1750s, but also in previous decades, the Musko-gees and Choctaws benefited greatly by using the English and the French against one another. If one European power did not satisfy their needs, they threatened to turn to the other. In 1755, for example, after failing to gain concessions from the English, many of the Muskogee head men, including Malatchi, the pow-erful chief of the Cowetas, went to Mobile to hear what kind of trade and presents the French offered. The Choctaws were equally adept at using this strategy. Though allied with the French, the Choctaws regularly threatened to switch their loyalties to the English because the English promised them "considered presents."[43]

If they courted the Choctaws and held the Muskogees with gifts, the English also tried to win the affection of interior groups by offering favorable prices in the regular trade.[44] In his 1772 tour of the Muskogees' country, David Taitt, an English agent, encountered a village leader who wistfully recalled the days when French competition inspired the English to offer good prices for hunters' skins. In those days, the English had "sold Stroud and duffle Blankets at Six pound leather each and every thing else in proportion, and took their buck Skins at five pounds and doe at three."[45]

By 1772, such favorable terms were only memories. After their defeat in 1763 in the Great War for Empire, the French departed the Southeast, leaving interior groups with no recourse but to trade almost entirely with the English. Though the trade was nominally divided between Carolina, Georgia, and Florida, this division did not constitute a form of competition that worked to the Choctaws' and Muskogees' favor. Rather, like the Catawbas of 1700, the Muskogees and Choctaws now found themselves surrounded on all sides by English colonists, forts, soldiers, and settlers. Just as the Catawbas had had to learn the perils of total reliance on the English for manufactured goods, so now the Muskogees, Choctaws, and Cherokees, the last strong southeastern Native American groups, would learn the same lesson.

Signs of this new reluctance to provide gifts surfaced immediately after the English took over West Florida in 1763. Hundreds of Muskogees and Choctaws accustomed to enjoying hospitality assumed the new commander would keep his "house constantly open to them, giving them victuals whenever they ask it, and the government making them annually considerable presents." For his part, the commander, Major Robert Farmar, bitterly complained that this was a "vile custom," a "most disagreeable custom," and assumed that it was one introduced by the French.[46]

At a conference held in Mobile in 1765, Farmar and Governor George Johnstone suggested that the Muskogees cede land to help the English raise the food needed to feed native visitors. At the next conference, held this time in Pensacola, the English again demanded land cessions. The Muskogees continued to demand presents. Clearly, there was a serious gap between Muskogee expectations and English intentions.[47]

If gift giving was being abandoned in West Florida, a colony most vulnerable to attack, it was rapidly dying in the older and stronger colonies of Georgia and South Carolina. After 1763, these latter colonies relied less on persuasion and gifts to establish peace and encourage commerce and turned increasingly to harsher measures, including sheer coercion. Unlike the infant and isolated colony of West Florida, which routinely devoted 20 percent of its budget for "Indian Expenses," Georgia and South Carolina gradually phased out the practice of gift giving.[48] Rather than give presents, these colonies, especially Georgia, turned to a strategy of debt collection to obtain what they wanted most: southeastern Native Americans' land.

After the French departed, the deerskin trade fell under the almost complete control of a few traders living on the border of South Carolina and Georgia, at Silver Bluff and Augusta. Located at Silver Bluff, George Galphin "possessed the most extensive trade, connections and influence, amongst the South and South-West Indian tribes, particularly with the Muskogees and Chactaws." Through his network of hirelings, clerks, and traders, Galphin engrossed a substantial percentage of the leather production of interior peoples. From Silver Bluff, his packhorsemen drove packtrains of one hundred "good size, well-made, hard-hoofed, handsome, strong and fit" Cherokee packhorses to the interior of Muskogee country. Moving at a cruel pace, whipping the horses till they nearly dropped, Galphin's packhorsemen, some of whom were African Americans, raced westward, determined to reach Muskogee hunters before any of Galphin's competitors.[49]

Galphin's traders included many of the most ruthless and exploitative men in the Southeast, and they routinely used devious means to cheat the Muskogees. The most common stratagem involved alcohol. Taitt, writing in 1772, witnessed how a trader, Frances Lewis, "met with the Indians (last night as they came into Town [Tuckabatchee] with their Skins from hunting) and Supplyed them plentifully with rum on purpose to get what skins they had brought in, and deprive the other Trader of any part of them."[50] The Tuckabatchees lost their skins, and the town's resident trader was left without any means of covering the cost of credit already extended to the hunters.

Francis Lewis was only one of many hirelings of George Galphin, and Galphin was but one of several licensed and countless unlicensed traders of the mid-eighteenth century. Together, they directed what amounted to a river of alcohol into Muskogee and Choctaw country. They did this so that they could, at very low cost, dramatically increase the flow of skins, manufactures, horses, and other commodities passing through their hands. James Adair, a veteran trader, described the practices of his less honorable colleagues: "Many Traders . . . have made a constant Practice of [carrying] very little Goods, but chiefly, and for the most part intierly Rum from Augusta, from whence as soon as the Indian Hunters are expected in from their Hunts, they set out with small or large Quantities of that bewitching Liquor according to their Ability. Then some of the Rum Traders place themselves near the Towns, in the way of the Hunters returning home with their deer Skins. The poor Indians . . . are unable to resist the Bait; and when Drunk are easily cheated."[51] In his report on the trade, Edmond Atkin related how rum merchants tracked hunters into the woods to ply them with rum. The celebrating hunters quickly found themselves stripped of "the fruit of three of four Months Toil . . . without the means of buying the necessary Clothing for themselves or their Families. . . . Their Domestick and inward Quiet being broke, Reflection sours them, and disposes them for Mischief."[52] Like so many officials before him, Atkin urged that the state step in to regulate the trade more closely lest abused southeastern Native Americans strike back.

While creating a state of economic dependency and debt among the Muskogees and Choctaws, rum traders made enormous profits. Moreover, the rum traders' practices served as the precondition for the next level of exploitation. Having used rum to create debt, they now sought to exploit debt to gain land. Galphin and the merchants of Augusta exercised considerable power in determining prices and arranging for the payment of southeastern Native Americans' debts. In 1772, it was these traders, the "Augusta rum traders," who insisted that the Cherokees and Muskogees cede land. This cession was the first of many to come as a result of the market's shift toward monopoly, and it served as a precedent for subsequent cessions.[53]

Another cost of the rum trade, internal conflict, occurred at the village level. After consuming alcohol, men were prone to violence. Alcohol explosively touched off internal conflicts that otherwise might have remained suppressed. As the English agent David Taitt reported in 1772, "The Abeckas desired that no more than ten Keggs of Rum might be brought to each Town by their Traders and the Tallapuses desired only four, as some of their men had been lately killed in Rum drinking and others greatly burnt.[54] Village chiefs vainly attempted to maintain order. Fatal fights among Muskogee men frequently erupted and disrupted village life.

As the Muskogees and Choctaws struggled to curb the socially destructive results of the rum trade, they were also facing an ecological crisis much like the one the Yamasees and Catawbas had faced generations earlier. The deer population could withstand only so much pressure before yields would drop, and the drop could be dramatic. This fact had already been demonstrated time after time, first in Virginia, then in Carolina, most recently in the Cherokee country, and now in the hunting grounds of the Choctaws and Muskogees. At the end of the seventeenth century, Virginia's deer population was in such critical condition that the government established a closed season. By the middle of the eighteenth century, deer were becoming scarce in Catawba and Cherokee country.[55] During the second half of the eighteenth century, Muskogee hunters, as William Bartram noted, began to find "deer and bear to be scarce and difficult to procure." In response, many Muskogees, taking advantage of the sparsely settled frontier to the south, migrated to Florida, where game remained plentiful and a hunter could "enjoy a superabundance of the necessaries and conveniences of life."[56] Most Muskogee and Choctaw hunters, however, did not have this option. In order to continue harvesting the same number of deer, they had to extend the season and range of their hunt. Their prolonged absence undermined traditional village life, but even more disturbing was a trend that prevailed among young men. No longer content to stay with their clans in winter hunting camps, they roamed far and wide over the countryside seeking deer to kill and, increasingly, horses to steal. Needless to say, these practices brought them into violent conflict with neighboring southeastern Native Americans and Georgia settlers.

In the mid-1760s, conflicts over hunting lands erupted between Muskogees and Choctaws, and these conflicts escalated quickly into a serious war between the two groups. This war, which caused the deaths of hundreds on both sides, was the direct result of economic pressures caused by the deerskin trade. It was also abetted by the English.[57]

If the Choctaw-Muskogee war weakened both combatants and left the English unscathed, it did not fundamentally alter the history of the deerskin trade. Nor did it lessen the economic distress suffered by Muskogees and Choctaws alike. At most, the conflict temporarily relieved some of the pressure on the deer population in contested borderlands.[58] The future of the deerskin trade remained dim. Locked into an economic relationship that increasingly worked against their interest, Muskogees and Choctaws were discovering their true position in the world market. It was to be a very bitter lesson. They were learning that they were extremely vulnerable, economically dependent, and now destined to lose much of what they had heretofore preserved so remarkably, creatively, and energetically. For the first time, their contact experience came to resemble that of other southeastern Native Americans. For the first time, their economic relations with Europeans became very destructive to both economic and village life.

With the decline of the practice of gift giving, Choctaws, Chickasaws, Cherokees, and Muskogees could not avoid going into debt if they were to obtain arms and cloth and consume other goods. Unlike the merchants of Carolina, who could quickly diversify in response to market forces by literally plowing the profits made in the deerskin trade into plantation slavery and staple crop production, southeastern Native American hunters possessed few economic options, no liquidity, no capital, and no control over credit. They could not afford to let the deerskin trade languish, or they would lose access to necessities such as clothing and weaponry. In the words of one mid-century observer, commercial hunting provided "the only means the Indians have to get everything else they stand in need of."[59] Although the Muskogees had avoided the perils of trading with the English longer and more successfully than many other southeastern Native Americans, they could no longer do so. By the end of the eighteenth century, Muskogees were bound to a threatened staple export, increasingly encumbered by debt, and economically dominated by strangers.

THREE

Intimate Strangers, Hostile Neighbors

Consider the remarkable biography of the Anglo-American woman Hannah Hale. As a young girl living in Georgia in the late eighteenth century, Hale was taken prisoner by a band of Muskogee warriors. They brought her to live in the village of Thlathlagulgau on the Tallapoosa River. Eventually assimilated by the Muskogees, she married one of the village headmen. In 1799, when her parents attempted to have her repatriated, Hale resisted. She had flourished in her adopted homeland. She had given birth to five children and acquired considerable property: "one negro boy, a horse or two, and 60 cattle and some hogs." Hale freely elected to remain in Muskogee with her new family.[1]

Hannah Hale's career illustrates how the colonial encounter involved much more than the deerskin trade and the Muskogee economy. The colonial encounter altered the social, demographic, religious, and cultural landscape as well, bringing nonnative men and women to live in the midst of the Muskogees. They came from England, Scotland, Ireland, France, Spain, Germany, and West Africa. They came as Jews, Catholics, Anglicans, Lutherans, Methodists, Moravians, Baptists, Muslims, and practitioners of the religions of West Africa. They came as captives, traders, packhorsemen, travelers, naturalists, spies, interpreters, cowherds, runaway slaves, missionaries, thieves, backwoods riffraff, spinners, weavers, settlers, smiths, government officials, soldiers, and agents. They altered the way the Muskogees thought, ate, worked, dressed, lived, and died. As individuals and small groups visiting or living in specific villages, they introduced the Muskogees to the great cultural variety of the Atlantic world. Intermarrying with the Muskogees, the newcomers fostered a group of multicultural individuals who would gain significant power and introduce serious levels of internal conflict within Muskogee.

Before discussing the impact of these multicultural offspring, we should consider that of their nonnative parents. African Americans, for instance, brought practical skills to Muskogee. Because their distinctive religious tradition communicated a perspective that was critical of Anglo-American civilization, it may have affected the course of the Muskogees' spiritual life.

Most African Americans who came into contact with Muskogees did so by working in the deerskin trade or by fleeing slavery and seeking refuge in Muskogee. An individual named Ketch pursued both avenues of contact. After serving for years as a translator in the deerskin trade, Ketch came to dwell among the Muskogees as an escaped slave. In his story, we catch a glimpse of the way contact with the Muskogees could strengthen resistance to slavery and fuel the desire for freedom.

Ketch belonged to John Galphin, the brother of the great deerskin trader of the mid-eighteenth century. In his youth, he picked up a Muskogean language. This would have been easily accomplished because the Muskogees frequently visited Silver Bluff and some Muskogees lived on Galphin's plantation as slaves.[2] Because Ketch eventually served as one of the Galphins' most important interpreters in the deerskin trade, he witnessed life among the Muskogees firsthand. Indeed, he was well known among the Muskogees, especially the Cussetas and Cowetas, who referred to him as "Galphin's Negro" and relied on him to convey their most important diplomatic speeches.[3] It is very likely that Ketch shared his experiences with his fellow slaves at Silver Bluff, and they probably recirculated the stories to other slaves on other planta-tions. Ketch also tended cattle on the Georgia/Muskogee fron-tier, helped construct buildings for a trading post, and, after Gal-phin's death, participated in the Revolutionary War as an officer's servant. After the war, he fled servitude: "Ketch left his master and went into the Creek Nation," where he lived as an "Indian negro."[4]

The stories and motivations of other runaways are less well known, but it is clear that Ketch was neither the first nor the last African American who came into contact with the Muskogees. Despite their fear of slavecatchers and the serious possibility that the Muskogees would not protect them, many African Americans fled slavery and sought refuge in Muskogee. Between 1732 and 1752, the *South Carolina Gazette* "contained advertisements for the return of no less than . . . 679 Negro slaves."[5] After Georgia capitulated to slaveholders' pressures and opened its territory to slavery in 1750, African American slaves began running to Mus-kogee with greater frequency. In Muskogee, according to one outraged official, "they lead an idle life and have an Idea of being free."[6] An indeterminable number of African Americans came to live among the Muskogees, marrying Muskogee men and women, adopting Muskogee culture.

Free African Americans among the Muskogees probably found a life much better than the degrading and oppressive one they would have led in Carolina or Georgia.[7] African Americans who were slaves of the Muskogees certainly found a better life than they would have as slaves elsewhere in the Southeast. Before the 1820s, African American slavery among the Muskogees was fundamentally different from the institution among Anglo-Americans and much milder than that practiced by the Cherokees or even the Choctaws. This was not because the Muskogees were somehow more enlightened or noble. It can probably be traced to the fact that the Muskogees had not yet adopted, and indeed strongly resisted adopting, intensive, staple crop commercial ag-riculture. They did not work their slaves hard or maintain rigid status distinctions based on color or ethnicity. As a consequence, a Muskogee's African American slave could own property, travel freely from town to town, and marry into the family of his or her "owner." In many cases, the children of a Muskogee's African American slave were free. African American Muskogees could become the most respected "old beloved woman" or even a chief.[8]

To a degree significantly greater than the Cherokees to the north, the Muskogees intermarried with African Americans. Regarding this difference, the Cherokees and Muskogees would later joke with one another in the following manner: "A Creek said to a Cherokee . . . 'You Cherokees are so mixed with whites we cannot tell you from whites.' The Cherokee . . . replied: 'You Creeks are so mixed with Negroes we cannot tell you from Negroes.'"[9] Muskogees married African Americans for many reasons, including practical ones. African Americans were highly valued as new members of any village for they knew and could teach some of the skills and techniques that the Muskogees deeply desired to learn: "how to repair guns and traps, to shoe horses, to improve agricultural methods [for new crops], to spin and weave, to make butter, to build houses, barns and wagons."[10]

While African American mechanics, tanners, carpenters, and blacksmiths brought a wealth of practical knowledge, African American preachers, worshipers, storytellers, root doctors, and visionaries exposed the Muskogees to one of the most dynamic forms of Christianity emerging from the crucible of southeastern cultural contact. This exposure may have contributed to the emergence of the Redstick prophetic movement for at the heart of African American Christianity was a spiritually inspired critical view of Anglo-American civilization. By stealing away to worship together in their invisible institution, African American slaves located an extraordinary space of life, joy, and healing. African Americans living in colonial Georgia and Carolina learned through visions, prayers, and prophecies that there was a mighty God on the side of the oppressed and that fiery judgment would strike the unjust. The new African American religion succored an oppressed community and nurtured resistance to a brutalizing system. In this nascent African American church, African Americans learned to think, sing, and act in tune with another world that was already in existence. They took the master's religion and altered its emphases, tone, and spirit, producing African American Christianity. Conversion was both a colonial and a counter-colonial process.[11]

A theme in African American Christianity present throughout the colonial period was apocalypticism, the forecasting of the final doom of the world. For instance, in 1710, the Reverend Francis Le Jau, an Anglican missionary in the Goose Creek area of South Carolina, was deeply disturbed to find a local African American community captivated by apocalyptic teachings:

> The best scholar of all the negroes in my parish and a very sober and honest liver, through his learning was like to create some confusion among all the negroes in this country. He had a book wherein he read some description of the several judgements that chastise men because of their sins in these latter days, that description made an impression upon his spirit, and he told his master abruptly there would be a dismal time and the moon would be turned into blood, and there would be dearth of darkness and went away.

Le Jau, as the official and sanctified interpreter of matters religious, attempted to put an end to these unauthorized speculations: "When I heard of that I sent for the negro who ingeniously told me he had read so in a book. I warned him not to put his own constructions upon his reading after that manner, and to be cautious not to speak so, which he promised to me but yet would never show me the book."[12] Perhaps passages from the Book of Revelation or a Hebrew prophet inspired this visionary.

It is significant that the African Americans who worried Le Jau had ample contact with Native Americans, including some Muskogees. At the time Le Jau wrote, the Goose Creek region provided Carolina's greatest deerskin traders, and there was a continual circulation of people, including indigenous burden bearers, back and forth between the coast and the interior. With this circulation of people, there occurred an inevitable exchange of cultural knowledge. Through their contacts with African Americans, Muskogees were continually exposed to an apocalyptic religious tradition that promoted resistance.[13]

Seventy years after Le Jau wrote, the center of the deerskin trade had moved hundreds of miles westward to Silver Bluff. Located on the Savannah River and just below the major trading path from Carolina to the Lower Muskogees, Silver Bluff was animated with the comings and goings of Muskogee hunters, Irish, Scottish, and English traders, African American slaves, cowboys, and packhorsemen, British colonial officials, land speculators, and frontier farm families. Like Goose Creek of the 1700s, it was a borderlands region where Native Americans, Europeans, and Africans frequently and freely mixed, and Galphin himself made no effort to hide his children by Native American and African American women. Perhaps it was this kind of intense intercultural contact, particularly the close association of enslaved African Americans and free Muskogees, that encouraged a novel form of creativity among the African American population. Sometime between 1773 and 1775, African Americans on Galphin's plantation helped found the Silver Bluff Baptist Church, the first separate African American church in North America and "mother church of several far-flung Baptist missions."[14] Famous African American preachers, David George and George Liele, began their careers at Silver Bluff. In this context, it is worth noting that one of the early preachers at the Silver Bluff church was Henry Francis, a man with "no known African ancestry," but clear Native American ancestry.[15]

Contacts between Muskogees and African Americans and the opportunity for significant cultural and religious exchange increased as time went by. After the American Revolution, African American slavery among the Muskogees became more common, providing yet another channel of intercultural exposure.[16] By the end of the eighteenth century, English travelers frequently encountered African American slaves in Muskogee.[17] With African

Americans came apocalyptic teachings. While visiting the Upper Muskogees in 1812, two German Moravian missionaries asked permission to preach to the African American slaves of a prominent Muskogee chief and close friend of Anglo-American officials. The chief refused it, saying, "They [the slaves] had already been made sullen and crazy by those who had preached to them. Many of them were inclined to be influenced by neighboring Negroes much like Phil." Phil preached of divine retribution and urged African American and Native American residents of Muskogee to anticipate a fiery, decisive judgment against the powerful. Such prophecies angered the chief, but they may have been broadcast to and more warmly received by Upper Muskogees already involved in the Muskogee prophetic movement. Muskogee rebels might not have identified with the specifically Christian contents of Phil's sermon, but the form, apocalyptic, was one they adroitly employed.[18]

While African American men and women certainly played an important role in bringing their cultures, skills, and religious visions to Muskogee, the nonnative individuals who had the most decisive effect on the Muskogees' lives were English or Scottish traders. These traders were almost completely without exception male. Their importance as cultural intermediaries went far beyond the material goods that they brought to the Muskogees through trade, for they usually also became part of the village by marrying a Muskogee woman.

Anglo-American traders were considered by Muskogees and Anglo-Americans alike to be a coarse and unprincipled group of men. "The Traders from Georgia," according to a mid-eighteenth-century observer, were "a monstrous set of Rogues for the major Part of whom the Gallows groans." Edmond Atkin portrayed them as "the loosest kind of People . . . held in great contempt by the Indians as Liars." James Adair, himself an English trader, damned his peers as "mean reprobate pedlars," and Caleb Swan vilified them as "the most abandoned wretches that can be found, perhaps, on this side of Botany Bay."[19]

To give some order to the sexual liaisons between these rough characters and Muskogee women, the Muskogees developed a casual, profane form of marriage. The casual marriage was more or less a matter of expediency and, in some areas, was known as "a make haste marriage." Arranged between a male visitor and the elder males and females of the woman's clan, such a liaison entailed few obligations and could be easily terminated by either party. From the founding of Carolina in 1670 to Removal in 1836, casual marriage provided the major form of bond between Muskogee women and European traders.[20]

The Muskogees also practiced a much more secure marital bond, one that was embraced by a small minority of traders. When men and women married seriously, it was a sacred event requiring a whole sequence of symbolic-material actions. These varied in detail but seem to have involved four critical phases: the invitation; provisional acceptance; a trial period; and public affirmation. The male traditionally issued the invitation by sending to the home of his beloved a proposal and a gift. The gift usually consisted of food, furs, or bear oil—that is, something produced by males and closely associated with the hunt. With the influx of European traders and their goods, the gift category broadened to include blankets, manufactures, and other articles of clothing.[21] These goods, though nontraditional, still represented materials brought in almost exclusively by males and thus were readily substituted for forest products such as skins or bear oil.

After receiving the gifts, the woman, almost always consulting with the clan elders, might accept the proposal. The couple was then considered provisionally married. During the next year, the man had to help his betrothed in the fields, in effect showing respect for the sphere of horticultural production, which Muskogee women largely controlled.[22] If all went well for a year and the couple still liked each other, "they become an honest married couple when the nuptial ceremony is performed."[23] The wedding involved the whole town. Having involved their clans, their friends, and the townspeople, the seriously married couple could ill afford to make light of their bond or violate its sanctity by committing adultery. Terminating the bond was possible, but only at the Busk. However, there was "seldom an instance of their separating after they have children."[24]

By continuing to live with the same woman year after year, giving presents to her and her clan, tending her garden, and fathering children, the regular traders, whether they intended it or not, became seriously married in the eyes of the Muskogee villagers. They believed the marriage had "taken" and began watching his behavior carefully. After that point, it mattered little what the trader thought or intended. He had involved himself in tight communal bonds that were difficult to break.

The Anglo-American traders whose marriages to Muskogee women displayed great loyalty and longevity became almost fully assimilated by the village or town where they lived. There they built a warehouse to store goods, and, generally speaking, they did not like to leave it unattended for long periods of time. Unlike Muskogee men, Anglo-American traders did not go on long hunts in the fall and winter but tended to stay put, perhaps tending to a small farm or some stock of pigs, horses, and cattle. As their holdings increased, they became more and more attached to the village where their property was located. In the opinion of James Adair, while the ordinary packhorsemen, traders, and hirelings drifted through Muskogee like so many "Arab-like pedlars," the "regular traders" enjoyed more stability. If they persisted and maintained good relations with the villagers, they could achieve a very comfortable life-style. Known as "Indian countrymen" by Anglo-Americans, these traders learned the "Usages and Laws" of the Muskogees. Adair knew "white people . . . who have become Indian proselytes of justice, by living according to the Indian religious system." He further implied, with no derogatory meaning, that it was incorrect to continue to term them "christians." They had gone beyond their natal orientations and youthful training, abandoned patrilineal culture, and learned to live as Muskogees.[25]

The constant presence of Scottish, English, and African American people among the Muskogees inevitably had important cultural and material consequences. The newcomers introduced novel languages, technologies, cosmologies, and cultural practices that became key elements in an emerging culture forged in the crucible of colonial contact. Along with this unprecedented cultural formation came a new group of multicultural individuals produced by intercultural marriage. The children of English traders and captives and African runaways were too numerous to ignore. Many of the children of English traders were economically privileged; they were to play an increasingly important role in Muskogee economic, social, and political development.

Labeled "half-breed" by Anglo-Americans, these bicultural men and women may be thought of as a nascent southeastern "métis" people. (The word "métis" is French for "mixed" or "in between" and was applied by the French to the multicultural children produced by the fur trade in the Great Lakes region. The term does not carry the negative connotations of the English "half-breed.")[26] These southeastern children of the deerskin trade and plantation economics were truly people in between, a borderlands people who could claim Native American, African American, and European American ancestors.[27] By birth, vocation, and life-style, the southeastern "métis" embodied the cutting edge of the great material, social, and political transformations reshaping Muskogee. Children of the deerskin trade, many métis men and women became traders themselves.[28] Already in the 1780s they were leading a life that departed from that of their fellow Muskogees. Those who had European fathers typically possessed more private property than other Muskogees. They hunted less and farmed more. They were the men and women who started owning and working African American slaves. They were the ones who hoped to pass down their possessions to their children. As a result, they were the people who downplayed matrilineal clan identities and elevated the father's relationship to his son.

In addition to owning the great majority of the Muskogees' African American slaves, these métis displayed an increasing attachment to stock, especially horses and cattle.[29] The introduction of stock raising represented a major economic innovation among the Muskogees, but it was one well suited to their lifestyle. Aside from requiring little attention, horses and cattle flourished in Muskogee's landscape, where they could be observed foraging with deer. By the 1770s, a horse in the Muskogee tongue was called *echoclucco,* meaning the "great deer."[30] Cattle, in contrast, were received less enthusiastically. Unfenced, they raided fields and trampled crops, invariably prompting bitter protests from villagers. Because cattle were owned privately, not collectively, their presence created tension in many villages and signaled the emergence of an incipient class division.[31]

The métis began playing a prominent role in Muskogee development around the middle of the eighteenth century, and by the last quarter they had gained even more power. If we consider the chronology of contact, this timing makes sense. Intermarriage between Anglo-Americans and Muskogees had begun in the initial phase of English contact (1670–1715). Because this was the first and founding generation of the Muskogee-English deerskin trade, the offspring had not yet become historically significant. During the second phase (1715–50), the métis became slightly more significant, but still not powerful. Before 1750, cultural contact and the deerskin trade seem to have been successfully assimilated by the Muskogees. The society's traditional patterns bent, but the Muskogees by and large controlled their own affairs.

However, with the third phase (1750–83), a great transition began. The métis became more visible and assumed active roles in the deerskin trade as "Indian factors." Moreover, with changes in Georgia's laws, African Americans began arriving in significant numbers, as runaways and as traders' slaves, adding yet another cultural dynamic to Muskogee life. By 1783, some sort of threshold was crossed, and a new phase began. For the first time, the métis dominated Muskogee politics. New forms of subsistence and kinship reshaped Muskogee society and moved many of its members away from hunting and horticulture and toward a yeoman-farmer life-style. Such economic, political, and cultural changes and challenges would help bring about the Redstick prophetic revolt.

The career of Alexander McGillivray is emblematic of the rise of the métis and their effect on Muskogee politics.[32] Born in Little Tallassee in 1759, McGillivray was a very important "second-generation" métis, the son of a Scottish trader and a Muskogee/French métis mother. Like several other métis, he inherited political status from his mother's clan (the Wind Clan) and economic power from his father (a leading Loyalist trader). Educated as a young man in Charleston and thoroughly literate, McGillivray rose to power in great part because of his trade connections, but also because he revitalized the strategy of playing off European powers against one another that several generations of Muskogees before him had used.

After the Revolutionary War, the Muskogees established connections with Spanish Florida and Anglo-American Georgia by dividing themselves into two major factions, each emphasizing one alliance.[33] On the one hand, those Muskogees dominated by Alexander McGillivray maintained the connection with the Spanish, or, more precisely, with the British-manned trading firm operating out of Spanish Florida. On the other hand, an oppositional faction led by chiefs Eneah Miko of Cusseta and Hopoithle Miko of the Tallassee town of Chattacchufaulee sought trade with U.S. citizens in Georgia.[34] Throughout the eighteenth century, factionalism had helped the Muskogees avoid exclusive dependence on one patron, gain gifts from various European governments, and establish multiple outlets for Muskogee skins. In the late eighteenth century, however, the factions bitterly attacked one another. The stronger faction, centered around Alexander McGillivray, directed violence toward the weaker one, introducing "a new element of compulsion" in Muskogee politics.[35]

Traditionally, Muskogee leadership had divided itself into two major kinds of chiefs, the war and the peace chiefs. The respective power of these chiefs covaried with the situation at hand, the war chief's authority coming to the fore in times of conflict with enemies, the peace chief guiding civil government in ordinary times: "Each town has its chief or *mico,* and some experienced war-leaders. . . . The micos are counsellors and orators. . . . The warriors and leaders . . . conduct the scouts and war-parties."[36] In representing this political order, we might say its performance in history described an ellipse, a curve of political praxis generated from the influence of two "chief" positions. Sometimes the arc of leadership and action moved closer to one office and away from the other, and sometimes it hovered equidistant from each. In any case, action was always conditioned by reference to both nodes of power, never, even in times of war, by only one chief.[37]

After the Revolution and the termination of open conflict, the peace chiefs had expected once again to exercise superior authority. In terms of our metaphor, they expected the curve of power to arc toward their position and proportionately away from that of the war chiefs. However, the war chiefs resisted the cultural imperative and refused to yield power. Their refusal was inspired by the métis Alexander McGillivray. More than any other single person, McGillivray enjoyed access to and control over the flow of goods and gifts coming into Muskogee. As a silent partner of the largest deerskin trading company of the day (Panton, Leslie and Co.) and the Spanish government's main agent among the Muskogees, he served as a powerful middleman in the deerskin trade and a key player in imperial politics. Both the company and the government paid for his services and supported his authority with gifts and a regular supply of goods. No other chief could so amply reward his friends or so materially punish his enemies.

After the American Revolution, McGillivray used his economic power to restructure Muskogee politics. According to a contemporary observer, McGillivray "effected a total revolution in one of their most ancient customs, by placing the warriors in all cases over the micos or kings, who, though not active as warriors, were always considered as important counsellors." McGillivray's action did not go unchallenged; it was resisted by Hopoithle Miko and others throughout the 1780s. Just as they opposed placing total reliance on the Spanish, they strongly criticized attempts to centralize power in a Muskogee National Council and "pronounced M'Gillivray a boy and an usurper." In 1783, Hopoithle Miko and Eneah Miko signed a treaty at Augusta with the Georgians. The land cession that the treaty authorized was rejected by the National Council. At McGillivray's direction, Hopoithle Miko's "houses were burnt in his absence, and his corn and cattle destroyed." [38]

In sum, in the late eighteenth century, factionalism was becoming dysfunctional, and some métis leaders were overthrowing long-standing political arrangements. Though factionalism enabled Muskogee leaders to exploit to their own advantage the conflict between the Spanish and the Americans, late eighteenth-century factionalism plunged the Muskogees themselves deeper into conflict, forcing them to fight over the fundamental shape of their political order. The violence between McGillivray and Hopoithle Miko certainly may be viewed as a foreboding of the future. It augured the way the Muskogees would be torn apart in the civil strife of 1813. It stopped short of civil war, however, probably because McGillivray and Hopoithle Miko determined to put aside their differences and stand together to face the grave external threat presented on their frontiers in the form of the advancing Americans, especially the land-grabbing Georgians.

In 1787, Georgians killed some Lower Muskogee men to retaliate for crimes committed by Upper Muskogees. These murders alienated the Lower Muskogees and other Muskogees from their "friends" the Georgians and led to a rapport between the two major Muskogee factions. The Muskogees temporarily repressed "their internal disputes, and united all their efforts, under the great chief [McGillivray], against the frontiers."[39] Rather than fight each other, they decided to negotiate with the U.S. federal government to prevent future outrages and encroachments. In 1790, Hopoithle Miko and McGillivray traveled to New York and signed a treaty with President George Washington. Within three years, McGillivray was dead. With his death, play-off politics died, and, after 1790, the United States effectively dominated the Muskogees politically. The Muskogees could no longer compel the invaders to give them presents.

The United States supplanted gifts of friendship with ordinary commerce. Such a strategy had been attempted by earlier colonizers, but the Muskogees had always managed to compel the French, British, and Spanish to give gifts. Gifts signified respect, however grudging, for the Muskogees' power. In the new situation of U.S. domination, gift giving was repressed and its meaning distorted. Because the Muskogees were far weaker than the United States, any gift they received was considered by Anglo-Americans to be charity donated to an inferior. Far from defining a tributary relationship, these gifts took the form of alms, and any Muskogees who asked for a gift was termed by Anglo-Americans a "beggar." In short, the United States was determined to force on the Muskogees an ideology that not only repressed the logic of gifts and the egalitarian society that it nurtured but also asserted that the Muskogees could become fully "civilized" only by becoming identical to Anglo-Americans. Until the Muskogees learned how to earn their living through commercial agriculture, the United States would consider them spoiled children. Anglo-Americans would think they were justified in taking the Muskogees' "vacant" lands.

PART II

Crisis and Creativity

F O U R

The Gaze of Development

"Here the soil is a dark clay, covered with long grass and weeds, which indicates a rich soil." Thus Benjamin Hawkins, writing in 1799, described Muskogee land along the Alabama River, land that later became known as the Black Belt. Descriptions of Muskogee land are plentiful in Hawkins's "Sketch of the Creek Country." Along the Flint River, "the growth of timber is oak, hickory, and the short leaf pine; pea-vine on the hill sides and in the bottom, and a tall, broad leaf, rich grass, on the richest land. . . . The whole is very desirable country." Near the Tallapoosa, on one of its large feeder streams, "the timber is red oak and small hickory; the flats on the stream are rich, covered with reed; among the branches the land is waving and fit for cultivation."[1]

In 1796, Hawkins had been sent by George Washington to bring a "plan of civilization" to the Muskogees and alter their society in fundamental ways. To a remarkable degree, Hawkins occupied the power vacuum created by Alexander McGillivray's death a few years earlier. Using his power as U.S. agent, Hawkins assumed a Muskogee title that had been invented for McGillivray, *Isti atcagagi thlucco,* which, translated, meant "great beloved person." *Isti atcagagi* (beloved men and women) were respected elders who counseled chiefs. By modifying the title with the adjective *thlucco* (great), the Muskogees signified that McGillivray exercised unrivaled power. As the Muskogees' *Isti atcagagi thlucco* and the U.S. government's representative, Hawkins enjoyed special authority to call regional and national councils of chiefs, to distribute the government's annuities to Muskogee headmen, and to mete out justice to criminals. As an enlightened educated agrarian, he lectured the Muskogees on farming and built a model plantation to encourage them to attend to stock, spin cloth on the loom, and rely on commercial agriculture to clothe and feed their families.[2]

Wherever the eye of the U.S. agent turned, it appraised Muskogee's fitness for agriculture, always noting where "improvement" had taken place and calculating how the land might provide greater profits to his native charges. The Agent observed that mossy shoals provided food for stock; a "never-failing stream" appeared "fine for mills"; red earth indicated the presence of iron ore; large stones were "fit for mill stones"; some soils were "well suited for wheat"; others were good for tobacco or even cotton.[3] In short, everywhere he looked, Hawkins saw a landscape of great potential. In his eyes, Muskogee was an area begging for "improvement."

Such an appraisal was not unique with Hawkins. When traveling through Muskogee, other Anglo-Americans had perceived a rich land ripe for cultivation and settlement. Writing in 1791, an earlier representative of the United States, actually a spy, Caleb Swan, enthusiastically described Muskogee's economic potential. According to Swan, the rivers "might be navigated with large boats." On streams, an "abundance of small waterfalls" meant that there were "mill-seats of constant water to be had, in all parts of the country." The land was "well watered," "well timbered," and dotted with "useful mines and minerals." Indeed, Swan felt the region's agricultural potential unlimited: "The country possesses every species of wood and clay proper for building, and the soil and climate seem well suited to the culture of corn, wine, oil, silk, hemp, rice, wheat, tobacco, indigo, every species of fruit trees, and English grass." With rhetoric that echoed that of early promoters of New World colonization, Swan asserted that the "inviting, fertile and extensive country" near the Muskogee town of Tallassee was "capable of producing every thing necessary to the comfort and convenience of mankind."[4]

Nearly twenty years before Swan had made his observations, William Bartram traveled through Muskogee "discovering and collecting data for the exercise of more able physiologists." He described "large rich savannas of natural meadows" and "wide spreading cane swamps" that were "incredibly fertile." He discerned that coastal areas, "when properly drained and tilled, would be suitable for rice." Like Swan, Bartram also spotted a specific region of Muskogee that promised unlimited wealth; Bartram located his planters' paradise in northern Florida (southern Muskogee). He contemplated what progress might bring:

> almost every desirable thing in life might be produced and made plentiful here, and thereby establish a rich, populous, and delightful region; as this soil and climate appears to be of a nature favourable for the production of almost all the fruits of the earth, as Corn, Rice, Indigo, Sugar-cane, Flax, Cotton, Silk, Cochineal, and all the varieties of esculent vegetables; and I suppose no part of the earth affords such endless range and exuberant pasture for cattle, deer, sheep, &c.: the waters every where, even in the holes in the earth, abound with varieties of excellent fish; and the forests and native meadows with wild game, as bear, deer, turkeys, quail, and in the winter season geese, ducks, and other fowl; and lying contiguous to one of the most beautiful navigable rivers in the world, and not more than thirty miles from St. Mark's on the bay of Mexico, is most conveniently situated for the West India trade, and the commerce of all the world.[5]

This great commercial destiny remained unrealized only because the region lacked "industrious planters and mechanics." Bartram linked their absence to the presence of native peoples. It is telling that even a thinker as sympathetic and responsive to the Muskogees as this Quaker naturalist could not refrain from engaging in a fantasy of English settlement and commercial development. The realization of this fantasy would almost certainly require a reduction, if not a complete denial, of Native American sovereignty.[6]

Other Anglo-Americans directly attacked native sovereignty in the name of improvement. Caleb Swan considered the Muskogees' presence a troublesome obstacle to development. The Muskogees, he felt, spent far too much time in hunting and far too little in "agriculture and the pursuit of mechanic arts." He was deeply and personally annoyed to see Muskogee's land unexploited: "It might give pain to a traveller, who now must view [Muskogee] but as a forlorn rude desert, which with a little labor might be made to 'blossom like the rose.' "[7]

By Swan's reckoning, the Muskogees' refusal to farm was a violation against reason. It was almost as if Swan felt that the land itself cried out for Anglo-American farmers to rescue it from neglect: "At present it is but a rude wilderness, exhibiting many natural beauties, which are only rendered unpleasant by being in possession of jealous natives." Disregarding the fact that Muskogee sovereignty was guaranteed by treaties with the United States and Spain, Swan also ignored the Spanish possession of Mobile. Swan asserted without hesitation, "The country . . . must, in process of time, become a most delectable part of the United States; and with a free navigation through the bay of Mobile, may probably, one day or other, be the seat of manufactures and commerce."[8]

Swan's opinions articulated well the prevailing sentiments of Anglo-Americans and especially those of leading officials, at both the state and the national level.[9] In the late eighteenth century, Anglo-Americans were invading western territories on a massive scale. Just north of Muskogee, thousands of them took over Muskogee and Cherokee hunting grounds as well as the old Shawnee homeland and created the new states of Kentucky (1792) and Tennessee (1796).[10] Farther to the north, settlers swarmed across the Ohio River, invading lands belonging to the Kickapoo, Miami, and other groups. By 1803, they had formed the new state

of Ohio. To the west of Muskogee, Anglo-Americans began settling along the Mississippi River. By 1798, nearly five thousand
Anglo-Americans, thirty-five hundred African American slaves,
and two hundred free African Americans occupied the Mississippi Territory.[11] Even closer to Muskogee, Anglo-Americans migrated with their horses, cattle, and stock to the rich cane and
grasslands above Mobile, forming communities known as Tensaw and Bigbe, of which more later.[12]

Though fearing attacks from Muskogees, Cherokees, and
other native peoples, settlers did not hesitate to squat on good
land, even if it meant moving uncomfortably close to native populations. Rather than limit their own advance, frontiersmen determined that it was the original inhabitants who "must" and
"will be circumscribed" and be confined to shrinking areas of
land.[13]

Native American sovereignty (and U.S. law) was similarly ignored by southern states such as Georgia. In 1795, Georgia un-
scrupulously and illegally offered to sell millions of acres of Muskogee, Chickasaw, and Choctaw land to speculative companies.
Though the "Yazoo Sale" and other grand colonization schemes
quickly collapsed, the migration of Anglo-American settlers continued apace.[14]

These migrations, invasions, and speculative schemes incarnate
an early and originary version of what American historians term
"Manifest Destiny."[15] After the Revolutionary War, victorious
Anglo-Americans believed that most of the North American con-
tinent should belong to them, and they determined to settle it.
As early as 1784, Thomas Jefferson imagined and sketched the
borders of fourteen imaginary Trans-Appalachian states. He
nominated these western states "Sylvania, Illinoia, Michigania,
Saratoga, Cherroneus, Pelisipia, Metropotamia," and so on.
While the names were sometimes fanciful, the intent was not.
Soon afterward, Congress, with the Northwest Ordinance
(1787), provided the political framework for transforming Na-

tive American lands into territories and territories into states. By incorporating the West, the United States would eventually gain thirty-one new states.[16]

While the phrase "Manifest Destiny" aptly describes the overarching ideology by which American officials justified their nation's continental imperialism, the concept becomes less useful when attention is turned to the grass-roots level of yeoman farmers looking for land. In describing and analyzing the particular ways settlers themselves related to Native American lands and Native Americans, to Muskogee and the Muskogees, a different approach is needed. We must inquire how Anglo-American settlers brought to bear on Muskogee and its people a historically specific way of seeing, a practice of viewing and evaluating that I call *the gaze of development*.[17]

The gaze of development was that cultural and economic grid and logic through which Anglo-Americans unrelentingly processed all land. It was traditional, taken for granted, unreflectively applied, and extremely practical. Originally derived from the unprecedented early modern expansion of European towns, cities, and Old World markets, this gaze or vision was by the late eighteenth century second nature to Europeans and European Americans. Centuries of draining swamps, clearing forests, building roads, planning and planting towns, producing stable crops, and trading them on an international market had trained Europeans and their descendants to view land as an assemblage of resources open to human manipulation and commercial exploitation.[18]

As heirs to this tradition, Bartram, Swan, Hawkins, and many others unhesitatingly applied the old vision to the new land. They never saw Muskogee's fields and streams in the ways that the Muskogees saw them, animated with a thousand nonhuman spirits, some dangerous, some seductive, some friendly. From the European and Euro-American perspective, the land was aching for development. Everywhere the eye turned, the gaze of development weighed the land's potential for improvement, calculating how best to turn this soil to use, to utilize this mineral for manufacture, this stream for commerce.[19]

As their eyes fixed on and classified the streams and soils of Muskogee, Euro-Americans like Swan and Hawkins were simply reapplying old habits of perspective, calculation, and evaluation that they and their ancestors had earlier applied with such profitable success to Georgia, Carolina, Virginia, Ireland, and the Old World itself. Just as those earlier exercises in colonization involved a peculiar form of violence, so too did this more recent one. This was a violence against the land—more precisely, a religious assault against the spirits of the land, the spirits of the streams, the spirits of the forests. To Anglo-Americans like Swan and Hawkins, Muskogee was spiritually void, inert, passive, safe. According to their imagination, the land was silent, mutely awaiting improvement and plantation.[20]

Although Hawkins, like almost all Anglo-American settlers, imposed the gaze of development on Muskogee, he attempted to inculcate this vision within the Muskogees themselves. His mission, the task set for him by Congress and the president, was to determine if Native Americans could learn to live, think, and work like ideal Anglo-American settlers, if they could adopt the gaze that appraised nature primarily in terms of its economic value for commercial agriculture and intensive husbandry.[21]

Hawkins invested his whole heart in his mission, leaving the U.S. Senate (Hawkins was one of the first two senators from North Carolina) and moving to Muskogee in 1796.[22] He remained there until his death in 1816. Because his dedication suggests that he believed very strongly in the experiment, it seems fitting to describe him as a kind of enlightened missionary of agrarian civilization, a champion of the gaze of development.

Like Jesuit, Dominican, and Capuchin missionaries who brought Catholicism to the New World, Hawkins initiated his mission by traveling among the people, learning some of their language, and familiarizing himself with their customs.[23] After a couple of years, he moved to a "log hut" in Coweta Tallahassee, a village close to Coweta on the Chattahoochee river. Here Hawkins, as principal temporary agent, located his first agency. Through example and teaching, he gave practical "instruction to" his "red charge, in plowing, raising stocks of hogs and cattle, in gardening, fencing, spinning and weaving, in lectures on the government suited to the relative situation of my hearers, acting as a practical physician and lecturing on physic." By 1799, Hawkins had established a large "garden well cultivated and planted with a great variety of vegetables, fruits and vines and an orchard of peach trees." The agency also included a blacksmith (another was located in Tuckabatchee) to make plows and other iron goods for the Muskogee, services that proved very popular. The intent was "to introduce a regular husbandry to serve as a model and stimulus, for the neighboring towns who crowd the public shops here, at all seasons, when the hunters are not in the woods."[24]

Aside from his own example, Hawkins lifted up that of his métis subagent, Alexander Cornells (Oche Haujo). Cornells was related to important English and métis traders and to the most important chiefs in Tuckabatchee, including Tustunnuggee Thlucco (big warrior), who became principal chief in 1802. Across the Tallapoosa River from Tuckabatchee, Cornells, who owned nine slaves, built what Hawkins considered a model farm: "the fences well made and straight, his garden 150 feet square, well spaded, laid off and planted with the variety usual in good gardens. . . . He is very attentive to all improvements . . . and has now prepared a field of two acres for cotton." Located half a mile from this farm, the subagency, which was also under Cornells's direction, included a blacksmith, a post rider, and accommodations for travelers. Thus, Cornells became a notable and controversial player in Muskogee affairs, and the subagency became an important locus in the plan of civilization.[25]

Ideologically, it is clear that the aims and intents of the plan of civilization put into practice the expansionist policies officially promulgated by high government officials, including George Washington, Henry Knox, and Thomas Jefferson. Yet Hawkins also practiced the modern and self-conscious pedagogy of a modern reformer. His work, though completely neglected by historians of education, aligns with some of the most innovative pedagogy of the late eighteenth and early nineteenth centuries.

Specifically, Hawkins's work in Muskogee followed with astonishing fidelity the shape of "experiments" performed by Johann Heinrich Pestalozzi (b. 1746) in Switzerland. This important educator, a contemporary of Hawkins's, focused his efforts on training European peasants for industrial work. He aimed to inculcate habits of discipline, thrift, and sobriety in the populace. Pestalozzi's pedagogy strongly emphasized practical exercises as a mode of educating children, and he especially valued the careful labors involved in spinning and gardening.[26]

Though directed at a different population, Hawkins's pedagogy was methodologically identical to that of a Pestalozzi. Where this famous reformer "civilized" peasants through new techniques of teaching, Hawkins used the same methods to "civilize" Muskogees. A striking similarity was the signal importance that Hawkins's plan gave to working models, for example, the farm as a teaching device.

Like Pestalozzi's experiments in Switzerland, Hawkins's first agency failed to take hold; the millennium of enlightenment did not arrive in Muskogee. The agent's plan aroused considerable resentment. Hawkins apparently realized that his project was in trouble from the very start. As he reported in 1797, the Muskogees did not like it: "The Indians have had it seriously under deliberation to ref[use offers] of husbandry and Smiths. . . . They told me they did not understand the plan, they could not work, they did not want ploughs, it did not comport with the ways of the red people, who were determined to persevere in the ways of their ancestors. They saw no necessity why the white people should change the ways of their ancestors." Writing in 1799, Hawkins admitted, "the agent entertains doubts, already, of succeeding here in establishing a regular husbandry, from the difficulty of changing the old habits of indolence, and sitting daily in the squares, which seem peculiarly attractive to the residenters of the towns."[27] In other words, the reformer encountered resistance from the very people he had come to enlighten. Though he offered "a model and stimulus" for regular husbandry, the plan literally and figuratively failed to move the folk.

Indeed, it was Hawkins who had to move, beating a retreat eastward toward civilization. Moving from the Chattahoochee to the Flint River, Hawkins moved farther from the heartland of Muskogee and closer to Georgia. Claiming land provided to the federal government by the Treaty of Coleraine (1796), Hawkins built his new agency where the Flint River crossed the historic trade route between Anglo-Americans and the Lower Musko-gees. The new agency was but two or three days from the Oconee River and Milledgeville, a thriving commercial and political center for the state. Based on the strengths of this new location, Hawkins felt the new agency's prospects for success "infallible." Since he had recently been commissioned principal agent on a permanent basis, he determined to build a much larger and more impressive model of civilization.[28]

If the first agency was a small farm, the second deserves to be termed a plantation. Like a plantation, it was a compact settlement that organized a wide range of subsistence and commercial activities in one community of artisans and slaves under the guidance of a single patriarch: "The agent has a large farm under regular cultivation and raises corn, wheat, rye, barley, oats, rice, cotton and flax and all the fruits and vegetables which can be procured from the northern states. . . . There is a Saw and grist mill, a Blacksmith shop, a tanyard, hatters shop, boot and shoe-maker, a tinman and cooper, cabinet workman and wheelwright, a staiemaker, a weaver." Several dozen slaves cleared and plowed fields, constructed cabins, assisted artisans, and performed other manual tasks at the agency.[29]

Unlike a plantation, however, the agency received heavy federal subsidies and did not have to turn a profit. This meant that the agency was less oriented toward the market, not dependent on cash crop production, and free to allocate energies and personnel to the civilizing mission. To the latter end, Hawkins employed "An instructor in spinning and weaving, and a School-master and a house for the Indians who visit at the agency for amusement and instruction. There are two Looms at the agency, one of them appropriated to instructing the Indians in weaving, the other occasionally in weaving cloth from the thread brought by the Indian spinners." [30] Hawkins also used two blacksmiths, who were public employees, to steer the Muskogees toward agriculture and away from hunting. The blacksmiths (one located at the agency, the other at Cornells's subagency among the Upper Muskogees) repaired plows free of charge but charged for the repair of guns and traps.

In sum, the agency provided an intense laboratory for remaking Muskogee society. In terms of material culture, it emphasized the homesteading skills and techniques of spinning, weaving, plowing, and making fences. Economically, it stressed the importance of producing marketable goods and knowing the value of a dollar. Hawkins paid Muskogee women for hickory oil, cotton thread, bushels of corn, tobacco, fowls, eggs, butter, cheese, groundnuts, peaches, turkeys, hand-woven baskets, fans, and homespun cloth. Hawkins urged Muskogee men and women to plant cotton and peaches and raise livestock, not only horses and cattle, but also hogs, goats, and even sheep. By offering a market for farm products, Hawkins intentionally encouraged "a knowledge of weights and measures, money and figures." [31]

By encouraging the shift to a life based on intensive husbandry, Hawkins and U.S. policymakers hoped to change Muskogee culture and society radically and make their land available to Anglo-American settlers. As the hunt declined and commercial agriculture intensified, the Muskogees would find it possible to live within a much smaller compass. They could pay their trade debts by selling unneeded "waste" land to the United States. If men stayed home more, they would certainly participate more actively in the life of their women and children, and the nuclear family would supplant clan ties. As the clans weakened, clan vengeance, an uncivilized practice, would be abandoned. The Muskogees would abandon the traditional practice of reciprocal retaliation and accept due process. At the same time, because the people would now practice agriculture and especially stock raising on a much more intensive scale, villages would have to disperse or "settle out" to care for their crops and stock better. This life-style also entailed a moral revolution. As families controlled more property, they would cease thievery and learn to respect Anglo-American principles of ownership and inheritance. Ultimately, the Muskogees would become good yeoman farmers, settlers with a slightly darker skin and some quaint ethnic memories. The men would display "the manners of a well bred man," the women the "neatness and economy of a white woman."[32] This was Hawkins's dream.

It was a dream dreamt to keep a nightmare at bay. Hawkins was convinced that, if the Muskogees did not transform themselves into "white" people, they would have no decent future in the Southeast, in a society increasingly dominated by the plantation system and slaveholders.[33] Since the Muskogees and other native groups offered an alternative way of life from those prescribed by slavery and an alien territory where runaway slaves might find refuge, slaveholders opposed the presence of free native peoples controlling their own land in the Southeast. As South Carolina and Georgia colonists devoted themselves ever more deeply to slavery, vastly increasing the African American and Anglo-American population and greatly expanding staple crop production, they tried to absorb the Muskogees and other southeastern groups into the binary racial system or push them out of the Southeast altogether. In short, planters and frontiersmen gave the Muskogees and other groups three options: move west of the Mississippi, become slaves like the majority of African Americans, or be killed.[34]

In the face of these terrible options, Hawkins and other enlightened Americans championed a fourth. Native Americans could assimilate and become "white." While it might have appeared more benign and carried greater moral authority than the others, the assimilationist plan was nonetheless hostile to Native American particularity. A dream of Anglo-Americans, the assimilationist plan intended to dilute the last drops of Native American blood in an ocean of European blood and, in the sanguine words of Thomas Jefferson, "finally consolidate our whole country to one nation only."[35] Instead of serving to explore and affirm existing differences and generate new, precocious forms of difference, the plan embraced incorporation, finality, unity, closure, the removal of the problem of cultural opposition, the termination of contact.

The assimilationist disregard for the integrity of Muskogee culture was perhaps nowhere more openly expressed than in the way Hawkins opposed native models of gender relations. Governmental planners such as Hawkins wanted to replace matrilineal social relations with patrilineal family relations. By attacking matrilineal relations, Hawkins was denying the validity of essential social and cultural patterns long established among the Muskogees. This reveals the hegemonic or domineering character of the plan of civilization, its inability to allow Muskogee self-determination. The plan of civilization would tolerate intermarriage, but only as defined from the official Anglo-American perspective. Marriage was to be patriarchal, patrilineal, and nuclear or independent of clan ties. As the champion of this plan, Hawkins felt that he had to resist any sexual involvement with Muskogee women, and he displayed self-restraint.

Unlike most Anglo-American men living in the Muskogee country, Hawkins refused to take a Muskogee wife. In fact, according to his letters, journals, and writings, he refused to engage in any romantic or sexual liaisons with Muskogee women. There is no question that he had ample opportunities and considerable interest. He was hardly in Muskogee a season when Muskogee women tried to involve him in a "make haste marriage":

> The mother of Mrs. Barnard called at my lodgings and requested I would accept her daughter, a young widow, during my residence here [at Timothy Barnard's farm on the Flint River], or as much

longer as I thought proper, recommending her for her cleanliness and attention to the white people, and for being the mother of three beautiful children, and that she could speak Creek and Uchee.

Hawkins turned the offer down, or, rather, seized it as an opportunity to advocate civilization and the overthrow of Muskogee matrilineal family relations and clan ties:

I do not yet know whether I shall take one of my red women for a bedfellow or not. But if I do, if it is for a single night, and she has a child, I shall expect it will be mine, that I may clothe it and bring it up as I please. . . . The wife must consent that I shall clothe them, feed them and bring them up as I please, and no one of her family shall oppress my doing so. . . . The red women should be proud of their white husbands, should always take part with them and obey them, make the children obey them. . . . She must promise me this, her mother must promise it to me, and all her family.

In response, the mother of Mrs. Barnard "remained silent, and could not be prevailed upon to acquiesce in the conditions proposed. She would not consent that the women and children should be under the direction of the father, and the negotiation ended there."[36] On this vital issue, the two cultures were at absolute loggerheads.

In a letter written to an Anglo-American female friend, Hawkins described an intimate encounter with another Muskogee woman:

Very early one morning she came to my bed side, and sat down. . . . "My visit is to you. I am a widow. . . . I have a fine stock of cattle, I wish them to be secured for my use and for my son. . . . If you will take direction of my affairs, the Chiefs have told me that you may settle my stock where you please and it shall be safe. When you go to Tookaubatche you will have a home, maybe I am to[o] old for you, but I'll do any thing I can for you. . . . If you take a young girl into the house I shall not like it, but I won't say one word; maybe I can't love her, but I won't use her ill. . . . When you was in the upper towns last year I come twice to see you, and drest myself. You took me by the hand and asked me to sit down. I wanted to speak to you then, but I could not. I said then I would never have an Istechate (red man)."

Hawkins savored her speech and appearance:

> I immediately rose up in my bed and took her in my arms and huged her, my hands wandered to certain parts the most attractive and she resisted not. Which were they? The milk pots. She was about 23 years of age, plump built, not tall, of coper colour, full breasted, her face regular, with the appearance of neatness in her dress. . . . I replied to her, huging her in my arms, you shall be gratified. You may return home. . . . If you desire to call me *chaehe* (my husband) do so.[37]

Despite Hawkins's attraction to this woman, the agent consistently refused to enter any liaison that might involve him in matrilineal social ties and interfere with "the plan of civilization." He consistently shunned the attempts to Muskogee women to bind him to themselves, their clan, their people, their traditions.

The dynamic here was not just psychological. In this case, the personal was also political; Hawkins's chaste behavior embodied at an individual level the new set of power relations between the United States and Muskogee in the late eighteenth century. By 1800, the United States possessed sufficient material, economic, and demographic strength to overwhelm the Muskogees. Indeed, even a single state, Georgia, had little to fear from the Muskogees and much to gain by exploiting their neighbors' relative weakness. Georgian officials routinely threatened the Muskogees with terror and destruction. As early as the 1780s, the Georgians felt there was nothing wrong in holding chiefs hostage and forcing them to sign treaties ceding land. In short, on a macropolitical scale, the relationship between the United States and Muskogee was one of domination or nonreciprocity, of Anglo-American "fathers" ruling over Muskogee "children."

Hawkins reproduced this pattern on the individual level of his everyday interactions with the Muskogees, including those with Muskogee women. Though the Muskogee women offered him modes of contact and participation that he found hard to resist, he did resist. Through sexual restraint and various other means, including the writing of hundreds of letters back east to his educated friends, he preserved the same patrilineal Anglo-American identity he had before he entered Muskogee.[38] Hawkins, in short, was human. He could not easily overcome his cultural perspective any more than the Muskogee women could. Like them, he was reluctant to give up the key values and expectations that had shaped his identity. He could move and change, but there were real limits to how far and how fast he would go.

While acknowledging the positive intentions of Hawkins's methods and ideology, it is important to stress how much of his educational work merely reinforced economic developments already present in Muskogee. As one of Hawkins's rivals noted, the U.S. agent greatly exaggerated his material impact. Writing from Paris in 1802, Louis LeClerc Milfort, who had been a close companion of Alexander McGillivray, scoffed at the claims contained in one of Hawkins's annual reports, which was reprinted in the *Gazette de France:* "With respect to the five thousand peach trees [Hawkins] claim[s] to have distributed, the author has no doubt forgotten, or never known, that the Creeks have such an enormous quantity of peach trees that one encounters them at every turn. After this, one may judge the importance of this gift."[39]

The Muskogees probably knew almost every crop, animal, and technique featured at the agency before it was established. Much of European material culture had already been introduced by traders and other immigrants. Well before Hawkins arrived, Richard Bailey, Robert Grierson, Joseph Cornells, and Timothy Barnard farmed land in Muskogee. Throughout the eighteenth century, an irregular stream of runaway slaves joined the Muskogees and undoubtedly informed them of recent farm innovations. "Wherever [African Americans] are," Hawkins observed, "there is more industry and better farms."[40]

Further, the sort of life-style preached by Hawkins had already taken hold among significant sectors of Muskogee society and in particular geographic regions of Muskogee. Without Hawkins's help, in the last quarter of the eighteenth century, the métis off-spring of European traders and Muskogee women had adopted practices associated with the yeoman farmer life-style. They had turned increasingly to stock raising, market crop production, sedentary living, patriarchal family relations, formal education for children, greater independence from clan and village, and a more substantial commitment to acquiring private property, including slaves. Among some Muskogees, the frontier-settler way of living supplanted the more mainstream horticultural-hunting strategies. In the Upper Muskogee country, for example, relatives of the late Alexander McGillivray tended ample stock, fenced their fields, and owned more slaves than any other group of Muskogees.[41] In short, they were pioneering well before most Anglo-American pioneers arrived.

Along the peripheries of Muskogee territory, this pattern was even more pervasive, particularly to the southwest in the forks of the Alabama and Tombigbee rivers. Here, the development of the river bottom settlements of Tensaw and Bigbe, again completely independent of any U.S. agent, began during the era of French control, accelerated with English occupation after 1763, and became significant with Spanish sovereignty over West Florida (after 1783).[42] During the latter phase, many of the more "wealthy half bloods" mingled with Anglo-American settlers in Bigbe and Tensaw.[43] Because both the métis and Anglo-American settlers owned slaves, this river bottom region mixed Muskogee, Anglo-American, and African American folk ways in a manner rarely duplicated in the Southeast.

Enjoying the access that Mobile provided to a much larger market, Tensaw and Bigbe produced a wide range of commercial products. Very early on, stock raising, which was not possible in many areas of West Florida (including Pensacola), became the centerpiece of the area's economy.[44] Black cattle thrived in the area because "wild grass and cane were here never killed by the frost." Other products included indigo, raw hides, corn, tallow, rice, pitch, bear's oil, tobacco, tar, timber, myrtle wax, cedar posts and planks, salted wild beef, pecan nuts, cypress and pine boards, shingles, dried salt fish, sassafras, canes, and staves.[45]

By any measure, the life-style of the river bottom métis represented a sharp departure from the ways of their cousins in the interior. Where their kin relied most intensely on the deerskin trade and annuities to obtain manufactured goods, the métis of the Forks settlements were dedicated pastoralists oriented toward the market.[46] Using the wealth that their trading fathers had gained in the deerskin trade, they had adopted a more capitalized mode of life. Indeed, without the U.S. agent's guidance, they had made the precise material, cultural, and economic shifts that Hawkins sought to inculcate among all Muskogees. They had positioned themselves on the cutting edge of Muskogee's "improvement." They had anticipated and profited from the fundamental economic shifts that development imposed on the region and its peoples. (These were the very shifts that plantation agriculture would later consolidate.)

This is not to say that the affluent métis had ceased being Muskogees. To say that would incorrectly presuppose that only one style of life was truly Muskogee and that the Muskogees were incapable of innovation, adaptation, and even revolution. Nothing could be farther from the truth. During the eighteenth century, the Muskogees had innovated, adapted, and to a large degree revolutionized their lives by becoming heavily involved in commercial deer hunting and the deerskin trade. In the late eighteenth and early nineteenth centuries, they continued to do so by avidly adopting stock raising. There were (and are) no wooden people in Muskogee.[47]

In this context, it is interesting and important to stress that some remarkable Muskogees adapted to the decline of the deerskin trade without abandoning their traditional culture. Unlike the river bottom métis, they found ways to practice development without turning their backs on their ancestral ways. These Muskogees, present throughout the interior, performed pastoralist innovations without sacrificing their culture's bedrock principles of reciprocity and redistribution of wealth. Just because they raised stock, they did not necessarily become market-oriented, money-mongering individuals, much to the chagrin of Hawkins: "One chief, Toolk-au-bat-che Haujo, has five hundred [good beef cattle], and although apparently very indigent, he never sells any; while he seems to deny himself the comforts of life, he gives continued proofs of unbounded hospitality; he seldom kills less than two large beeves a fortnight, for his friends and acquaintances."[48] While this behavior scandalized Hawkins, it bolstered the mainstream ethic of hospitality, generosity, and redistribution.

Other Muskogees showed similar creativity within tradition in the way they handled African slavery, another key aspect of the pastoralist life-style. Rather than working their slaves to exact as much profit as possible from the land, these slaveowners were satisfied if the slaves produced enough to meet basic subsistence needs for themselves and their owners; beyond that, the slaves could do as they pleased.

This approach, what we might term the "minimalist" strategy, outraged Hawkins. He complained that Efau Haujo, one of the prominent chiefs, made "little use" of his "five black slaves." Similarly, Hawkins disapproved of the management styles of Sophia Durant and Sehoi McGillivray, two surviving sisters of Alexander McGillivray and inheritors of his slaves. "[Mrs. Durant] is industrious, but has no economy or management. In possession of fourteen working negroes, she seldom makes bread enough, and they live poorly. . . . Sehoi, has about thirty negroes, is extravagant and heedless, neither spins nor weaves, and has no government of her family." Rather than compelling their slaves to work, Mrs. Durant and Sehoi asked only that they provide "a little wood" in winter and "a scanty crop of corn" in summer. Moreover, these women allowed their slaves to host a great Christmas party that drew African Americans (and Anglo-Americans and Muskogees) from miles around for "a proper frolic of rum drinking and dancing."[49]

The minimalist or casual style of pastoral living revealed that the Muskogees could adopt many aspects of civilization without simply imitating Anglo-American settlers. Raising and exchanging cattle could reinforce reciprocity, clan ties, and communal obligations. Wealth could continue to unite rather than divide. Instead of adopting Anglo-American ways wholeheartedly, many Muskogees tried to maintain their critical distance, refusing to let the profit motive determine their life-style or the way they treated African American slaves. Muskogees like Mrs. Durant and her sister Sehoi tried to subordinate "civilization" to their own cultural codes. In this regard, it is interesting to note that the Muskogee women who learned to pick and card cotton and sell food to traders and travelers were actually intensifying, not abandoning, their traditional economic and social role as village-based providers. In short, they knew full well how to assimilate novel economic and subsistence challenges in such a way that innovations supported rather than undermined traditional cultural and social patterns.[50]

In contrast, the affluent river bottom métis of Tensaw and Bigbe did the opposite. Rather than subordinate the pastoral life-style to Muskogee culture and principles of reciprocity, they gave the market the upper hand and boldly departed from mainstream Muskogee cultural and social patterns. Rather than translate the pastoral style into a Muskogee vernacular, they learned to speak and act like Anglo-American people and to hold their own people in contempt. Because they hunted less and farmed more, they lived by different rhythms than the rest of the people and found fewer reasons to participate in the Muskogee ceremonial cycle. They might criticize it directly, expressing "contempt for the Indian mode of life."[51] Or their disaffection might be expressed in symbolic but very important ways.

Once again, the experience of Alexander McGillivray, the most famous métis, is revealing. After his death in February 1793, McGillivray did not receive the kind of funeral that marked the final passage of the great majority of Muskogees. If standard practice had been followed, McGillivray's corpse would have been interred "about four feet deep, in a round hole dug directly under the cabin . . . in the hole in a sitting posture, with a blanket wrapped about it, and the legs bent under it and tied together." As a warrior, McGillivray would have been "painted, and his pipe, ornaments and warlike appendages" deposited with him; the grave "covered with canes tied to a hoop round the top of the hole, and then a firm layer of clay, sufficient to support the weight of a man." His relations would "howl loudly and mourn publicly for four days." For months or even years, survivors might have feared the presence of his spirit at the site. Or the dread might have ceased if it was perceived by the community that his spirit had successfully completed the passage to the "realms of the Master of Breath."[52]

But McGillivray did not join his Muskogee ancestors in the sanctioned manner. Instead of receiving a traditional Muskogee burial, he was buried as a European by the region's leading merchant in its most important entrepôt. McGillivray's corpse was interred in the Pensacola garden of his Scottish business partner, William Panton.[53] His spirit was commissioned to Christ, his bones lost to the Muskogees.

The emergence of this Christian-inspired, European-modeled, market-oriented style and approach to life among the Muskogees heralded the dawn of a new and dangerously divisive social reality. For the first time, the Muskogees found themselves internally divided by economic class. The deerskin trade had introduced market economics several generations earlier, brought English traders to live in Muskogee villages and marry Muskogee women, and led to conflicts over hunting territories with other native groups. English-Muskogee marriages had produced a new bicultural people who began to dominate Muskogee politics in the last quarter of the eighteenth century. True class divisions, however, emerged only at the end of the century, when the wealthy métis began living like Anglo-American settlers. While the majority of Muskogees practiced subsistence horticulture and relied on the commercialized hunt to gain access to the market, this small minority of Muskogees met almost all their needs through commercial agriculture and husbandry. Using land commercially, they inevitably diverged from their more numerous cousins in significant ways. As we have seen, they distributed and inherited wealth in nontraditional ways, were far more dependent on the market for their livelihood, and were much more likely to emulate Anglo-Americans culturally and religiously. The economic and ceremonial practices of the "wealthy half bloods" set them apart from their Muskogee contemporaries. The affluent métis constituted a nascent class increasingly dedicated to development and self-development. They were a class oriented toward private land ownership, consumption, and accumulation.

The rise of class divisions in Muskogee society was an event of grave religious import for the Muskogee people. Because Muskogee religion, myth, and ritual supported the ethic of reciprocity, required the redistribution of wealth, and affirmed assimilation to the ancestors and their ways, the new class's refusal to honor this ethic, to practice redistribution, and to respect ancestral models for social life contradicted the Muskogees' deepest sense of what was right and proper. In short, class stratification introduced an enemy within, an enemy related by blood and heritage but differentiated by economics, ethics, education, and even aesthetics. Because it betrayed the ways of Native American ancestors and kin, this enemy threatened to undermine Muskogee religion and wreck the web of social and natural relations this religion evoked. This was a profound and unprecedented religious crisis.

If Muskogee religion was being undermined within, it was also beginning to be contested from without. As Anglo-Americans developed the frontiers of Muskogee, they brought, not just the plow, but the Bible, held high and thumped hard by the mobile, nimble-tongued evangelists of the Second Great Awakening. Lorenzo Dow, a famed evangelist, traveled the perimeters of Muskogee, preaching salvation at the Tensaw boat yards in July 1803 and the Flint River agency in 1811. In the first decade of the nineteenth century, the Methodist church assigned a circuit rider to Bigbe, and fervent camp meetings animated the community in 1813. Most significantly, in 1807, two German Moravian missionaries settled permanently at Hawkins's agency with the express purpose of Christianizing the Muskogees.[54]

The Moravians were very patient in their approach to Muskogee religion, taking the time to listen to Muskogee views and attempting to learn the people's language. Their example should alert us to the dangers of making sweeping generalizations about Christianity or its missionaries. Moravians, Quakers, and Shakers, to name but three small Protestant groups, practiced a respectful style of proselytizing to Native Americans.[55] Perhaps because they were critical of their own society, these particular groups were relatively open to contact and exchange with Native Americans.

Even gentle missionaries, however, could provoke bad feelings. In the 1730s, for instance, John Wesley, preaching to the native peoples of Georgia, urged a Yamacraw headman to convert to Christianity. Wesley had made arrangements to learn the Yamacraws' language and was not without sympathy for their situation.[56] Nevertheless, when Wesley tried to impose his theology on the chief, the headman voiced a strong rejoinder: "Why these are Christians at Savannah! Those are Christians at Frederica! Christians drunk! Christians beat men! Christians tell lies! I'm no Christian."[57]

Aside from this direct kind of rejection, the Muskogees practiced a less confrontational, but no less effective, form of resistance to Christian missionaries, a mode of resistance they employed with great effect against the soft-spoken but persistent Moravians. Rather than point out the hypocrisy of Europeans or exhaustively debate the merits of Christian civilization, they ingeniously pretended to accept the missionary's teachings, hoping to cut short his diatribe. Eventually, even the greenest, most "unseasoned" missionary caught on, gave up, and became silent: "Br. Burckhard had a long conversation with [an old Muskogee man], and then proceeded telling him of the great love of God through Jesus Christ. He was quite attentive and gave the usual Indian response. 'Yes.' This is their answer to all matters spiritual. They are most anxious to say 'yes' followed by a 'yes, yes, I know.' When asked if they really understood, it is 'yes, yes' as always."[58]

This form of passive resistance or feigned receptivity seems to have been a very common strategy of resistance among the Muskogees. Such dissimulation politely but effectively thwarted the missionizing European. Missionaries considered the Muskogees to be ignorant souls "thirsting to know the love of Jesus Christ." In the actual encounter with the ingenuous Muskogees, however, the missionaries met only dissimulating people who said they already knew all about Christ. Because the Muskogees refused to profess ignorance, the missionaries had no excuse to teach them their religion.[59]

Although institutionalized Protestant Christianity made no serious inroads in Muskogee before the 1820s, the very presence of Protestant missionaries in Muskogee signaled in its own way the increasing dominance of the United States over Muskogee. It was only in a context of cultural and political domination by the United States that these missionaries of Protestant culture and religion were able to secure a safe foothold on the borders of and sometimes in Muskogee territory. The missionaries' pulpits, in short, depended on underlying economic processes of development that rendered the Muskogees dependent and vulnerable to cultural imperialism.

Indeed, it seems a general rule that reformers like Hawkins in Muskogee, Pestalozzi in Switzerland, and Owen in Scotland appeared in history precisely when a formerly peripheral area of the world economy was being aggressively developed and more firmly incorporated by commerce and state. The reformer, with all good intentions and a sincere desire to help, promised the folk that they would benefit from the ensuing change. Passionately believing and hoping that the dystopia he knew in the old city could be evaded in the countryside, he dreamed of utopia and preached that a just society would be realized through hard work. In promoting industry and thrift, reformers inevitably glossed over the painful ruptures, asymmetric power relations, and intractable class contradictions produced by development. In the reformer's discourse, any social ills resulted because the folk stubbornly clung to old habits (collective memories, traditional practices) and did not fully embrace development. Hawkins, for example, argued that Muskogee's people suffered solely because they wanted "economy or management." They did not know how to utilize assets for maximum return. Even those métis who had acquired property failed to manifest the desired degree of "economy and neatness," and they especially failed to govern, use, and discipline their slaves adequately. As Hawkins saw things, the Muskogees had much to learn from his example. In governing their own African American slaves, Hawkins and his wife, Lavinia, were harsh taskmasters. Mrs. Hawkins had one slave whipped "50 lashes with a cowhide [strap]" for preaching without authorization.[60]

Despite Hawkins's sense of his own importance, it is certain that ongoing macroeconomic processes of development/underdevelopment preceded his arrival and would have continued without him. Nevertheless, even if Hawkins was not quite the engineer of progress he imagined himself, this does not mean that the reformer's presence was simply redundant or that his plan was insignificant. Quite the contrary, Hawkins helped the Muskogees become more fully aware and conscious of the contours of their specific historical situation, so aware in fact that, when in 1813 many Muskogees decided to revolt against Anglo-America's version of civilization, they would name Hawkins as one of their main enemies. In short, by 1813 Hawkins's pedagogy of development had become a potent force in Muskogee history, but not in the way he expected or intended.

The agency was intended as a practical model of regular husbandry. A pedagogical device of the sort that enlightened educators cherished, it was designed to promote a pastoral way of life. In many ways, the agency sought to demonstrate and produce a particular version of the future. But the agency, by the very fact that it provided such a concise and sharply focused presentation of a possible· future, invited criticism and evoked new levels of resistance. Here, we encounter a crucial fault line, a gap between intent and outcome, between author and audience.

To borrow anthropologist Clifford Geertz's conceptualization, the agency was both a model for reality and a model of reality. As a model for reality, the agency served as a blueprint for agrarian life. As a model of reality, the agency provided a simulation of Anglo-American civilization. In its latter capacity, the agency gave the Muskogees a picture of this civilization that enabled them to reflect on the meaning and implications of agrarian life.[61] Hawkins's agency provided a signal critical text for Muskogee readers.

As they visited the agency to trade, receive annuities, obtain justice (which Hawkins increasingly monopolized), or hear Hawkins's lectures on cotton culture, Muskogee observers encountered a highly contrived presentation of the meaning and form of Anglo-American civilization.[62] In one concentrated dose, they saw civilization's practices (slavery, sedentary life, cash crop production, patrilineal nuclear family), and they heard civilization's theory (hard work, moral behavior, honesty, no presents, private property, Protestant Christianity). This full presentation of the practice and theory of civilization better enabled the Muskogees to interpret the patterns of behavior and life-style practiced by affluent métis in Tensaw, Bigbe, and elsewhere.

Without the agency, the Muskogees would certainly have developed a critical perspective on the affluent pastoral métis. In the 1780s, Hopoithle Miko had already anticipated such a perspective when he opposed Alexander McGillivray, an early champion of development and commercial pastoralism. With the agency, however, it became possible for the Muskogees to greatly sharpen their critique. By looking at the agency, the Muskogees could better sort out conflicts between themselves and the affluent métis, conflicts heretofore confused with factional disputes or masked by their common heritage. The agency helped the Muskogees name the affluent pastoral métis traitors and identify them and their life-style with invading Anglo-Americans. Even as the agency intentionally championed development, it unavoidably nurtured a form of class consciousness.

The gaze and rhetoric of development, in short, encountered and evoked an unexpected rebound. "Yes, yes, yes" gave way to "No." From the underdeveloped Muskogees, people whom Hawkins termed spoiled children, there came swift and violent acts of popular justice directed against colonizing invaders and intimate enemies. From Muskogee, a land that Anglo-Americans considered silent and dead, there came a completely unexpected and baffling form of religious resistance. Thousands of Muskogees embraced a millenarian revolt that ravaged the plan of civilization and rejected the Anglo-American attack on the spirits of the land.

F I V E

The Resounding Land

In 1811 and 1812, a tremendous series of earthquakes shook much of North America and all of Muskogee.[1] Waves of energy flowed in and through the land, visibly rolling the ground and buckling its surface. In some places, gaping fissures opened, releasing jets of water, sand, and sulphur. The Mississippi briefly reversed its course, and other rivers and streams suddenly gained new falls. In western Tennessee, a fifteen-mile lake formed. Farther to the south, in Georgia, on 16 December 1811, "early at three o'clock two shocks of an earthquake were felt. The house[s] trembled and everything was in movement. The hens fell to the ground from their roosts and set up a pitiful cry. At 8 o'clock another but lighter shock was felt."[2] Still another quake occurred on 23 January.

Again, on the night of 7 February 1812, everyone in Muskogee was roused from sleep as the earth and all on it rattled and shook for a minute. For more than a week following, the Native American, African American, and European American residents of north central Georgia could "feel the trembling of the earth almost every night." At the Flint River agency, a pair of earnest Moravian missionaries thanked the "dear Lord that no damage was done." According to their counterparts at Springplace, Georgia, the Almighty God had "used concussions of the earth . . . as a warning to do away with the service to sin and listen to his voice."[3] Throughout the frontier, lapsed Christians recommitted themselves to their traditions, taking the tumult of the earth as a sign to repent and rechurch. The Muskogees (and other southeastern Native Americans) also understood the incredible series of quakes of 1811 and 1812 as a sign of deep spiritual significance, and they cast about for a meaningful and useful interpretation of the unprecedented events.

In shaping their interpretations, the Muskogee people, unlike the Moravians and other European Americans, could not turn to the Book.[4] As a Muskogee man put it, "white people have the old book from God. We Indians do not have it and are unable to read it." Even so, he averred, his people still possessed insight into the order of things: "The Indians know it without a book; they dream much of God, and therefore they know it."[5] Like traditional people in many societies, the Muskogees formed their responses to important events by rumormongering, engaging in animated discussions, circulating countless anecdotes, and dreaming new visions.[6] After the earthquakes, "flying tales daily multiplied and were exaggerated in all parts of the nation, told and received as truth by every one. . . . [These] tales had no Father for they were said to be told by first one and then another and no body could ascertain who, but the relators were at a distance in general and hard to be detected."[7] In many of these popular "Fatherless tales," the great Shawnee chief Tecumseh figured prominently. Indeed, according to some of the popular narratives, Tecumseh had stomped his foot and caused the earth to shake. In others, Tecumseh did not cause the earthquakes, but he prophesied how the Lower World would release awesome power, collapse the old order, and allow a new one to emerge.

To understand what the Muskogees meant by these claims, we must backtrack a bit to the autumn of 1811 when many Muskogees, particularly the Upper Muskogees living along the Alabama, Coosa, and Tallapoosa rivers, had begun to embrace a politics and ideology that would greatly influence how they were to interpret the earthquakes soon to follow. In September 1811, Tecumseh and prominent Shawnee prophetic shamans had traveled from their home in Indiana to visit Muskogee.[8] Promoting a bright vision of pan–Native American unity, they found avid listeners and strong allies among the Muskogees. In the previous decade, the Muskogees had witnessed the Anglo-American invasion escalate dramatically. Settlers had illegally squatted on Muskogee lands along the Oconee, Ocmulgee, Cumberland, and Tensaw rivers and legally occupied the millions of acres the Muskogees had ceded to Georgia. With settler encroachments, trade debts, political pressures from the United States, and border conflicts increasing daily, the Muskogees were ready for a new vision and strategy of resistance. Several additional factors made the Muskogees especially receptive to the Shawnees and their anticolonial message.

First, the Shawnees and the Muskogees had maintained strong, positive contacts for more than a century. In the late seventeenth century, some Shawnees had lived along the Savannah River; later, many Shawnees moved to the heart of Muskogee, forming a town on the lower Tallapoosa and intermarrying with Tuckabatchees. Based on the strength of these intimate ties, the two groups regularly sent emissaries back and forth between Muskogee and the Ohio country. In the latter part of the eighteenth century, Shawnee and Muskogee warriors hunted and fought together in Tennessee, Kentucky, and the Ohio country.[9]

Second, in very significant ways, the Shawnee experience in the late eighteenth century mirrored that of the Muskogees. Though the geography and climate varied, the political struggle was identical. In both regions, the self-designated "masters of the land" witnessed the invasion of thousands of Anglo-American settlers. These settlers disregarded treaties and transgressed boundary lines, and older chiefs, often bought off by the U.S. government, yielded to the demands of U.S. officials and continually made new land cessions. Game grew more difficult to obtain because of overhunting, competition from Anglo-American hunters, and loss of access to hunting grounds. Young warriors felt restless, frustrated, and futureless.[10] Aware of one another's struggles, the Shawnees and Muskogees nurtured channels of cross-cultural communication. From each other's stories, they learned just how massive the Anglo-American invasion was becoming.

Third, both the Shawnees and the Muskogees held an undying hope that the invasion of American settlers could be reversed with British help. Tecumseh maintained close contact with British officers at Detroit.[11] As for the Muskogees, they successfully maintained contact with the British military, even after the United States won its independence from England in 1783, in part thanks to the determined efforts of a British officer and adventurer, William Augustus Bowles.

Bowles married a Seminole woman, fomented revolt against the United States in 1788 and 1799, and declared himself king of an independent "Nation of Muscogee." His influence was greatest among the Hitchiti Seminole of Miccosooce in Florida, but he also gained supporters among other Seminole groups and those Muskogees living along the Chattahoochee River. Even Hopoithle Miko approved of some of Bowles's actions. Bowles condemned Alexander McGillivray and later Benjamin Hawkins, pillaged Panton's Apalachee warehouse, and declared "the ports of Alalhachitola, Okwetokne and Tampe free ports to all nations."[12] Through these and other actions, Bowles kept dreams of a triumphant British return alive in many Muskogee villages.

Even though they did not support Bowles, the Muskogees along the Coosa, Alabama, and Tallapoosa rivers savored the return of the British. As Caleb Swan observed:

> Their prejudice in favor of English men, and English goods, has been carefully kept alive by tories and others, to this day [1791]. Most of their towns have now in possession British drums, with the arms of the nation, and other emblems, painted on them; and some of the squares have the remnants of old British flags yet preserved in them. They still believe that the *"great king over the water"* is able to keep the whole world in subjection.[13]

According to George Stiggins, a métis Muskogee, his people "had a true magnetic predilection for the British." Like the Shawnees, most of the Muskogees "were ever partial" to the British, believing that "the English dealt with equitable justice and candor."[14]

As the scale of the U.S. invasion continued to expand and its pace quickened, Shawnees and Muskogees adopted similar political strategies. They not only looked to the British for aid but creatively promoted new forms of contact and cooperation among native groups. Acting independently of one another, the Shawnees and the Muskogees each attempted to unite their immediate neighbors in regional pan–Native American confederations fiercely opposed to any future land cessions to the United States. In the north, in 1807, the Kispokotha Shawnees, led by Tecumseh, urged Ottawas, Kickapoos, Chippewas, and Potawatomis to adopt two principles: "common ownership of all the remaining Indian lands by all the tribes, and a political and military confederacy to unite the tribes under [Tecumseh's] leadership."[15]

In the South, a similar political revolution was spearheaded by Muskogee chiefs. In 1803, at Ocheubofau on the Coosa River, the Muskogees, Cherokees, Choctaws, and Chickasaws agreed that they, "the four nations," would oppose further cessions; no nation was to sell land without the consent of the entire confederation. Repeatedly, in 1805, 1807, and 1810, the principal chiefs of the Muskogees (Hopoithle Miko, Tustunnuggee Hopoi, and Tustunnuggee Thlucco) implored the four nations to present a united front.[16]

Despite their persistent efforts, the Muskogees never successfully formed a pan–Native American union. The United States, through the influence of its agents, opposed any practice or movement that encouraged Native Americans to hold their lands in common. Such a form of land tenure made cessions and sales more difficult to obtain, and, above all, the United States wanted more land cessions. In 1803, the secretary of war instructed

Hawkins, "It would be much more desirable to see them dividing their respective territories among the peoples. . . . Each town should have complete controul over their lands."[17]

The idea of confederation and common land tenure was also undermined by conflicts that divided southeastern Native Americans themselves. During the 1770s, Choctaws and Muskogees had fought a bitter war against one another. The rift between them remained strong and soon widened. In 1805, the Choctaws, compelled to pay debts to Florida trading companies, ceded four million acres to the United States in exchange for $50,000. By acting independently, the Choctaws had rejected the foundational principles of the confederation. Even worse, in their treaty with the United States, they ceded lands east of the Tombigbe, lands claimed by Muskogees. When the Choctaw treaty (the Treaty of Mount Dexter) was ratified by Congress in 1808, the outraged Muskogees realized that their dream of a southern confederation was a failure. They lamented that "the Chaktaws . . . stole our rights and sold them to the U.S. . . . Our own color are playing tricks with us about our lands."[18]

Meanwhile, in the north, Tecumseh's proposal for a pan–Native American confederation received a mixed response. Many Shawnees refused to join his cause, but a significant number of Wyandots did. Determined to prevent future land cessions, the Wyandots, especially the younger men and women, found Tecumseh's arguments persuasive. They also responded favorably to the teachings of Tecumseh's brother, the Shawnee prophet Tenskwatawa. Ethnohistorian R. David Edmunds notes that, "for five years, from 1805 until late in 1809, [Tenskwatawa's] religious teachings were the magnet that attracted large numbers of tribesmen first to Greenville and then to Prophetstown."[19] The shaman mediated new spiritual powers that enabled political experiments, including Tecumseh's pan–Native American union.

Bolstered by the support of the Wyandots and seeking yet additional allies, Tecumseh traveled south to involve southern tribes in a grand movement of pan–Native American cultural rebirth and political solidarity. He won few supporters among the Chickasaw and Choctaw nations. His success among the Muskogee people was much greater. When Tecumseh and prophets trained by Tenskwatawa reached Tuckabatchee in September 1811, they gained a warm welcome from many Muskogees and an attentive hearing from leaders who had vigorously championed the idea of pan–Native American unity.

The Shawnee delegation, which included Kickapoos and other northern Native Americans, arrived just as the huge general annual meeting of the Upper Muskogees began. Since this meeting may have included as many as five thousand Muskogees, the Shawnees' timing could not have been better.[20] Another unexpected factor greatly enhanced the northerners' chances for success at this meeting; Benjamin Hawkins attended the conference in an effort to press for a federal road that was to be built across Muskogee. Several months earlier, Hopoithle Miko had rejected the president's request for the road in the strongest possible terms:

> You ask for a path and I say no. . . . I am glad the President has asked us without doing it first. . . . I have a little path here that the white people make use of and my people are so mischevious that I have continued complaints of my people interrupting them. . . . What land we have left is but large enough to live on and walk on. The officers must not be going through out lands to hunt paths. . . . I am an old man and speaker of our warriors. . . . I altho' an Indian have a little sense yet—the great god made us and the lands for us to walk on. . . . I hope it [the road] will never be mentioned again.[21]

Under orders from an impatient secretary of war and a development-minded president, Benjamin Hawkins, attending the general meeting of September 1811, demanded Upper Muskogee acquiescence. Hawkins's rhetoric was inflexible: "The period has now arrived when the white people *must* have roads to market and for traveling wherever they choose to go through the United States. The people of Tennessee *must* have a road to Mobile, and the post paths *must* become a road for travellers and both of these roads will be used by troops of the United States in marching from post to post as the public good may require" (emphasis mine).[22] The Muskogees at the conference resisted these demands, and Hawkins finally had to promise certain lucrative payments to the town chiefs: one thousand spinning wheels, one thousand pair of cotton cards, a few tons of iron, and the right to collect tolls along the new road. These payments won the day, and the Muskogees yielded.

Without question, Hawkins's action chafed against the Upper Muskogees. They feared that a new road would cause conflicts between Anglo-American travelers and Muskogees and bring new dangers to their homelands. By forcing the road on the Muskogees, Hawkins unwittingly provided a useful object lesson for Tecumseh and the Shawnees to exploit. Hawkins had vividly demonstrated how the American government was determined to override Muskogee sovereignty and interests.

Against this backdrop, Tecumseh's call for pan–Native American resistance must have seemed most timely and provocative. According to nineteenth-century historians who interviewed witnesses, Tecumseh reminded the Muskogees of "the usurpation of their lands by the whites, and painted in glowing colors their spirit of encroachment, and the consequent dimunition, and probable extinction, of the race of Indians."[23] This aspect of Tecumseh's message resonated strongly with Muskogees, who had a vibrant oral tradition that delineated precisely which lands had been lost.[24]

Only a few years earlier, they had witnessed a major land cession. In 1805, the Muskogees had ceded 2,225,194 acres of land to Georgia, yielding the lands between the Oconee and Ocmulgee rivers. Settlers immediately started crossing the Ocmulgee, moving toward the Flint. In response, Hopoithle Miko, "the oldest and most distinguished micco in the land," took his people's cause to the "Great Father" Thomas Jefferson:

The Muscogee land is become very small. . . . When a thing began to grow scarce it is natural to love it. . . . What we have left we cannot spare, and you will find we are distressed. . . . What I mean is some encroachments on this side of Ocmulgee. I hope you will suffer no more to be made. . . . Our agreement was plain. . . . This line is violated, and the Stock is drove over on our land. . . . My people hunting on those parts, tell me there is fields cultivated and houses made on our land. . . . Your people frequently come over firehunting and kill our game, they come on hunting bees on our land, and fall our trees, all game on our land is ours.[25]

Despite Hopoithle Miko's plea for justice and Benjamin Hawkins's efforts to protect the Muskogees' territorial rights, the settlers continued to encroach from the east (Georgia), the southwest (Bigbe), and the north (Tennessee and Kentucky). To Anglo-American settlers and slaveholders, it mattered not that "time out of mind [the Muskogees] had claims to the hunting grounds, north of Tennessee, that their old camps were to be seen there long before a white man crossed the mountains."[26] Settlers continued to hunt, cut cedar, and drive stock on Muskogee land.

By 1811, the Muskogees had collectively witnessed the loss of millions of acres of hunting lands. They had good cause to fear that they would lose everything. They knew well how little Anglo-Americans respected their rights and had even formulated a special name to describe the excessive territorial lust of Americans. Americans were *Ecunnaunuxulgee*, "people greedily grasping after all [Native American] lands."[27] Thus, Tecumseh's warning to Muskogees struck a raw and vital nerve.

Yet Tecumseh did more than touch a sore spot; he greatly shamed the Muskogees by contrasting "their sedentary . . . occupations [spinning and farming] with the wild and fearless independence of their ancestors."[28] Calling for pan–Native American solidarity, he urged the Muskogees to join in a grand movement to protect Native American lands from invasion.

Tecumseh's timely and powerful message garnered many Muskogee supporters, and, in subsequent months, several Muskogee leaders journeyed to Indiana and visited Tecumseh, Tecumseh's brother Tenskwatawa, and other northern prophets. As a partial result of the violent earthquakes of 1811–12, the movement gained many more converts. The shaking of the earth encouraged many Muskogees to engage in a grass-roots debate concerning their future. In countless discussions and stories, the Muskogee people sounded the times and formulated their own strategies for future action. Like Tecumseh, the resounding land issued a cosmological and political message.

Muskogees, as they usually did in times of crisis, turned not just to their chiefs but to their regular doctors (*alikchaki*), medicine makers (*hilís háyaki*), and knowers (*kithlas*). Experienced medicine makers could discern and treat the spiritual causes of diseases.[29] A select number of them, apparently only males, underwent rigorous training, gained esoteric knowledge, practiced clairvoyance, and could travel to secret realms of reality. They served as the priests or shamans of the town, and one of them might become the high seer, a very powerful person in Muskogee society. According to Bartram, who provides the fullest description, the high seer or shaman enjoyed

> communion with powerful invisible spirits, who [the people] suppose have a share in the rule and government of human affairs, as well as the elements, that he can predict the result of an expedition; and his influence is so great, that they have been known frequently to stop, and turn back an army, when within a day's journey of their enemy, after a march of several hundred miles; and indeed their predictions have surprized many people. They foretel rain or drought, and pretend to bring rain at pleasure, cure diseases, and exercise witchcraft, invoke or expel evil spirits, and even assume the power of directing thunder and lightning.[30]

Among the Alabamas, the seer lived in a special skin hut and performed a remarkable divination ceremony. Bossu provides a rare description of this shamanistic performance: "He enters the hut completely naked and utters words, understood by no one, in order to invoke the spirit. After that, apparently in a complete trance, he gets up, shouts, and moves about as the sweat pours from every part of his body. The hut shakes, and the spectators think this is evidence of the presence of the spirit."[31] Because they communed with extraordinary powers, the services of seers, knowers, shamans, prophets, and medicine makers were most valued in extraordinary times, times of crisis (war, disease, drought, famine).

In 1811–12, the resounding earth had forcibly reminded the Muskogees of the fragility of This World and reconfirmed the awesome power of the Lower World, the realm of the great serpent and all primordial powers of destruction, chaos, and rebirth. Accordingly, the prestige of shamans and knowers, adept travelers in the other worlds, rose dramatically. As the earth itself manifested crisis and unprecedented violence, the visions of shamans and knowers acquired greater currency and cultural power.

In this context of seismic crisis, political turmoil, and popular debate, there appeared among the Upper Muskogees a shaman with a powerful vision that initially captivated many Muskogees. Captain Sam Isaacs, a conjuror-cum-*kithla,* related his vision of "diving down to the bottom of the river and laying there and traveling about for many days and nights receiving instruction and information from an enormous and friendly serpent that dwels there and was acquainted with future events and all other things necessary for a man to know in this life."[32] As Captain Isaacs revealed, it was the powerful Tie-Snake who recklessly shook the earth and unleashed a new force for recreating the world. On the basis of this vision and the special knowledge and power that it provided him, but also because he had traveled north and visited Tecumseh and the Shawnee prophets, Isaacs acquired the veneration of a large number of people, perhaps several hundred.[33] For a while in 1812–13, he was widely regarded as the Upper Muskogees' greatest shaman.

Nonetheless, Captain Isaacs, like every shaman and medicine maker, was far from invulnerable. Because a shaman consorted with great powers, the people expected him to produce good things for their benefit. Just as the Muskogees expected most forms of wealth to be communally redistributed, they required sacred power to be socialized in the form of healings, positive outcomes in war, and successful crops. No matter how intriguing the shaman's vision, the people demanded practical fruits. The rainmaker must deliver rain, or he jeopardized his life; the medicine woman must cure, or she found herself in danger. In short, every claim to special power was subjected to intense social review, and the scrutiny was proportionate to the power claimed.

Furthermore, because the shamans' power derived from their privileged access to strange and otherworldly spiritual powers, they opened themselves to the charge that they consorted with malevolent spirits. Should their power prove counterproductive to the life of the people, they might be denounced as malicious conjurors and threatened with execution. This happened to Captain Isaacs. Having served as a great shaman in a time of crisis, he proved himself to be a traitor.

In the summer of 1812, the town chiefs, pressured by Benjamin Hawkins and obligated by the Treaty of New York, had put to death eight Muskogee men and flogged seven for crimes against Anglo-American settlers in the Ohio country, on the Duck River, and in Muskogee itself.[34] One of these men had fled to a white town of peace headed by chief Hopoithle Miko and claimed sanctuary by sitting in the chief's seat in the square ground. Nevertheless, the man was pursued and shot while on the seat by William McIntosh, a Coweta warrior and leader of the Creek National Council's police force. The following spring, the town chiefs were again compelled to punish their own people. After Hawkins learned that seven families were murdered near the mouth of the Ohio, he demanded that the "outrage . . . be settled immediately."[35] Captain Isaacs and his warriors hunted and killed one woman and several men, including Oostanaulah Kecoh Tustkey, himself a shaman who had visited the Shawnees.

While it is virtually impossible to reconstruct precisely what happened next, it is clear that these assassinations marked a turning point. From this point on, Isaacs's influence in the prophetic movement was nil. Younger leaders came to the fore, bitterly attacking Isaacs, the town chiefs who had approved the executions, and the warriors who had performed them. Despite a very sketchy historical record, these younger leaders can be identified with some confidence. They included the new Auttaugee prophet warrior Josiah Francis, the Coosaudee war chief–shaman Cussetaw Haujo, a shaman and interpreter named Paddy Walch, and the Upper Muskogee warrior Jim Boy.

Joseph Francis was the son of a Coosaudee woman and an European trader-blacksmith. In addition to Muskogean languages, he could speak English fluently. From his home in Auttaugee on the Alabama River below the juncture of the Coosa and the Tallapoosa, he actively traded with the Pensacola firm of Forbes and Company. Like so many residents of Muskogee, he was deeply in debt to that company and concerned that the company and the United States would collect payment by forcing additional cessions of Muskogee land. Francis was a *hilís háya* (medicine maker) and accordingly became known by the name Hillis Hadjo. During the early phases of the prophetic movement, he definitely exercised shamanistic powers and taught others, including Cussetaw Haujo, methods of divination. Cussetaw Haujo, also known as High-Headed Jim, was later identified as "one of [the rebel faction's] greatest warriors and prophets."[36] Paddy Walch "was a great Indian linguist speaking the creek alabama chickasaw and choctaw languages fluently." This linguistic ability reflects Walch's birth in western Muskogee. His adopted father, James Walch, was a Tory who fled to Muskogee during the Revolutionary War. Like shamans had always done, Paddy Walch made men invincible in battle.[37]

As their numbers multiplied and war chiefs joined their cause, the critical shamans boldly attacked Isaacs, denouncing him for killing his own people and polluting a sanctuary town.[38] They impugned the source and morality of his spiritual power. Such an attack carried great political import for a leader's authority was respected only so long as the community judged that the leader's action suited the precise play of spiritual powers shaping the current situation. By identifying the serpent of Isaacs's vision as a "diabolical spirit," the critical shamans asserted that Isaacs should no longer be respected. Instead of serving to restore a safe and sacred balance, Isaacs represented a threat to the community; he recklessly used the "power to injure and destroy any one he pleased." Because he consorted with an aquatic spirit, the critical shamans may well have identified Isaacs as one of the highly feared class of spiritual beings known as water cannibals, dangerous killer beings that resided on the bottoms of deep rivers and ate their human victims.[39]

In contrast to Isaacs, the critical shamans claimed a relation to a spiritual power that indisputably worked to produce proper balance, purity, and good order. In their religious teachings, they placed less emphasis on the great serpent and much more on *Essaugetuh Emissee,* "the Holder of Breath," Breathmaker, the Maker of Breath, the Giver and Taker of life.[40] Where the serpent belonged to the Lower World, this god was associated with the Upper World. The serpent was morally ambivalent. It was a symbol of raw creativity, and it was a source of chaos and conjury. In contrast, the Breathmaker was the good spirit that "extends above all things and . . . hath created them."[41] Yet, in 1813, the Maker of Breath also inspired revolution, transforming the critical shamans into prophets of rebellion against the town chiefs and U.S. officials. These religious inspirations and innovations deserve a closer look.

In 1813, the Muskogees were confronting a difficult complex of political changes and cultural challenges, internal conflicts and economic crises. Like their ancestors before them, the Muskogees relied on those powers that they experienced as most real to reveal what the people should do to survive. Muskogee politics was radically restructured by the spiritual powers of the land itself. Though the gaze of development denied these powers, it was in response to primordial powers such as the Great Serpent and the Maker of Breath that the Muskogees determined what was to be done.

Between 1812 and 1814, the Maker of Breath inspired the critical shamans and disclosed to them the great revelation that the time was ripe for anticolonial revolt. Speaking prophetically, these shamans declared to the people that the cosmos itself opposed the colonial invasion and despiritualization of Muskogee. If the earth shook, it was because the Maker of Breath could no longer stand the evils that Anglo-Americans forced on creation and on the people of the land. The Maker of Breath, the land, the cosmos, and the ancestors demanded that the Muskogee people repel the invaders—and their native collaborators as well. Thus, it was the spirit of order, not the spirit of chaos, that motivated the prophetic shamans to lead a political rebellion. Invoking the power of order and balance, the shamans gained great political authority and led the Muskogees in revolt, a revolt to restore proper balance to a terribly imbalanced reality.

According to the prophetic shamans, a sacred history was unfolding in Muskogee, and its first act required the assassination of Captain Isaacs.[42] Empowered by their spiritual vision and acting out of political outrage, the critical shamans declared that fire (a power of the Upper World) must purify Isaacs's body and the community of the spiritual pollution that he had introduced. If this purification was not performed, the prophets warned, the people would suffer greatly.

At this juncture, some Upper Muskogee chiefs, trying to restrain the prophets, sent a messenger with a taunting speech demanding evidence of their shamanistic powers: "You are but a few Alabama people. You say that the Great Spirit visits you frequently. . . . Now we want to see and hear what you say you have seen and heard. Let us have the same proof you have had." The prophets killed the messenger. Led by Hillis Hadjo (Josiah Francis), they "attacked Capt. Isaacs . . . killed him, his nephew and three more of his party." They then urged swift gestures of popular justice against several other Upper and Lower Muskogee chiefs, an unprecedented act tantamount to a revolution in Muskogee political life. Among those singled out were several of the U.S. agent's friends, including Oche-Haujo Cornells, Tustunnuggee Thlucco, and William McIntosh. The shamans demanded the death of every man involved in the execution of Muskogees: "every chief and warrior who aided to execute the murderers, then the old chiefs, friends to peace, who had taken the talks of Col. Hawkins, from whom the orders for punishing the murderers came, then Mr. Cornells, because he was the interpreter, and if they could, at the same time, to put Colonel Hawkins to death."[43]

The prophets immediately succeeded in driving off the chiefs of Autossee and other towns, and they killed four chiefs in Coosa and five in Okfuskee. It is significant, but not too surprising, that the prophets transformed the execution of "friendly" chiefs who collaborated with Anglo-Americans into a religious rite of purification, a ritual sacrifice. In Coosa, the friendly chiefs, apparently unaware of their imminent danger, were directed to sit down by a group of prophets. The prophets then circled and danced around the chiefs. Suddenly, the head prophet "gave a war whoop" and attacked, killing as many chiefs as possible with war clubs, bows, and arrows.[44]

The power of the prophetic shamans grew quickly. By early July, it appeared to a trader on the scene that "the wole of the upper towns have taken up the war Club." The war clubs, painted red, served as key symbols of the prophetic movement, and the warriors who wielded them became known by Anglo-Americans as "Red Clubs" or "Redsticks." The Redstick rebellion spread so fast that the Upper Muskogee chiefs were caught completely off guard. Even Tustunnuggee Thlucco's men were abandoning him and joining the war party. Upper Muskogee chiefs had incorrectly considered the prophetic movement innocuous—"a sort of madness and amusement for idle people." They had convinced Hawkins, their benefactor, that "the Alabama prophets were foolish people only to amuse young people."[45]

When events proved otherwise and their own people turned against them, the chiefs were ill prepared to respond. Put on the defensive, the friendly chiefs turned timid and were unable to act decisively. Fearing the prophets' wrath, the condemned chiefs "fortified themselves at Tookabaubatchee," laying in seventeen hundred bushels of corn in case of a siege and requesting that Hawkins and Georgia provide military aid.[46] In early July 1813, the prophetic shamans and hundreds of warriors surrounded Tuckabatchee. Claiming "the power to cause an earthquake," they had determined to purge their land of accommodating chiefs and domineering U.S. agents.[47]

Just as the rebellion shocked the Upper Muskogee chiefs,[48] it alarmed Georgian settlers on the Ocmulgee River. The key military man in the area, Major General David Adams, reported that people talked "of breaking from this frontier." Adams was himself worried. He considered ordering "the people to fort" because he had received a frightening report from a trader who had good contacts among the Upper Muskogees. According to the trader's story, a single prophet had instructed the Upper Muskogees "to make a hundred arrows," presumably in preparation for war. Next, the prophet had directed warriors "to kill off any of their own People if they do not take up the war Club." Claiming that he had a letter from the commanding officer of the British at Detroit, the prophet directed the Upper Muskogees to send "ten or twelve horses out of every town" to Pensacola, where they would receive "arms and ammunition" from the Spaniards or the British. Once these arms were in hand, the trader warned, "they mean to fall upon the frontier of Georgia; the Alabamas and ten towns of the Chactows mean to fall upon the Tensaw and Bigby." Needless to say, this report was one that Adams conveyed to Georgia governor Mitchell immediately, along with an urgent request for instructions and support. Sensitive to the political stakes involved in this crisis, Adams also informed the governor how frontiersmen cursed their officials: "I am blamed for not doing something to satisfy the frontier people—your excellency is blamed and Hawkins also."[49]

As for Hawkins, he too was astonished at the prophetic movement's intensity and rapid growth. Nevertheless, he acted immediately, attempting to end it as soon as possible and with the least bloodshed. He hoped that the Upper Muskogees could settle things among themselves so that the United States need not become directly involved. He directed the chiefs, particularly Tustunnuggee Thlucco, chief of Tuckabatchee, to make battle and attack the prophets before the rebellion spread. Simultaneously, he sent runners to the prophets' party, urging them to abandon their course and warning them of potential U.S. military involvement: "You may frighten one an other with the power of your prophets to make thunder, earthquakes, and to sink the earth. These things cannot frighten the American soldiers. . . . The thunder of their cannon, their rifles and their swords will be more terrible than the works of your prophets." Hawkins extended an olive branch, but couched within the offer was a crucial qualification—"If you are friendly you have nothing to fear. If the white man is safe in your land, you are safe."[50]

The prophets and their party, now led by the veteran opponent of Hawkins's meddling Hopoithle Miko, claimed that they intended Anglo-Americans no harm. Hopoithle Miko said firmly, "I am not at war with any nation of people, I am settling an affair with my own chiefs."[51] The conflict was not with Anglo-American invaders but with red traitors, internal enemies. Other rebels reinforced Hopoithle Miko's statement, but with much less concern for diplomacy made it clear that they were ready for all opponents.[52] In any case, whether Anglo-Americans came or not, the town of Tuckabatchee was destined to fall on the eighth day.

The symbolic significance of this timing would not have been lost on any Muskogees. As a multiple of the number four, the number that stood for the cardinal directions and all creation, the number eight was sacred. Moreover, eight days was the normal length of time to perform the *poskita* or Busk ceremony in important square grounds, including Tuckabatchee. Finally, the number eight was associated with the shaman's "star," Venus. During the time of Venus's inferior conjunction, the planet leaves its position in the morning or evening sky, disappears for nine nights and eight days, and then reappears in the opposite sky. Shamans considered this cycle as emblematic of their own passages to and from secret spiritual realms. Since shamans led the movement, it is not surprising that they asserted that the eighth day of the siege was "the day the town was to be sunk by the prophets."[53] Accordingly, on 22 July 1813, the rebels attacked Tuckabatchee. The "peace" party fled to Coweta, guarded by Lower Muskogee warriors from towns along the Flint and Chattahoochee rivers. Thus began the Muskogee civil war.

The events leading to this war had been significantly and unmistakably shaped by spiritual processes, authorities, and controversies. Earthquakes encouraged the Muskogees to tell stories about the awesome power of the amoral Great Serpent and imagine that the world was about to be destroyed. By describing his visions of and conversations with the Serpent, a shaman named Captain Isaacs temporarily captivated the Muskogees' attention. However, when Isaacs betrayed his own people, he was denounced and executed by a new generation of shamans. The actions of these shamans reflected deep involvement with and acute awareness of spiritual powers. Just as they interpreted earthly events through the symbolic template of sacred stories about the Maker of Breath, so they now acted politically in a way directly patterned after their most sacred rituals.

S I X

Muskogee Millenarian Initiation

The Muskogee prophetic rebellion was a religious movement that powerfully and authentically addressed and dramatized the deepest concerns of thousands of Muskogees at a critical juncture in their history. These people found their very existence profoundly threatened, and, to meet extraordinary economic, political, and cultural crises, they responded with bold and extraordinary spiritual creativity. The pattern of action that informed the revolt was modeled on traditional rites of passage and world renewal ceremonies. The Redstick millenarian movement of 1812–14 was an initiation ceremony performed on a grand collective scale.

Throughout the spring, summer, and fall of 1813, the prophetic rebellion grew. Expanding beyond its initial base among the Alabamas, the movement rapidly attracted thousands of participants from dozens of towns on the Alabama, Coosa, and Tallapoosa rivers. A few hundred inhabitants of the Chattahoochee region also joined the prophets. At its apogee, the prophetic faction probably incorporated seven to nine thousand men, women, and children. In the sacred symbols, ritual actions, cosmological meanings, and inspired purposes of this movement, at least half of Muskogee's Native American population found something of compelling power and appeal.

An industrious people, the Alabamas produced surpluses of corn for distribution among the upper towns and trade downriver with settlers in Mobile. Despite their profitable economic relationship, the Alabamas strongly disliked Anglo-Americans. In 1800, some Alabama villagers had moved beyond the Mississippi because they were disgusted with settler encroachments on their hunting lands.[1] A year earlier, in the Alabama village of Auttaugee, Hawkins had observed a singular custom that hinted at the Alabamas' true feelings about Anglo-Americans: "as soon as a white person has eaten of any dish and left it, the remains are thrown away, and every thing used by the guest immediately washed."[2] This custom suggested a deep concern for purity and the maintenance of symbolic boundaries separating Native Americans from Anglo-Americans.

The separatist values encoded in Auttaugee custom were absorbed and later promoted by the métis prophet Hillis Hadjo. Hadjo had grown up in Auttaugee. He became one of the prophetic leaders of the Redstick movement by stressing the value of strengthening cultural boundaries and purifying Muskogee of Anglo-American influence. His message was immediately popular in his home region. In addition to winning the support of Alabamas, the new teaching attracted Koasati people, who had also seen kin move west to escape Anglo-American control, and Shawnees, who responded favorably to Tecumseh's and the prophets' call for concerted resistance.

While this initial group of supporters was ethnically non-Muskogee, the movement soon incorporated the great majority of Muskogees proper living on the Tallapoosa, Coosa, and Alabama rivers. This included inhabitants of the towns of Autossee, Woccoccoie, Foushatchee, Columee, Hoithlewaulee, Ecunhutke, Muclassee, Tallassee, Hookchoi, Hookchoioochee, Ocheobofau, Tuskegee, and Okfuskee, the villages of Pucantallahassee, Nuyaka, Tookaubatchee Tallahassee, Emuckfau, Toohtocaugee, Auchenauulgau, Opithlucco, and Okfuscoochee, and many smaller settlements that consisted of only a few families. In addition to the shared cause of resisting Anglo-American domination, each community, clan, and family probably had its own motivations for joining the rebellion. Tallassees had long opposed the political meddling of the U.S. government and its agents. Their aged chief, Hopoithle Miko, vehemently opposed Hawkins and offered sanctuary to Muskogee men accused of crimes by the Creek National Council. The head warrior of Tallassee, a métis trader named Peter McQueen, was deeply in debt to Forbes and Company; he may have viewed revolt as the Muskogee people's best means of escaping further land cessions. In Okfuskee and Hoithlewaulee, relatives of men and women who had been executed by the Creek National Council craved for retaliation. The chance to express and perhaps realize these and many other hopes and desires encouraged dozens of Muskogee communities to join the Redstick movement.

A small minority of Upper Muskogees did not join the revolt. Most of them were concentrated in an area upstream on the Coosa River far from the Alabamas and the center of prophetic activity. Many of the people living in towns of Aubecooche, Nauchee, and Coosa opposed the revolt at a very early date and then fled to escape reprisals. Also opposing the revolt, but much closer to the center of prophetic strength, was the town of Kailugee and its satellite village Hatchechubba. In July 1813, several of these people were killed, and their hogs, cattle, and fowls were destroyed by the prophetic faction. The survivors fled to the town of Tuckabatchee.[3]

Tuckabatchee, a town of six hundred people located near the confluence of the Coosa and Tallapoosa rivers, did not join the revolt, and this was deeply resented by the prophets. Tuckabatchee was the most prestigious town among the Upper Muskogees because it possessed sacred ceremonial brass plates and was the annual meeting place of the Creek National Council, an organization of chiefs that dealt with matters of concern to the entire Muskogee people. Most distinctive about Tuckabatchee, however, was the degree to which it had been influenced by Benjamin Hawkins. In Tuckabatchee, Hawkins had his greatest success among the Upper Muskogees in promoting the plan of civilization. Here, the U.S. government funded an assistant agent, a blacksmith, a dwelling house, and a kitchen. Hawkins himself visited Tuckabatchee annually to attend and address the meetings of the Creek National Council. Most important, Hawkins won the allegiance of Tuckabatchee's métis chiefs by buying their produce and meat, by giving advice, and by providing gifts of money, cotton seed, sheep, peach stones, and looms.

While this may explain why they ultimately did not side with the prophets, it does not mean that the chiefs of Tuckabatchee or its inhabitants were completely opposed to the movement from the beginning. Despite their substantial economic ties to Hawkins and their own complicity in the treaty-mandated executions of Muskogees, these chiefs initially hesitated to oppose the prophets. Before the prophets signaled him out for execution, Tustunnuggee Thlucco, head chief of Tuckabatchee, contemplated joining the rebellion. He had spoken extensively with Tecumseh in 1811 when the latter visited Tuckabatchee. According to an Anglo-American trader, Tustunnuggee Thlucco had been strongly "inclined to take the talk" of the Shawnee resistance leader and was "as hostile as any." However, from the moment he was condemned by the prophets, Tustunnuggee Thlucco had no choice but to join the "friendlies." The town itself became identified as a "friendly" town, and in the early summer of 1813 it served as a refuge for scores of Upper Muskogee chiefs fearing for their lives. Meanwhile, those Tuckabatchee people who wished to side with the prophets left town and joined the rebellion.[4]

Additional Upper Muskogee communities that were internally divided included the Alabama River town of Coosada, the Coosa River town of Wewokee, and the Tallapoosa River towns of Tuskeegee, Tallassee, Hookchoi, and Hillaubee. All these towns eventually became Redstick strongholds. (Wewokee warriors were to distinguish themselves in battle against the United States.) One of Hillaubee's affiliated villages, however, did not follow the lead of its *i:talwa,* refusing to join the rebellion. This decision owed something to the influence of the village's nearby neighbors, the Cherokees, who urged the Hillaubee people to avoid fighting against Anglo-Americans, and to the presence of the wealthy Scottish trader Robert Grayson and his large métis family. The Grayson family had hundreds of head of cattle, seventy-three African American slaves, thirty horses, and eleven workers busy spinning and weaving cotton grown on their land. In early August 1813, the pro-prophetic faction attacked the village, killed twelve of its inhabitants, took Grayson's slaves, slaughtered his cattle, and forced the inhabitants to flee to the Cherokees for safety.[5]

Like the Hillaubee dissidents, the great majority of Muskogees dwelling on the Chattahoochee River did not side with the prophets. Nevertheless, many Lower Muskogees sympathized with the Redstick cause, and several hundred actually joined the rebellion. Located fifty miles below Coweta, the town of Eufaula came close to "taking the rebels' talk" and joining the revolt. As late as the end of September 1813, emissaries of the prophets were visiting Lower Muskogees, bringing them red arrows and war clubs and encouraging them to join in an attack on Coweta. These emissaries promised that "if the red people would unite nothing could withstand them." Although this prophecy ultimately did not convince the Eufaulas to join the revolt, it did persuade the Yuchis. A distinct ethnic group living on the Chattahoochee River, the Yuchis had been deeply alienated from their Anglo-American neighbors in the mid-1790s when a band of Georgians under Captain Benjamin Harrison destroyed the Yuchi village of Padjeeligua and killed sixteen of its inhabitants. Moreover, the Yuchis on the Chattahoochee must have known about the prophetic movement at a very early date because some of their close kin lived in the Shawnee town of Sauwanogee on the Lower Tallapoosa River. When the time to choose sides came, hundreds of Yuchis abandoned their main town on the Chatta-hoochee River and joined the Redsticks.[6]

Lower Muskogee chiefs and Hawkins worked hard to dissuade or coerce other Chattahoochee towns not to join the Redsticks. A prominent Lower Muskogee chief such as William McIntosh of Coweta had tremendous incentive to prevent his people from defecting. Because of his leading role in executing Muskogee men and women charged with frontier crimes, McIntosh's name fig-ured prominently in the prophets' list of chiefs to be killed. Like McIntosh, the chiefs of Coweta, Cussetuh, and other Lower Muskogee towns held the prophets in contempt and feared the consequences of war with the United States. Responding to the Redstick challenge in July and August 1813, these chiefs gath-ered a force of more than five hundred warriors, fortified the large Lower Muskogee towns of Coweta and Cussetuh, attacked the Upper Muskogee villages of Chattachufaulee and Nuyaka, sent two hundred warriors to rescue the Upper Muskogee chiefs trapped in Tuckabatchee, and brought that town's women and children out of danger to Coweta.[7]

The Lower Muskogee chiefs and Hawkins were successful in preventing a massive defection of the Lower Muskogees to the cause of the Redsticks for one key reason. Lower Muskogee towns directly neighbored Georgia and thus were subject to in-stant and harsh reprisals from Anglo-Americans. Where political geography probably emboldened a group like the Alabamas or the Koasatis, it gave the Lower Muskogees reason for fear; the Lower Muskogees had to weigh much more seriously and im-mediately the potential costs of warfare with the United States. Twenty-five years earlier, the state of Georgia had warned the Lower Muskogees that they would pay heavily for any hostile acts committed by the Muskogees: "should any act of hostility, or depredations be committed on our people by your nation, be perfectly assured we will not hesitate to do ourselves ample jus-tice by carrying War into your Country, burning your Towns, and staining your Land with blood, you will be compeled to fly for refuge to some other Country."[8] In the quarter century after issuing this warning, Georgia had grown much stronger, and the prospect of incurring its wrath certainly gave pause to the Lower Muskogees. Rather than risk annihilation, they remained loyal to their chiefs and eventually chose to oppose the Alabama prophets. As a very nervous (and relieved) Benjamin Hawkins wrote in July 1813, "The Fanatical fright seems to subside a little among the Lower Muskogees and all of them apparently are again friendly."[9] He and the chiefs of the Lower Muskogees had managed to prevent the Redsticks from gaining the additional support of three to four thousand adult Muskogee men and women.

Of course, as late as the summer of 1813, Hawkins still believed that the rebellion would soon subside among the Upper Muskogees. He mistakenly assumed that it had originated in an outburst of irrational fanaticism. In fact, the revolt enjoyed the committed support of adult men and women ripe and ready to rebel against the Anglo-American invasion and its agents. Contrary to Hawkins's belief, these were people deeply committed to a comprehensive program of religious purification and ritual renewal modeled on rites of passage for individuals and the annual Busk ceremony. Rebel Muskogees sought collective renewal and would sacrifice much to achieve it.

As among traditional peoples elsewhere, the Muskogees identified participation in rites of passage with a movement toward freedom, maturity, and responsibility. For instance, among the Muskogees, the transition from girlhood to adult womanhood occurred at first menstruation.[10] The initiate would be isolated in a separate structure away from the village, attended by elder women. She was secluded because she was in profound contact with the sacred power of fertility. She needed to learn about her new identity, and she could do this best away from ordinary life. Finding herself ritually located on the margins of the human world, she also gained an altered perspective on her culture. By contacting sacred powers, she learned that her culture was a finite order precariously pitched in a great wilderness. While this new knowledge was tremendously humbling and even shocking, it gave the Muskogee initiate mature respect for the fragility of human cultured existence. Having transgressed the limits of her culture through contact with the sacred, she now knew that she bore responsibility for giving life to the culture. Before initiation, she was a child; she returned to the people a new woman. Having contacted the spirit of the wilderness, she returned to live consciously and freely as a cultured being who could assume mature responsibility.[11]

The passage of a boy into manhood was also ritualized. Among the Cussetas, male initiation took place between the ages of fifteen and seventeen years. Secluded for four days under the guidance of *Istepuccauchau thlucco* (the great leader), a group of boys drank a purifying tea that intoxicated and maddened them. "The fourth day they go out but must put on a pair of new moccasins (Stillapica)." For one year, the boys could not eat deer, turkey, fowl, peas, and salt. "During this period they must not pick their ears, or scratch their head with their fingers, but use a small stick." This taboo was identical to one that applied to menstruating women. To achieve still greater purity, "for four moons" the boys "must have a fire to themselves to cook their food, and a little girl, a virgin, may cook for them but their food is boiled grits." With each new moon, the boys repeated the initial four-day ceremony of "physicing" or purification. Each time, they received additional special knowledge regarding manhood from the great leader. At the end of the year, they came out of their house, gathered corn cobs, burned them to ashes, and, with these, rubbed their body all over. Their initiation into manhood was completed.[12]

Among the Alabamas, the passage into manhood was not so prolonged. Alabama boys became men through contact with blood. The blood was produced externally through a profound encounter with other life forms. The transition from boyhood to manhood occurred when the boy obtained an enemy's scalp or killed his first deer or bear. The boy could not eat any of the first kill of game; thus, he learned that he hunted not for his own glory but for the sake of the people. The boy might also be beaten by clan elders, a terrifying and humbling event not re- peated at subsequent kills. In sum, among Muskogees, profound experiences of contact with vital blood entailed a loss of inno- cence and fracture of the child's identity. At the same time, how- ever, these events inaugurated a new identity for each individual and marked for the entire community the assumption of new powers for a new generation.

In a similar way, but on a much larger scale, the collective ex- periences of colonial history challenged the colonized peoples of Muskogee to assume a new identity as a people. Demographic collapse (1540–1640), the deerskin trade (1670–1812), and then the development of Muskogee (1763–1812) created an un- precedented level of change. It forced the Muskogees to confront the limits of their own culture, to undergo a radical critique of their way of life.

The colonial critique, however, did not annihilate the culture, nor did it evoke a reactionary fixation on "tradition." Rather, the colonial critique, like initiation, evoked human creativity and the painful passage to fuller and more mature life where a new form of freedom and a new sense of responsibility ennobled and deep- ened Muskogee existence.[13] Like initiation, colonial contact pos- itively heightened the Muskogees' appreciation of their respon- sibility to and for their culture.

Contact and development exposed Muskogees to the Euro- pean "civilized" way of life with its emphasis on literacy, money, property, commercialized agriculture, slavery, and stock raising. In so doing, contact encouraged intense self-reflection. Having seen some of their own people adopt the European way of life as a viable and sustainable option, the Muskogees found that they could make a choice. They could let history take its course and gradually become more and more like Anglo-Americans or Afri- can Americans, or they could explicitly and consciously chose to pursue the "red" road evoked by conscious and critical resistance and informed by spiritual interpretation.[14] In any case, because of their full exposure to civilization, they found that they had to choose how they wished to live; they collectively realized that they could freely shape and reshape their relationship to their culture, their ancestors, the land. Where before they had identified themselves ethnically as Tallasees, Okfuskees, Toowassas, Autossees, Yuchis, and so on, they now consciously, creatively, and self-critically became "red people" in the New World of global contact. They did this by improvising a grand collective rite of passage that signified the shift from one kind of identity to another.[15]

To signify their surrender of their old colonized identity, the prophets first urged the Muskogees to perform acts of negation by shedding the old and confining skin of colonial civilization. They had to strip away the old identity in order to make way for the new. The prophets challenged the people to renounce key leaders, things, practices, and symbols associated with dependence on Anglo-American civilization. Specifically, the rebels dispensed with ornaments of silver, brass, glass, and beads, implements of husbandry, hoes and axes, and other trade goods. Warriors attempted to rely less on guns and more on bows and arrows. Furthermore, rebels performed many violent acts, killing friendly chiefs and slaughtering livestock. Led by prophets, they killed cattle, hogs, and fowl belonging to friendly chiefs and Anglo-American traders. Slaughtered livestock was left to rot, or the meat was smoked and taken to rebel camps. Even more significant, the rebels killed their own livestock and abandoned their cornfields, and rebel women burned fine muslin dresses that they had purchased from traders.[16]

To Anglo-Americans such as Benjamin Hawkins, these acts of renunciation seemed purely destructive: "The declaration of the prophets is to destroy every thing received from the Americans, all the Chiefs and their adherents who are friendly to the customs and ways of the white people." The rebels' radical actions baffled Benjamin Hawkins: "One thing surprises me they have totally neglected their crops and are destroying every living eatable thing. . . . They are daily persevering in this mode of destruction."[17]

Yet this mode of destruction was oriented toward something positive beyond destruction. Acts of destruction were necessary as a kind of prelude, an opening phase within a larger transformation drama. By killing cattle, the Muskogee rebels severed the worn-out and debilitating colonial connection. By performing material acts of renunciation, they purified themselves of old identities and cleansed themselves of polluting symbols, spirits, and substances.[18] In a striking way, these acts of destruction and renunciation were homologous with those sometimes performed before the Busk. As in the Busk ceremony and other initiation rites, the consumption of salt and salted meat was abandoned. Before the Busk in some villages, people collected "all their worn-out cloaths and other despicable things, [swept and cleansed] their houses, squares, and the whole of the towns, of their filth, which with all the remaining grain and other old provisions, they cast together into one common heap, and consume[d] it with fire."[19] Similarly, in the prophetic movement, acts of destruction prepared the people for contact with sacred powers. By renouncing their dependence on Anglo-American civilization, the people readied themselves for the assumption of a new collective identity.[20]

The encounter and initiation, appropriately, took place in the woods. It was in the forests, not the village, that the Muskogees had always sought contact with wild spirits. The woods, though familiar to Muskogee men and women, was the untamed, undomesticated space beyond human control. Here, one encountered wild animals, enemies, and dangerous spirits. Yet this was also the place where medicine men and women located herbal cures and wild foods, hunters and warriors purified themselves, and shamans received visions.

Among several Muskogee groups, a springtime ceremony called *poski* required men to spend four days and nights in the woods purifying themselves. The men fasted, eating only unsalted bread, drinking an emetic medicine, and taking sweat baths. Such a ceremony brought luck in hunting. The Alabama, Koasati, and other groups performed the *ayihilká* ceremony before warfare. Similar to the *poski,* it involved fasting, sweating, and drinking ritual medicines. Men customarily performed this ceremony in the summer. Among the Koasati, the *ayihilká* ceremony was also linked to the training of shamans. Shamans received their powers through long days of fasting and seeking spirits in the forest.[21]

In the woods, something powerful and invincible fed and released life, letting deer out of a cave that they might be harvested by men and sending children to women that the people might survive. The Hallowing King spoke truly when he said, "Our life is dependent upon the woods."[22] In the spring and summer of 1813, as rebel Muskogees sought purification and renewal, they moved out of the towns into the woods to small camps. Here, they also constructed new settlements for each of the three main regional subdivisions among the Upper Muskogees (Alabamas, Tallapoosas, and Abekas). For Alabamas, Eccanachaca (the "holy ground") was built on the Alabama River in July 1813, under the direction of Redstick prophetic leaders, at a location "made sacred by the great spirit." For Tallapoosas, another settlement was built near Autossee on the lower Tallapoosa, and a third, Tohopeka, was built on the middle Tallapoosa and occupied by Abekas from Okfuskee, Nuyaka, and other nearby towns.[23]

This movement away from their towns dramatically relocated the rebels in space. As in other religions, movement in space was correlated with a passage toward sacred transformation and fulfillment. Like a pilgrimage, this movement into the woods used space and human movement in space as a concrete means of altering the people's relation to the sacred; the sylvan movement effected a fundamental reorientation of the people. By resettling in the wild woods where so many of their rites of passage occurred, Muskogees embraced communal rebirth, their collective initiation into the New World identity of "red people." Real Native Americans, as they imagined, came from the woods, so it was to the woods that they withdrew to be reborn.

Life in the woods depended to a great extent on the substantial contributions of the thousands of women involved in the movement. When the rebels withdrew to the woods, they abandoned their corn, squash, and bean fields. To compensate for the loss of these domesticated foods, men and boys hunted deer, turkey, and small game more intensely and slaughtered hogs and cattle. These efforts, however, were far from sufficient and increasingly conflicted with the men's need to prepare for war. In the first few months in the woods, the rebels survival depended primarily on the efforts of women. Women greatly increased their gathering of wild summer foods such as persimmons, muscadines, berries, china briar roots, and the seeds of the chenopodium plant and cockspurgrass. As time passed and hundreds of rebel men died in battles, the dependence on women's gathering skills grew. That the rebels survived through summer, fall, and spring without access to their regular crops is a testimony to the sustained gathering and processing efforts of thousands of Muskogee women and girls fulfilling their social role as *hómpita háya* (food makers).

While women satisfied most of the material needs of the rebel camps, men fasted and prepared for war. Most significantly, they danced. It is not surprising that dance played an important role in the Muskogee millenarian movement, for dance had always been important to all Muskogees, and, according to William Bartram, they knew "an endless variety of steps."[24] By integrating dance into their daily lives and their ceremonies, the men and women dramatically expressed and transformed their most important social, natural, and spiritual relations. Men commemorated ball play with the ball dance, war with a war dance. Other dances were less serious, more geared toward entertainment. In the old people's dance, the performers wore phallically shaped gourd masks and behaved like clowns. In the mosquito dance, the women pricked the male dancers with pins. Women exclusively performed the snow, fox, and snake dances. Countless other popular dances were named for animals.[25]

Given the importance of dance in Muskogee life, it was inevitable that the rebels would dance. Given their vast repertoire, they could have selected a familiar dance and given it new meaning. By doing so, they would have bolstered traditional identities and revitalized their existing culture. Such a strategy was apparently not radical enough, however. The times, which were threatening and promising, required an extraordinary dance performed with unprecedented energy. On the verge of receiving a new identity, the Muskogee rebels felt more than ever the need to dance a radically new dance, to move their bodies in a new way in and into a new space/time. As Loretta Czernis has noted, "Tribal peoples have always believed in dance as a sacred force, generating the power to reverse existing orders," to destroy an oppressive historical situation and recover a golden age or inaugurate a new mode of being.[26] So it was with the Muskogee rebels in 1813.

The dance of the Indians of the lakes was not a native Muskogean dance, and herein lay much of its appeal. Because it was an "import," this dance satisfied the rebels' needs for a radically new and unfamiliar dance. But what made it superior to all other indigenous and nonindigenous dances was its particular history. The dance had arrived rather dramatically in Muskogee in the fall of 1811 with Tecumseh and the Shawnee prophetic delegation. Hence, it was uniquely associated with the anticolonial resistance movement and its spiritual authority.

The dance was a war dance of the type performed by Shawnee warriors before leaving their home villages to attack an enemy.[27] This preparatory dance featured three major movements: a slow rather formal initial phase performed by a core group of honored warriors; a more animated second phase performed by an individual warrior who acted out his glorious victories and cajoled his fellows to seek vengeance; a final climax movement that involved the entire party in a very loud mock battle. This tripartite dance was observed and described in 1786 by a military officer visiting the Shawnees:

> Eight or ten of the most active men stripped themselves quite naked, except the breech cloth, painted their bodies so as to have a horrid appearance; armed with tomahawk and scalping knife, they formed a circle, danced moderately to a mournful tune for ten or fifteen minutes, gave the war-whoop, and sat down together on seats placed for the purpose. They now hung their heads—a dead silence for a short time; one gets up, dances and capers to the music—repeats his exploits, the injuries they had sustained, urging the others to be strong, and rise and revenge themselves upon their enemies. At length, they are roused, one after the other, until all get up, when they commence the most tremendous yelling, jumping and figuring about in imitation of shooting, scalping and tomahawking, exerting themselves exceedingly, until a signal is given for silence.[28]

The Shawnee prophets taught a variant of this war dance to the male Muskogees assembled at Tuckabatchee. As one horrified Anglo-American observer noted, after Tecumseh had spoken, the Shawnee delegation "leaped up with one appalling yell, and danced their tribal war-dance, going through the evolutions of battle, the scout, the ambush, the final struggle, brandishing their war-clubs, and screaming in terrific concert and infernal harmony fit only for the regions of the damned."[29] Despite this impressive demonstration, initially only about forty Muskogee men adopted the dance. Muskogee warriors were used to dancing not before but rather after battle.[30] Yet, aside from connoting war, the dance conjured other associations, and, for this reason, its popularity rose quickly. The dance held special significance because it originated in the remote interior of North America. Because of its origin, the Dance provided a most fitting means of expressing and invoking authentic Native American difference. Dancing this dance effectively socialized the prophets' visions.[31] Where fasting shamanistic prophets had traveled to Upper and Lower Worlds,

Muskogee warriors vigorously moved their bodies to create an Other World. By dancing a new dance, they would negate colonialism and cross the threshold into a new moral and political order. By following the northern custom, the Muskogee rebels vigorously claimed an aboriginal identity and power sufficiently pure to offset and overcome the overcivilized condition.

More than any other ceremonial act, belief, or practice, dancing the dance distinguished the male rebels from those Muskogee men who remained friendly with Anglo-Americans. The dance was fully identified with the rebel movement. Wherever the prophets went, they performed the dance. They performed it at ritual executions of friendly chiefs and before battles. They even performed it during battles in the face of cannon.[32]

Disclosed in new settlement patterns, increased reliance on gathering wild foods, and the performance of the dance, the identity celebrated in the Redstick movement was not uncritical, naive, or illusory, escapist, stiff, one-dimensional, or reactionary. Rather, it was processual, dynamic, self-critical, innovative, fluid, acutely aware of contradiction. This is the case because the new identity presupposed a terribly painful and ineluctable awareness of its own negation, an acute consciousness of real this-worldly forces that would deny native peoples their political independence and right to remain in Muskogee. The Muskogees had witnessed the consequences of colonialism. It is hard to imagine any group of Muskogees who did not know the story of how their ancestors' lands had been stolen, settled, and developed by invading Anglo-Americans. Muskogee men had long complained that hunting was growing more dangerous and less productive, and now the *Ecunnaunuxulgee* were demanding more land cessions. Muskogee hunters told stories about the great influx of Anglo-Americans traveling the new federal road to the Bigbe area and beyond.[33] Many Muskogees were familiar with Hawkins's plan, his refusal to give gifts and to intermarry. Perhaps they had seen the settlements of the river bottom métis and noted how they forgot their poorer kin. Runaway slaves told villagers how

Anglo-Americans treated their African American slaves, and they also told stories describing a fiery judgment to come. In any case, Muskogees knew Atlantic civilization and could never forget it. It was around them, it was in them, it was part of them.

SEVEN

The Invasion of Muskogee

Surging with new power in the spring of 1813, the Muskogee prophetic faction went on the offensive. Taking up the red battle club, the rebels planned initially to purge the Upper Muskogees of friendly chiefs; then they would attack the Lower Muskogee towns of Coweta and Cusseta and unify the peoples of Muskogee against the forces of colonialism.

However, as we shall see, citizens of the United States refused to let the movement take its own course. Frontier settlers in Tennessee, Georgia, and Mississippi, interceding at a critical juncture, violently provoked the Redsticks. They forcibly and perhaps intentionally transformed the civil war between Redsticks and friendly Muskogees into a confrontation between the Redsticks and the United States. This decisive action occurred just as the Redsticks were besieging Tuckabatchee in July 1813.

The prophetic faction had directed a large party of warriors to Pensacola to demand badly needed arms, powder, and ammunition from the Spanish authorities. The delegation, which hoped to obtain "five horses loads for every town," was led by major prophets and leaders of the resistance movement (Jim Boy, Hillis Hadjo, and Peter McQueen). After pressuring the governor of West Florida, Don Mateo González Manrique, they received around "1,000 pounds of gunpowder, a quantity of lead, and a quantity of food and blankets, but no guns and or repairs for those they brought with them."[1]

As the rebels headed north, American spies in Pensacola immediately alerted U.S. and territorial officials of their movements, and the militia of Washington County, Mississippi Territory, moved to intercept them. The militia consisted of around 180 men, including many of the Tensaw métis. On 27 July 1813, at Burnt Corn (a place where two trails met about forty miles northeast of the Bigbe settlements), the militia attacked a dozen rebels. The startled warriors fled into the surrounding swamp, leaving their packhorses behind, and the militia, congratulating themselves on an easy victory, began dividing the loot.[2]

According to an early Anglo-American historian of the Muskogee civil war, in battle situations Muskogees "would not give one swamp or cane field for forty forts." In the swamp at Burnt Corn, the warriors regrouped and rallied when other nearby Redsticks responded to the gunfire and joined them. The Redsticks painted themselves for battle, "fired a few guns from the creek swamp and a general stampede was the result." The exposed militia, finding themselves surrounded, "were panic struck and made a quick and rapid retreat."[3] Only eighty militiamen remained to fight approximately one hundred Redsticks; the militia soon retreated.

This skirmish, though it terminated in their favor, was one the Redsticks had neither intended nor anticipated. According to their testimony, the Redsticks had never thought of being attacked by an army, and considered the militia's action entirely unprovoked.[4] Thus, it seems plausible that, up until the Battle of Burnt Corn, the rebel Muskogees were not fixed on actual war with Anglo-American armies.

Until the Battle of Burnt Corn, the prophetic faction, despite making many bold and provocative claims about "trying the strength of the Americans," had not killed any U.S. citizens.[5] As late as 4 July 1813, a Moravian observer could write that the "agitators have been cautious not to harm the whites."[6] Though they attacked the chiefs friendly to Anglo-Americans and intended to destroy the artifacts of civilization, the prophets did not kill the Anglo-American traders living in their midst. A close examination of historical documents reveals that the prophets carefully avoided claiming that they would take the war outside Muskogee, qualifying every threat involving Anglo-Americans: "*If* they could," they would kill Hawkins; "*if* [Anglo-Americans] came *among them* . . . they would be ready for them" (emphasis mine).[7]

Considering these explicit strictures, cautious behaviors, and qualified statements and their genuine shock at the Burnt Corn ambush, it seems fully plausible that many of the rebels had hoped to avoid an immediate military confrontation with the United States. At a minimum, they intended to avoid direct conflict with the United States until certain preconditions had been fulfilled: "1st they were to put to death all who assisted the Chiefs to give satisfaction for the murders at the Ohio. 2nd all the old Chiefs friendly to peace and those who refused to join the prophets, by this means to unite the nation in one opinion then wait for Tecumseh."[8] The latter proviso, waiting for Tecumseh, meant that a good number of the rebels understood that their actions were linked to a much larger drama that might or might not require them to attack Anglo-Americans. If Tecumseh succeeded in the North, then and only then would the Redsticks go on the offensive. One of the rebels' plans, intercepted by a trader, makes geographic sense. The Upper Muskogees would "fall upon the frontier of Georgia; the Alabamas . . . upon the Tensaw and Bigby."[9] However, if Tecumseh failed or British support was not forthcoming, it was likely that a majority of the Redsticks would have prudently avoided the military conflict with the United States. Though inspired with new power, they were also flexible and pragmatic.

In contrast, since the métis of Bigbe and Tensaw were the rebels' primary target, they had every reason to hope that a general war involving the United States would erupt. This perhaps explains their active and highly visible role in the Burnt Corn ambush. Rather than wait for the Redsticks to attack their Tensaw homes, métis leaders such as Dixon Bailey rushed to spill first blood. It is interesting to observe that this action was widely condemned by many settlers; they felt that Bailey and the militia had moved "too hastily." Instead of attacking the Redsticks, many of the citizens of Washington County felt that "it would have been better to have made use of conciliatory measures towards the Creeks; that they thereby might be overruled and perhaps averted hostilities."[10]

Although such a sentiment may have reflected the views of ordinary frontier settlers, wealthy U.S. citizens were eager to cause a general war. Anglo-American planters did not feel that they had to wait for the rebellion to spill out of Muskogee in order to take action. They felt entitled and compelled to crush the rebellion within Muskogee. Indeed, we can argue that many prominent planters feared that the Redsticks might *not* attack U.S. settlers. A peaceful resolution of the rebellion would leave no pretext to crush the Muskogees and absorb greater portions of their land.

Land speculators throughout the region, Georgia politicians and planters, and Tennessee slaveholders and farmers positively itched to open Muskogee's rivers and trails to commerce. They desired to claim, settle, and plant its rich soils. For its part, Tennessee wanted direct road and river routes to the Gulf. Well before the war, Tennessee let all parties know that it "must be gratified" in its wish to navigate the Coosa River and transport its produce to Mobile.[11]

When the Muskogee civil war broke out, frontier leaders realized that they could finally get what they wanted and more. They could meddle in the civil war, transmute it into a general war between the United States and the Redsticks, and gain the wealth of the Muskogees' land. What the frontier leaders had to do was provoke both U.S. citizens and Redstick rebels. They had to arouse their own people through rhetoric and antagonize the Redsticks through "unprovoked" acts of military aggression.

Loathe to imagine how peace would rob them of potential wealth, elite citizens in Tennessee spoke constantly of Muskogee depredations and greatly exaggerated the threat posed by the Muskogees to U.S. citizens. In May 1812, a full year before the Muskogee civil war erupted, the *Nashville Clarion*, responding to the murders of frontier settlers on the Duck River committed by Muskogee men, declared that the Muskogees "have supplied us with a pretext for dismemberment of their country."[12] Another Tennessean, the prominent land speculator, lawyer, and slave-holder Andrew Jackson, provided additional hot rhetoric to feed the spirit of war, writing the following: "When we make the case of Mrs. Manly and her family and Mrs. Crawley our own—when we figure to ourselves our beloved wives and little prattling infants, butchered, mangled, murdered, and torn to pieces, by savage bloodhounds, and wallowing in their gore . . . we are ready to pant for vengeance. . . . The whole Creek nation shall be covered with blood."[13] Acting quickly, Jackson's friend William Blount, the governor of Tennessee, successfully "got some [Muskogee] blood." It was hoped, Thomas Hart Benton said, that Tennessee could "keep the war alive."[14]

Tennessee's bid for war, however, failed. In 1812, Georgia took a stab at causing a general war. Georgia filibusters invaded East Florida and attacked the Seminoles of Alachua. Though the Seminoles still maintained a tenuous connection to the Upper Muskogees, the Seminole-Georgia conflict remained regional and did not directly involve the Upper Muskogees.[15] It was not until the July 1813 skirmish at Burnt Corn that the frontier leaders, thanks in part to the self-motivated actions of métis settlers fearing for their own lives, succeeded in drawing the Muskogees into open military conflict with the United States. The militia's unprovoked attack against the prophetic faction within Muskogee guaranteed that a full-scale Redstick-U.S. war would occur. After Burnt Corn, the prospects for peace closed.

From the outbreak of the Muskogee civil war to the skirmish at Burnt Corn, the Redsticks had planned to attack Coweta.

Coweta was a town closely associated with dominant friendly chiefs, trade with the United States, and the influence of Benjamin Hawkins. By winning Coweta, the Redsticks hoped to unify the Muskogee people behind the prophetic faction. After Burnt Corn, however, this primary objective was temporarily deferred; clan vengeance demanded an immediate retaliatory strike against the métis and Anglo-American settlers of the Bigbe area: "The families of the killed and wounded and those who were plundered of the [Spanish] Governor's present forced the leaders to change the attack [from Coweta] to that of the half breeds and their assistants."[16]

In addition to the exigencies of clan vengeance, the rebels had other reasons to attack the Bigbe settlements. The mere existence of these settlements had long angered the Upper Muskogees. The Upper Muskogees, and, more particularly, the Alabamas, had contemplated wiping them out as early as 1789. Only the adamant opposition of the McGillivray family, which just happened to own a plantation in Tensaw, prevented the attack.[17] Subsequent years saw a rapid increase in the size of the Bigbe and Tensaw settlements and a concomitant rise in the level of tensions. From a population of 750 Anglo-Americans and African Americans in 1801, the settlements grew more than threefold to a total population of 2,600 in 1810 (1,400 Anglo-Americans and 1,270 African Americans). The first grist mill was built in the area in 1812, the first cotton gin in 1813.[18]

With the expansion of Anglo-American settlements came increased intercultural conflict and political wrangling. In 1811, for instance, a zealous U.S. collector at Fort Stoddert (just above Mobile on the Tombigbee River) insisted on stopping Alabamas traveling on the river to make them pay duty on imports from and exports to Spanish Florida. The Muskogees, who had traded with Mobile since its founding more than a century earlier, complained to Hawkins that the United States failed to practice what it preached. The United States did not allow free navigation of all American waters.[19]

As early as spring 1812, Anglo-Americans in the Settlements feared that the prophetic faction led by Captain Isaacs would descend on them. In March of that year, a Mississippi official reported that "considerable consternation pervades the upper settlements—particularly in the forks of the Tombigby and Alabama; of an immediate attack upon them from the Creek Indians."[20] Fortunately for the settlers, the prophetic faction was not yet strong and still committed to deferring direct conflict with U.S. citizens.

After blood was spilled at Burnt Corn, however, the Muskogee war chiefs and prophets could no longer restrain their warriors. They would finally "allay a thirst of long standing desire to fight that part of the country for imposing on them for many years." As they moved down to kill the "half breeds and their assistants" responsible for Burnt Corn, the Redsticks "were informed the former were at Mim's Fott . . . and they directed the attack accordingly."[21]

On Lake Tensaw, settlers had built a stockade around the house of Samuel Mims. The stockade was but one of many makeshift forts thrown up by U.S. citizens fearing war or Redstick reprisals for Burnt Corn.[22] In late August 1813, the fort housed around 400 Anglo-Americans, African Americans, métis, and friendly Muskogees. Of this number, 120 were militia. At noon on 30 August, the Redsticks, numbering 750, surrounded the fort. In the ensuing action, magic played a key role. Shamans claimed to make several warriors invulnerable to their enemy's fire.[23] This action was nothing new; Muskogee warriors had always sought and received powerful war medicines from their shamans. What was relatively new, at least to Anglo-American observers, was the bold way the Redsticks departed from the "Indian mode of warfare" and attacked "a regular fortification."[24]

They definitely surprised the fortified settlers and appeared to have had the cooperation of some of the African Americans within the fort: "Siras, a negro man, cut down the pickets."[25] Nevertheless, the Redstick attack did not issue in an immediate victory or massacre. The battle lasted several hours, and at one point the Redsticks actually withdrew. At this point, the African Americans fighting alongside the Redsticks urged them on. The warriors renewed the attack, setting fire to the houses. By sundown, the Redsticks had finally conquered the fort. Because "the Master of Breath . . . ordered [them] not to kill any but white people and half breeds,"[26] they spared many of the fort's African American inhabitants, but they showed no mercy to Anglo-American and métis people. At least 247 of the fort's inhabitants lay dead.[27]

The battle also cost the Redsticks dearly. Half the 750 rebel warriors were killed or wounded.[28] Indeed, this so-called Indian massacre was probably one of the most damaging days in the entire history of Muskogee warfare. Reeling from their losses, the Redsticks held their prophetic leader, Paddy Walch, to blame, for he had failed to neutralize Anglo-Americans' bullets as promised: "The prophets [had] told them in a hard fought battle they would loose two only and a very severe one three at most." Had the Alabamas not protected Walch, who was one of their chiefs, the rest of the rebels might have condemned and executed him as a malicious conjuror.[29]

In a much larger sense, the Battle of Fort Mims cost the Redsticks far more than the lives of their warriors or the prestige of a shaman, for this battle guaranteed that the United States would invade Muskogee. As news of the battle spread throughout the frontier, fiction, fantasy, and hysteria absorbed and overwhelmed fact. As U.S. citizens retold the event, the six-hour battle transmuted into an instantaneous and total massacre; the death toll soared from 250 to 400, perhaps 600. The men, women, and children, it was loudly broadcast, were indiscriminately slain and their bodies mutilated in the most horribly unspeakable manner. Frontier leaders feared that, if the United States did not act, the Redsticks, backed by the British and Spanish, would perform more "massacres," and a massive slave insurrection would erupt.[30]

Given such a pretext, the South's planter elite could finally legitimate the long-desired invasion. It mattered not that the people in the Forks settlements had no legal right to be there and squatted on the land without any authority of government. All that mattered was that Muskogees had killed Anglo-Americans. In Nashville, prominent citizens called for a war to "exterminate the Creek Nation and abettors." Tennessee's governor William Blount declared that the time had arrived to "teach those barbarous sons of the woods their inferiority." In a letter written a month later, the governor further explained that Tennessee welcomed war, for it would clear Muskogee (and perhaps Florida) of native peoples and open a millennium of "general improvement of the face of the country."[31] On 20 September, the Tennessee Legislature authorized an army of thirty-five hundred for the purpose of invading Muskogee. By late October, Georgia had twenty-five hundred in readiness. In November, the Mississippi Territory's force of twelve hundred men under General Claiborne was in the field. Throughout the region, the slogan "Remember Fort Mims" moved thousands of soldiers to invade Muskogee.

The Anglo-American invasionary force exacted ample vengeance by crushing the Redsticks in a series of one-sided battles and by devastating Redstick towns and villages in what many historians have termed "massacres." During November, the invasionary forces attacked the Redsticks on several fronts, to the north, the northeast, the east, and the southwest. In the northeast, on 3 November, Tennesseans overwhelmed the Redstick town of Tallushatchee and killed about two hundred of its inhabitants, including women and children, and took eighty surviving women and children prisoner. On 8 November, Tennesseans attacked a rebel force of warriors besieging the neutral village of Talladega and killed more than three hundred Redstick men. To the northeast, on 18 November, one thousand East Tennessee militiamen, in the most notorious Anglo-American massacre of the war, destroyed a Hillabee town that had already surrendered to General Andrew Jackson. Commanded by an officer who had failed to communicate with Jackson, the militia killed sixty Hillabees, including women and children, and took more than two hundred prisoner. To the east, on 29 November, the Georgia army defeated a large group of Redsticks at the town of Autossee on the Tallapoosa River, killing at least two hundred. Although some women and children were killed in their huts, most survived the battle by hiding in caves along the bluff of the river. After their experiences at Tallushatchee and Hillabee, the Redsticks had learned to separate warriors from women and children so that, in the case of defeat, noncombatants would not be harmed or taken prisoner. When Redstick towns were attacked by surprise, most women surrendered without resistance; a few did fight desperately to defend their homes.

The strategy of keeping nonwarriors away from the scene of battle was applied again with success by the Redsticks in December 1813 at Eccanachaca.[32] Built on the Alabama River in July 1813 under the direction of Redstick prophetic leaders at a site "made sacred by the great spirit," Eccanachaca was supposedly protected by a sacred barrier that Anglo-Americans could not penetrate.[33] This barrier was undoubtedly related to the power that the Redsticks had encountered when dancing the dance of the northern prophets. The war dance had generated and disclosed the power of a new pan-tribal New World identity. Through dancing the new dance in the woods, the Muskogee millenarians had crossed into a new relation to their own culture, their history, the world. In their rituals of purification, fasting, and dancing, the Muskogee rebels had crossed a sort of threshold. They had become initiated and encountered new powers.

The prophets of the rebellion tested these new powers. As shamans of the new native power, they rejected the identity forced on their people by the reigning colonial power. The United States had attempted to use the plan of civilization to "circumscribe" the Muskogees. According to this vision, the Muskogees lacked what the citizens of the United States enjoyed: mature civility, true religion, literacy, and a rational system of justice. The

Muskogees did not yet deserve self-determining political sovereignty. The Muskogees deeply needed the help of the United States and its agents to become fully human. In short, the colonial order sought to impose a relationship of dependency between a putatively infantile native population and a supposedly wiser, more responsible Anglo-American parent.

Rejecting this negative assessment, the shamanistic prophets spoke of contact with a timeless excess of power. Invoking this power through the Maker of Breath, the shamanistic prophets affirmed the integrity of the Muskogee identity as "red people" living in a land created expressly for their race. Rather than allowing civilization to reduce them, the prophets imaginatively assimilated the signs of power of Anglo-American civilization. The prophet Hillis Hadjo, for example, symbolically assimilated all the powers of literacy and the Book. Though his people had no printed and bound books, he announced that the Breathmaker had personally instructed him in all "the branches of writing and languages perfect enough to converse write and do his own business. . . . He wrote a lengthy letter in Spanish (of which language he knew not a word) to the Govr. of Pensacola requesting him . . . to send arms and ammunition."[34] In short, Native American power, because it tapped the power of the Maker of Breath, could absorb all the forces of civilization, be they of the pen or of the sword. Anglo-American colonizing culture could be digested, its signs and modes of power tamed.

When the impure Anglo-American soldiers invaded the sacred Muskogee land at Eccanachaca, the Redsticks expected that the former would encounter a deadly impenetrable barrier, the liminal threshold that only the initiated could cross. The barrier, in short, would manifest the Native American power expressed in the new war dance and other rituals of rebirth. Like the dance, the invisible barrier's shape was supposed to be circular and its action anticolonial. Within this circular barrier, the Redsticks and the many runaway African Americans who joined them felt invincible.[35]

When, on 23 December 1813, 1,000 Mississippi Territory soldiers and 135 Choctaw warriors approached, Redstick women and children were conveyed across the river and hidden in the thick forests and canebrakes. When the invading army transgressed the sacred barrier, the dismayed and poorly armed Redstick warriors also fled. Thirty-three Redsticks were killed, including a Shawnee prophet and twelve African American supporters.[36] In their retreat, there was no shame, for it was the warrior's maxim to avoid any battle where an omen portended ill fortune. Though the Redsticks were disappointed in their prophets, it is unlikely that their confidence in the new power was completely shaken. They had avoided catastrophic losses. If anything, their faith was refined; the new power was real, but not easily manipulated; the power to be Native American remained outside history, outside the control of Native Americans themselves.

Soon after Eccanachaca, at Calebee Creek on 27 January 1814, a large Redstick war party fought the Georgia militia. Redstick resistance cost the Georgians dearly, but the latter prevailed. Seventeen militiamen died, and 132 were wounded. The Redsticks lost fifty warriors. These losses were serious, but, as it turned out, they were small when compared to those to come two months later at Tohopeka. Tohopeka, one of the three new towns organized by the prophetic leaders of the rebellion, was located in the Abeka homeland. Because they thought the place had never been inhabited, the prophets felt that it was a good place to make a new beginning. The site also possessed considerable strategic merits. The new town was surrounded on three sides by the Tallapoosa River. For this reason, Anglo-Americans gave it the name "Horseshoe Bend." On the land side, the Redsticks, guided by a brilliant war chief named Menawa, constructed a sturdy breastwork, making Tohopeka an exceedingly well-defended town. In March, Tohopeka held around four hundred women and children and one thousand warriors drawn from Abeka towns and villages such as Okfuscooche, Nuyaka, Hillabee, Eufaula, and Thlathlagulgua.[37]

On 27 March 1814, a force of fifteen hundred Anglo-Americans, five hundred Cherokees, and one hundred "friendly" Muskogees surrounded and attacked Tohopeka. Despite these odds, the Redsticks, securely protected by Menawa's breastworks, held their ground for several hours and inflicted serious casualties on Jackson's army. It is probable that they hoped to withstand the frontal attack until nightfall and then use their canoes to escape downriver under cover of darkness. They certainly had intended to ferry nonwarriors away from the scene of battle. They were denied these options, however, when some of the Cherokee men stationed on the outside of the bend forded the Tallapoosa, cut loose the Redstick canoes, and attacked Tohopeka from the rear.

Though the Redstick men resisted hard and long, only 25–33 percent of them possessed firearms. This was not because they refused to use European weapons. They simply did not have access to them. Throughout the revolt, the Redsticks attempted to procure firearms and ammunition from British traders in Florida. With only a few exceptions, however, these traders refused to extend credit to rebels or supply them with arms. As months passed, Redstick guns became inoperable, and their meager supplies of ammunition were consumed. At Tohopeka, the majority of warriors had no choice but to rely on bows and arrows, war clubs and knives. When they were exposed to direct fire from the rear, they were unable to prevent Jackson's army from penetrating the breastworks.

Redstick losses were staggering. Five hundred and fifty-seven Redsticks died on the field desperately defending their community, and it was estimated that 250–300 died in the water, attempting to escape. Later, some neutral Muskogees from a small village on the Chattahoochee told a U.S. official that they knew "of not more than ten men that had escaped from the battle at the horse shoe."[33] Not since the time of the Soto *entrada* had so much blood been shed in Muskogee. Never again would so many die in a battle between Americans and Native Americans. In all,

800 Redstick warriors had died, and 350 Muskogee women and children had been captured.[39]

The Battle of Tohopeka ended Redstick military action among the Upper Muskogees. After Tohopeka, the rebel forces were fragmented and confused, and no unified action was possible in Muskogee. Those who had survived were anxious for peace and sent runners to obtain terms from Hawkins. Some former warriors determined to turn over their principal leaders to the United States. A great many others, however, were unvanquished and unwilling to surrender. Around two thousand Redstick men, women, and children abandoned Muskogee and fled to Florida, where they became involved in subsequent Seminole wars against the United States.[40] In these conflicts, African Americans became even more prominent. Many runaway African Americans, including some who had fought with the Redsticks, also fled south. By July 1814, Benjamin Hawkins concluded that there was "no hostility existing" above Florida, the new locus for anticolonial resistance.[41]

In less than one year, from the Battle of Burnt Corn (27 July 1813) to the Battle of Tohopeka (27 March 1814), eighteen hundred Redstick warriors and several hundred Redstick women and children had lost their lives in the war with Anglo-Americans and their Native American allies. To this great loss of life must be added the "virtually complete" destruction of all hostile settlements in the Upper Muskogee country by American forces. American armies had burned nearly fifty villages and towns. Since the militia took or destroyed all foodstuffs, Redstick survivors were "reduced to extreme want."[42] A Georgia newspaper described their plight as "a most melancholy and affecting spectacle. It is impossible to describe the late sufferings of the hostile Indians. Many have been reduced by famine to mere skeletons, and others, from fear and hunger, divested of their reason. In a word, the face of the country is entirely changed—where there was once plenty, nought is now to be seen but poverty and wretchedness, devastation and ruin." Hawkins's description was equally bleak: "Look to the towns, not a living thing in them; the inhabitants scattered through the woods, dying with hunger, or fed by Americans."[43]

While the nonhostile Muskogees avoided famine, they too were in a difficult situation. During the war, the Lower Muskogee towns of Coweta and Cussetuh had served as the headquarters of the friendly Muskogees and housed and fed hundreds of refugees from places like Tuckabatchee. By the end of the conflict, the towns' food supplies were exhausted, and these people, like the Redsticks, had to depend on the United States for provisions.[44]

Writing on 23 April 1814, the chief U.S. military commander General Thomas Pinckney declared complete victory. Using theological and, more precisely, soteriological language, he interpreted the war's meaning. "Almighty God" had "blessed the arms of the United States" and granted its cause "complete success." The United States had "severely chastised" the "insolent," "infatuated," and "perifidious" Muskogees. Since "the loss of blood sustained by the citizens of the United States" had been "amply retaliated," the U.S. government was now "willing to spare the dispersed remnant of these miserable people, who may be sincerely disposed to atone for their former misdeeds."[45]

General Pinckney asked that the hostiles comply with four terms: (1) cede "so much of the conquered territory, as may appear to the Government . . . to be just indemnity for the expenses of the war; and as a retribution for the injuries sustained by its citizens, *and by the friendly Creek Indians*"; (2) tolerate the building of U.S. military posts and trading houses and allow the United States to use Muskogee's roads and rivers freely; (3) surrender the prophets; and (4) agree to "restrictions upon their trade with foreign nations, as shall be established by the government of the United States." In communicating these terms to Benjamin Hawkins, Pinckney stressed that the United States would not forget the friendly Muskogees' interests: "The United

States will not forget their fidelity, but, in the arrangements which may be made of the lands to be retained as indemnity, their claims will be respected, and such of their chiefs as distinguished themselves by their exertions and valor in the common cause, will also receive a remuneration in the ceded lands, or in such manner as the Government may direct."[46] Unfortunately for the friendly Muskogees, the memory of the United States was remarkably short. By August, when the Treaty of Fort Jackson was negotiated, the United States had forgotten the fidelity of their Muskogee allies, and the new military commander determined not to respect their claims or remunerate them for their services but to strip them of millions of acres of their lands.

When General Jackson arrived as sole commissioner, "he addressed a speech to the Chiefs, among whom there was but a single hostile one; marked his line which, he said, should not be altered." Jackson demanded that the friendly chiefs yield "nearly eight million acres" of land, land that Jackson himself described as "first rate." His demand outraged his former allies. The friendly chiefs "repeatedly urged the justice of their claims to losses, as promised in the terms of peace offered; and the general as often denied having powers to act on it."[47]

With the Treaty of Fort Jackson, Jackson apparently wanted more than simple indemnity; he wanted to perform a final act of closure. According to Hawkins, Jackson said he wanted "to prevent an intercourse between the Indians and the Spaniards and English in the Floridas." He wanted to create a boundary: "to have a border to know and separate his enemies from his friends." This would serve the government by connecting the settlements of Georgia with the Mississippi Territory and Tennessee and by enhancing U.S. commerce, development, and domestic security.[48]

The general's unauthorized and unjust behavior so forcibly struck Benjamin Hawkins that the latter wrote a letter urging the secretary of war to end Jackson's involvement in the negotiations.[49] The outraged chiefs also wrote a letter expressing their claims and stating their objections to the treaty that Jackson forced them to sign.[50] They urged that this letter accompany the treaty and considered it "their part of the treaty." Moreover, the friendly chiefs gave a gift of three square miles of land to General Jackson, the very man who unjustly took eight million acres of their land. The general, "impressed with this unexpected mark of national gratitude," accepted it on the condition that the land could be sold in order to clothe the "poor naked" Muskogee women and children. This modification was firmly rejected by the chiefs; Jackson would have to accept the gift as a gift and not turn it into charity toward the Muskogees. By giving Jackson a gift, the chiefs hoped to demonstrate with intentional irony that they, despite everything, remained "the masters of the land." As for the chiefs' document, Jackson promised that his own secretary would see that it arrived in Washington. As it turned out, the document was strangely omitted, mysteriously lost.[51]

In all, the United States took fourteen million acres from the Muskogees, the largest cession of land ever made in the Southeast. With remarkable speed, the ceded land was settled by thousands of squatters, including many veterans of the campaigns against the Muskogees. Propelled by soaring cotton prices and craving new soils to plant, the new settlers pushed in from all sides and immediately transgressed the new boundary line between the United States and the Muskogees. For example, near the Alabama River, Anglo-Americans "took forcible possession" of the rich fields and sturdy houses belonging to Alexander McGillivray's descendants. In their plea for justice, these métis, who had remained neutral during the war, described how the Anglo-Americans had "reproached us with our origins, insulted us with the most abusive language, and not content with that they have even proceeded to blows and committed private injury on our stocks and property."[52]

It is one of the great contradictions of this history that Anglo-Americans who united to fight the Muskogees had no sooner won victory than they began to fight each other over the land. With victory, the fault lines and class conflicts of Anglo-American society instantly revealed themselves.[53] Many of the new settlers would themselves be forcibly removed by their own government from the land they squatted. The land officer at Huntsville complained that the squatters "settled themselves on the Lands reserved for the use of schools, and that they are cutting down and destroying the timber in the most wanton and Shameful manner, and no doubt to the great injury of the public."[54] In a similar vein, the secretary of war wrote Hawkins in October of 1815:

> I understand that the land lately ceded to the United States, is rapidly settling by the whites. *This must not be permitted.* The effect of these settlements is to place the very worst part of our citizens in possession of the very best part of the public lands upon pre-emption principles. They settle all the choice spots, and form combinations to deter the purchasers from bidding for all the lands so settled and in that manner deprive the government of the possibility of receiving more than two dollars per acre.[55]

By 1820, eighty-five thousand Anglo-Americans and forty-two thousand African Americans had made Muskogee their home. Needless to say, the massive influx of Anglo-American settlers and African American slaves completely wrecked the deer-skin trade and other long-standing modes of intercultural contact and exchange. Anglo-American hostility and the spread of the cotton culture placed the Muskogees themselves in a precarious situation. Crowded in a small domain, the Muskogees soon found themselves stripped of their political sovereignty by the new state of Alabama (1819). During the 1820s, the state and federal governments demanded new land cessions.

Though the Muskogees continued to adapt to their ever-changing world, accepted Protestant missionaries in their midst, published laws, ran ferries and stores on the federal road, and vigorously defended the land they still held, the invasion of Muskogee continued its advance. It would not end until all Muskogees were forcibly removed by military guard from their land

(1835–36) and taken west to homelands selected by the United States.[56]

The forced removal of southeastern Native Americans was brutal. Underfed and exposed, one in ten Muskogees died en route. Three hundred were killed when the steamboat carrying them from Alabama to the Arkansas Territory sank in the Mississippi River. The total number of deaths greatly exceeded those suffered at Tohopeka. For the lives and lands lost, Muskogee men and women must have grieved deeply. They could easily have despaired, and surely some individuals did. Yet, as a people, they did not lose their will to live. Though they were forced to leave the land of their ancestors, some Muskogee towns had been able to take something central and powerful with them. They took something that had sustained their ancestors and would sustain them in the new land. Tuckabatchee people carried from Alabama to the west an ark containing sacred coals from their council fire. Each night of the journey the guardians of these coals used them to kindle a new fire and create fresh coals for the next day's travel. Additionally, six specially selected warriors carried Tuckabatchee's ancient copper plates, sacred items that traditionally were displayed only during that town's Busk ceremony: "Each one had a plate strapped behind his back, enveloped nicely in buckskin. They carried nothing else, but marched on, one before the other, the whole distance to Arkansas, neither communicating nor conversing with a soul but themselves, although several thousand were emigrating in company; and walking, with a solemn religious step one mile in advance of the others."[57] Once they reached their destination, the Tuckabatchees carefully buried the plates at the center of a new square ground and set the coals on a new hearth. The Muskogees began a new life away from Muskogee. As these significant gestures suggested, even as they embraced life in yet another new world, they remained oriented toward and sustained by their traditional sense of the sacred.[58]

PART III

Conclusions and Comparisons

E I G H T

Religious Renewal in the New World

If Anglo-Americans had not become involved and squelched the Muskogees' millenarian movement and civil conflict, what would the outcome of the prophetic movement have been? How would it have altered the Muskogees' relation to Anglo-American culture? At least three distinct interpretations deserve to be elaborated and evaluated. A romantic interpretation smoothly returns the Muskogee rebels to their communities and intense contact with Anglo-American civilization. A cynical interpretation locks them in permanent opposition. A third, deconstructionist interpretation locates the rebels in a critical middle ground between total return and total withdrawal.

First, according to the romantic interpretation, the rebels never intended to withdraw permanently from contact with Anglo-Americans and take up the life of their ancestors.[1] They intended not to escape Anglo-American civilization but to outstep it. As in most initiation processes, the moment of withdrawal was the prelude to a moment of return. By withdrawing temporarily from the ordinary order, the millenarian Muskogees gained a critical perspective on their lives, history, and culture. By dancing in the woods, they formed a sacred circle in which the people found new freedom and power, freedom and power to decide for themselves what they would do with civilization.

Rather than become its victims, through a dramatic ceremony of withdrawal and purification, they determined to become civilization's indigenous masters. According to the romantic interpretation, it is altogether likely that, after the intense phase of fasting, purification, and rebirth, and after doing battle with the "friendly" Muskogees at Tuckabatchee and Coweta, the "hostile" millenarian Muskogees, whether victorious or not, would have returned to their villages and resumed their normal lives. They would have returned, however, as different people, fully initiated, keenly aware of who they really were, and more determined than ever to defend and nurture their culture. Thus, even if Anglo-Americans did not disappear from Muskogee, the millenarian movement of 1813 would be—was already—a success. It had creatively transformed the Muskogees.[2]

This romantic interpretation, however, requires us to overlook the historical situation, the very condition and context of the dance itself. The historical situation may not have allowed such an outcome, and it is doubtful that the rebels were themselves so sanguine concerning their future. An alternative and more pessimistic interpretation would hold that the crisis seemed so deep to the rebels, the threat posed by agrarian slavery and Anglo-American development so total, that the millenarian Muskogees really intended to sever permanently their contact with Anglo-American civilization. According to this interpretation, the Muskogees faced (or thought they faced) total annihilation and therefore desperately sought a total revolution. They anticipated the miraculous in-breaking of a new world order and inevitably would be crushingly disappointed. Within this interpretation, the revolt can be understood only as a tragic event.

The latter interpretation may have some validity, but it appears overly stark, melodramatic, and insensitive to the processual aspects of the rebellion. Moreover, this interpretation surreptitiously gains much of its persuasive force because of events that occurred after the Muskogee civil war. These events narrow and overdetermine our reading of the Redstick movement. Because we know that the United States eventually intervened and defeated the rebel Muskogees and later (1836) removed almost all Native Americans from Muskogee, we are predisposed to assume that the resistance movement (and all Native American movements) had to end in tragic failure. Knowing how everything came out, we are tempted to oversimplify or ignore the complex dynamics expressed within the movement, its processual character and complex self-critical component. Instead of describing a creative movement of self-making and revolution, we are inclined to project a static, reactionary last stand.

Furthermore, since we are greatly influenced by a historiography that depicts (to far too great a degree) an antebellum South without Native Americans,[3] we are inclined to think that the southeastern Native Americans and the Cotton Kingdom were absolutely incompatible, that the Muskogees and all other Native Americans really had no future in the South and must have felt completely desperate. Recent revisionist ethnohistorical works, however, show that this was by no means the case; these works emphasize how southeastern Native Americans increasingly not only raised stock but also mingled with African Americans, successfully grew cotton for market, and adapted many other economic innovations.[4] Muskogee history could have turned out differently. Alternative futures, quickly repressed and now forgotten, once inspired (and terrified) historical actors, Native American, African American, and European American. Having survived for ten thousand years in the region, it is likely that most southeastern Native Americans deeply believed that they could adapt and survive whatever changes came their way. This conviction probably explains in part why the Cherokees, Choctaws, and Chickasaws and several thousand Muskogees rebuffed Tecumseh and did not join the resistance movement.[5] Though they knew the path ahead was treacherous, they determined to walk it carefully, avoid war with Anglo-Americans, and hold onto their land as much as possible.

As for the several thousand Muskogees who did rebel, we should not assume that they acted out of desperation or a sense of powerlessness. If anything, they rebelled because they more than any other southeastern Native Americans felt themselves very powerful and safe. Unlike the Cherokees, who had seen their land repeatedly invaded, the Muskogees had never been defeated by the English or European Americans. American invasionary armies had never leveled their villages and burned their cornfields, leaving old men, women, and children homeless. No group of Muskogees felt stronger or safer than the Alabamas, and it was the Alabamas who sparked the movement and provided its greatest prophets.

Finally, among the Alabamas and other Upper Muskogee communities, it seems that the young helped initiate the rebellion. Young chiefs and prophets, such as Tustunnuggee Emathla and Lecetau, the latter only eighteen years old, figured prominently in the movement.[6] The importance of these and other youths underscores how the millenarian movement served as a form of initiation. The movement provided many young men with an excellent chance to become adult men in the way they considered most valid, going to war for one's people. It also provided them with a vehicle to attack older chiefs whom they felt were squandering or jeopardizing their heritage, their land.[7] In its own fashion, the prominence of youth also suggests that the rebellion came not from world-weary despair but from renewed vigor, from fresh contact with resurgent Native American power and the dreams of a newly initiated people.

A third interpretation of the millenarian movement is necessary. We need an interpretation able to account for this youthful vigor and avoid either romanticism or cynicism. Such an interpretation may be constructed by drawing on and reformulating Arnold Van Gennep's portrayal of "rites of passage."[8]

The term "rites of passage" has gained enormous importance in anthropological and religious studies. Unfortunately, the scope of the term's application has been contracted in a significant way. When contemporary scholars think of rites of passage, they think first and foremost of ceremonies that mark momentous transitions in the life of the individual: birth, adulthood, marriage, and death. Scholars do not often think of *collective* social movements as rites of passage. Because such usage goes against the grain of contemporary practice, it needs to be articulated logically and empirically. The late Victor Turner provided the germ of such an articulation in one of his final writings. He reminded us that Van Gennep delineated two categories of rites of passage: "1. Rites that accompany the passage of a person from one social status to another in the course of his or her life, and 2. Rites that mark recognized points in the passage of time (new year, new moon, solstice, or equinox)." Turner continued, "The term has come to be restricted . . . to the former type, which are now sometimes called 'life-crisis rites.'" Significantly, Turner was "not in agreement with this [restriction]" and did not let it constrain his use of the term "rites of passage." Rather, he applied the term to a very rich array of social phenomena, including collective historical movements.[9]

In his study of the liminal or transitional phase of rites of passage, Turner remarked that millenarian movements bear striking homologies to rites of passage. If the traditional rite of passage is connected to crises in the human life cycle, the millenarian movement is connected to phases of history that impose great changes on people. Both rites of passage and millenarian movements enable their participants to reduce internal differences and increase solidarity (communitas). Further, rites of passage and millenarian movements require participants to perform actions symbolizing that they are betwixt and between ordinary social states (liminality). Homologies such as these led Turner to conclude that millenarian movements were essentially phenomena of transition.[10]

Following Turner's lead, we can interpret the Redstick movement as a rite of passage—specifically, a ceremony of collective initiation—performed on a grand scale. To be sure, it may have been an initiation ceremony on an unusually large scale, displaying a great many improvisational features, and fusing itself more openly with political agenda, but it is nonetheless recognizable as a rite of passage experienced on a collective level.[11]

To develop this interpretation, however, we will need to make one significant alteration in Van Gennep's analysis. Van Gennep's interpretation of initiation ceremonies presupposes a stable society to which the initiand returns in order to assume a well-defined adult status. While Van Gennep's analysis illuminates a great range of ethnographic data, it needs to be modified if it is going to advance our understanding of the Redstick revolt and Native American prophetic movements. For the colonized person undergoing millenarian initiation, no traditional reintegration is possible because ordinary society under colonialism is always already distorted by exploitative power relations. Millenarian initiation, unlike traditional rites of passage, could not terminate in the assumption of a whole or self-same identity; no full return to the ordinary world was possible. Something, someone, had to remain at least partially absent.

For the millenarian Muskogee rebels, no full return to the ordinary world was possible. At the same time, the millenarian Muskogees could not permanently withdraw. They eventually would have to relate to Anglo-Americans, and they knew it. The Muskogees had to move into uncharted cultural space where a complete return was impossible and a final escape equally unrealistic. According to this interpretation, the millenarians determined to take up life betwixt and between, in a liminal cultural space, neither totally outside nor totally inside. They had no choice but to live within the colonial order, but they nevertheless determined to negate its spiritual and cultural negativity while affirming a new kind of identity for themselves.

This interpretation would seem to be able to do justice to the negative or oppositional and positive or affirmative aspects of the movement. It acknowledges that the movement was in part a reaction to Anglo-American colonialism without claiming that it was simply a product of colonialism. Rather, the interpretation recognizes that the Redstick revolt was also motivated by positive experiences and hopes. In so doing, this interpretation illuminates the Redstick revolt and links it to the long history of Native

American religious movements in which religious creativity and cosmological hope were central.

Well before the Muskogee Redstick revolt, we find several Native American peoples engaged in large-scale and dramatic movements of rebirth centered on prophetic visions of a new age. Consider the evidence from the Eastern Woodlands. Before the Muskogee revolt of 1812–14, prophetic movements affected the Shawnees in 1805, the Iroquois in 1799, the Lenapes and Ottawas in 1763, the Cherokees in 1760, the Yamasees in 1715, the Tuscaroras in 1711, the Sewees in 1680, and the Powhatans in 1644 and 1622. If we also cast our nets toward those indigenous peoples who faced Spanish invaders in the Southwest, we encounter a prophetic resistance movement arising in 1616 among the Tarahumaras in the great Tepehuan revolt. In Spanish mission provinces in the Southeast, we encounter an important religious revolt shaking the Guale missions from 1576 to 1585 and again in 1597, followed by similar revolts in Apalachee in 1647 and Timucua in 1656.

A pattern of spirit-based revolt extends back to the first half of the sixteenth century, as is clearly indicated by the critical comments of the Chibchas of what is now Colombia. In 1541, their leader rejected the Spanish peace offer, saying, "You desecrate the sanctuaries of our gods and sack the houses of men who haven't offended you. Who would choose to undergo these insults, being not insensitive? Who would not omit to rid himself of such harassment, even at the cost of his life? Note well the survivors who await you, to undeceive you that victory is always yours."[12]

Comparative study of these revolts discloses some general patterns that bear consideration. First, as the timing of most of these movements reveals, full-fledged prophetic movements almost never occurred in the initial encounter between Native Americans and Europeans. Rather, they emerged after several generations of either direct or indirect contact. They emerged most often within the kind of unequal and exploitative relations that characterized full-fledged colonialism. Several of these movements, particularly the later ones in the Eastern Woodlands, occurred in a context in which Native American groups experienced a severe depletion of marketable game and a rapid loss of land to Europeans. Game depletion and land loss were concerns explicitly and prominently addressed by prophets among the Lenapes (Neolin), Ottawas (the Trout), Shawnees (Tenskwatawa), and Senecas (Handsome Lake). For instance, in 1763, the great Lenape prophet Neolin revealed that the Master of Life had told him, "Ye have only to become good again and do what I wish, and I will send back the animals for your food . . . . As for those [British] that come to trouble your lands, drive them out, make war upon them. . . . Send them back to the lands which I have created for them and let them stay there."[13]

Given the apparent link between painful contact experiences and the timing of these movements, some social scientists have assumed that the former caused the latter. They assert that contact produced among Native Americans a bitter experience of deprivation, "a negative discrepancy between legitimate expectation and actuality, or between legitimate expectation and anticipated actuality, or both."[14] Frustrated and threatened, suffering negative economic and political experiences, Native American groups responded to innovative prophets, radically transformed their cultures, and sometimes revolted.

In light of the insights produced by our case study of the Redstick revolt, this kind of explanation seems problematic for several reasons. It ignores the fact that these negative experiences were practically ubiquitous, experienced by almost all Native Americans. Thus, the theory cannot explain why other groups that suffered just as much or greater deprivation did not revolt. Additionally, deprivation theory focuses so narrowly on negative experiences that it neglects to consider that these movements may have been motivated by positive experiences, visions, and hopes, some derived from the contact context, others springing from renewed connection with tradition, and still others supported by new modes of pan–Native American cooperation. This is not to minimize the suffering caused by contact, but it is to affirm that these movements may not have been fueled solely by *ressentiment* or loss of cultural coherence. Colonialism may have been a necessary precondition of these movements, but colonialism and the deprivation that colonial relations produced were probably not the only causes. In addition to the experience of land loss and game depletion, we should also call attention to the impact and power of new visions, visions discerned through ecstatic contact with spirits of water, earth, and sky and amplified in communal discussions.

This approach, in contrast to deprivation theory, affirms the full humanity of Native Americans by assuming that they were much more than victims of history—they were also actors in it. Not only did they react and rebel against colonialism—they also innovated on tradition and initiated new ways of life within the world created by contact. Cognizant that tribal tradition alone could not provide adequate orientation, participants in these movements considered multiple options and energetically borrowed ideas and forms offered by nonnative neighbors (including Christians) and other Native American groups (often from a great distance). From Europeans, they may have appropriated Christian ideas concerning the sacred book and the Savior.[15] From other Native American groups, they borrowed purification practices. Of course, as they innovated, they took pains to ensure that the new religious forms meshed well with traditional indigenous forms. Among the Lenapes and Shawnees, the Christian ascent to heaven was correlated with the shaman's sky journey. The Sioux ghost dance of 1889–90, one of the most famous Native American new religious movements, clearly resembled the old sun dance. In all these movements, the participants were rigorously concerned with divining gestures and disseminating representations of a "path" that would lead to a meaningful future for themselves and their children. These kinds of divination emerged from traditional shamanistic travels as well as new kinds of pan–Native American contact and organizing; the dissemination process employed rumors, speeches, new dances, and "books."

Since their historical experiences were greatly negative, the divination of this path included and developed a sharply focused analysis of the specific social and economic practices that jeopardized the people's future. As they did among the Muskogees, prophetic shamans among the Yamasees, Cherokees, Lenapes, and Shawnees explicitly attacked commerce that led to economic dependency, consumption of alcohol, disruption of clan relations, and land cessions.[16] They linked disregard for the ancestors with a sterile or counterproductive fascination with "white" ways. In many, especially among those Native American groups that still wielded significant numerical or territorial power, the movement rose to the level of a thoroughgoing critique of colonialism. It was at this point that these movements manifested themselves as politically revolutionary.

In almost all these revolts, as in the Redstick movement, the critique of colonialism began at home with self-critique. This self-critique brought to consciousness major ways in which the people had collaborated with colonialist forces. In some of these revolts, not just collaborative practices were criticized and rejected but particular people as well. In the Lenape, Shawnee, and Muskogee revolts, prophets verbally and sometimes physically attacked the indigenous insiders who had accepted an Anglo-American understanding of civilization and were imposing it on their own people. As these prophetic movements gained popular support, there came into ever sharper focus a class of Native American people who had betrayed their people. These traitors appeared to be "red people" when judged by clan ties and culture, but, with the advent of prophetic discourse, it became possible to specify precisely how their collaboration with colonialist forces jeopardizes the people's future. These traitors, many of them chiefs, had agreed to land cessions, had delivered their own people over to European American agents for justice, or had personally profited from their mediating position in the rum, fur, and skin trades but failed to redistribute the wealth in accord with the mainstream ethic.[17] Within the millenarian movement, these chiefs were for the first time unmasked and named "malicious enemies." They were not scapegoats randomly selected but a class of internal enemies identified through critical vision. Violent attacks on these enemies appeared early and ferociously in both the Shawnee and the Muskogee revolts and relatively late and on a small scale in the Lenape prophetic movement.

This self-purge signals that these movements were very much concerned with internal developments and dynamics, not just with responding to "external" pressures. Among the Shawnees and the Muskogees, for instance, the prophets directed their greatest passion not toward vilifying European Americans but toward identifying and purging those natives who had betrayed tradition in order to pursue personal wealth. In these cases, we must reverse Marxist theory and assert with Edward P. Thompson that it was struggle that gave rise to class consciousness: "People find themselves in a society structured in determined ways . . . , they experience exploitation . . . , they identify points of antagonistic interest, they commence to struggle around these issues and in the process of struggling they discover themselves as classes, they come to know this discovery as class-consciousness."[18] Out of the profound spiritual struggle to sound and incarnate a viable identity in the colonial context, violent and unprecedented class conflict often ensued within these transformative movements. In sum attacks on colonial collaborators were the indigenous modes for articulating and deepening an emerging consciousness of class inequalities.

The internal struggle, which in the case of the Muskogees erupted in civil war, demonstrated yet again that prophetic movements were movements in which Native Americans reclaimed their power to shape their own future as they saw fit, in accord with their understanding of power. For participants in these movements, history was not understood from the perspective of passive victims confronting a monolithic and inevitable invasion.

Rather, they affirmed that their situation was partly their responsibility by asserting that it resulted from the action of traitors within, traitors who had neglected traditions or, even worse, actively advanced colonialist forces. Highly charged with a millenarian spirit, the prophets asserted that these traitors could be vanquished by the active intervention of a new kind of anticolonial warrior, a dancer guided by fresh contact with the sacred. Their millenarian perspective acknowledged that the European American invasion had created the conditions for new kinds of identities but asserted with even more vigor that it was now up to the people to decide which road they would walk, the road to destruction that would result from passive accommodation or the "red" road evoked by conscious and critical resistance and informed by spiritual interpretation. In short, millenarian prophets called people to imagine the outlines of and participate actively in creating a postcolonial future. Colonialism may have pushed but, even more important, the sacred pulled Native American peoples into a new religious world.

Though terms such as class consciousness, colonialism, and anticolonialism imply a political reading, we should not lose sight of the way these movements remain spiritual movements concerned with spiritual issues and organized as spiritual processes. Within these movements, acts of destruction, purification, and withdrawal were necessary, but they were necessary as a kind of prelude, an opening phase within a larger transformation drama oriented toward a higher subsequent phase and a new kind of status. In these movements, diverse Native American groups ritually rejected dependence on European Americans and symbolically affirmed the new pan–Native American identity enabled by prophetic visions.

In doing so, they were not simply reassuming an old identity that had been forgotten, although their prophets claimed that was precisely what they were doing. Rather than focusing on their commonalities, Native Americans before the arrival of Europeans, must have been most conscious of the plethora of highly diverse religious, linguistic, political, social, and cultural forms that divided them into a great number of ethnic groups. Though many of these groups were linked by broad cultural commonalities, complex political arrangements, and significant trade networks, the emphasis was probably on difference, not commonality. The situation changed dramatically when these diverse peoples were collectively misnamed "Indians" and then reconstructed as colonized subjects within a world system dominated by European nation-states. Though ethnic differences did not diminish or intertribal conflicts cease, very deep and widespread cultural and religious commonalities could not help but become more apparent. A new and quite powerful potential for cooperation emerged. As diverse Native American peoples found themselves linked by unprecedented types and levels of trade and more rapid forms of transportation, many groups engaged in diplomatic talks and attempted to unify their political strategies. As they found their economies revolutionized, land bases threatened, and cosmologies challenged as a result of contact with the invaders, it was almost inevitable that a self-conscious pan–Native Americanism would emerge. This prospect was realized most vigorously and dramatically in prophetic movements. In these movements, prophets beckoned diverse peoples to put aside their differences and forge a new common identity.[19]

In justifying pan–Native Americanism, several prophets employed a theory of racial polygenesis. Developed by Native Americans during the eighteenth century, this theory held that "red" people were fundamentally different from "white" people. This theory was promoted by a mid-eighteenth-century Cherokee prophet who said, "You yourselves can see that the white people are entirely different beings from us; we are made of red clay; they, out of white sand." The same theory was conveyed when the Shawnee prophet related that "the Great Spirit told them that this white man was not made by himself but by another spirit who made and governed the whites." The prophet concluded that Native Americans and European Americans should not live together. Similarly, Redstick leaders asserted that diverse peoples could unite and hold onto their lands by identifying themselves as "red people" in opposition to "white people." Thus, the prophets in many of these movements asserted that pan–Native Americanism was grounded ontologically.[20]

The development of theories of polygenesis is yet another example of the creativity expressed in Native American religious movements. In the Redstick revolt and other similar movements, Native Americans not only reacted and rebeled against colonialism but also innovated on tradition and initiated new ways of behaving and thinking within the world created by colonial contact. This religious creativity evinces the fact that Native Americans were not mute victims of history but vigorous actors within it. No more or no less than any other people in North America, Native Americans responded dynamically to their changing world and seized the novel possibilities it presented.

Here, we can invoke a metaphor used by historian James Merrell to describe the Catawbas' experiences in colonial South Carolina. As Merrell asserts in his studies of the Catawbas, contact brought Native Americans just as surely as it brought Europeans and Africans into a "new world." Merrell counsels historians to think of "a 'world' as the physical and cultural milieu within which people live and a 'new world' as a dramatically different milieu demanding basic changes in ways of life."[21] Because of contact with European diseases, the Catawbas experienced severe demographic losses. Because of contact with European traders, they acquired livestock and poultry, steady supplies of very useful materials, tools, and weapons (iron, cloth, glass, firearms), as well as novel luxuries (silk, rum). Because of conflicts with European settlers and armies, the Catawbas lost most of their land, retaining only a small reservation in Carolina. In short, because of these and other positive and negative experiences brought about by contact, the Catawbas had to learn how to survive in "a dramatically different milieu demanding basic changes in ways of life."

Along with African and European newcomers, the Catawbas entered a "new world."

Merrell invests a great deal of significance in the metaphor of a "new world." He believes that it provides a narratively powerful way of linking the story of Native Americans with the stories of Europeans and Africans in America. Since all these peoples found themselves in a new world, he argues, historians can no longer fail to integrate Native American history with the rest of American history. Whether Merrell's metaphor will alter historiography in the ways he hopes remains to be seen.[22]

Yet the metaphor gives rise to thought and might fruitfully be taken up by religious studies to foster a fresh perspective not just on the Redstick revolt but on Native American religious movements in general. Merrell's metaphor could be blended with one developed by the historian of religion William Paden. In order to advance the comparative study of religion, Paden argues that different religions be understood as inhabiting and constructing different life worlds. Scholars of comparative religion have the task of studying and comparing the plurality of "religious worlds."[23]

Blending the perspectives of the colonial historian James Merrell and the historian of religions William Paden, we can argue that the new world entered by Native Americans was also a new "religious world," a generative locus in which new gods revealed themselves and old gods were rediscovered, a creative time when new systems of purity displaced old ones and new myths and rites arose. This new religious world was one that emerged when various "primordial" religious worlds—Native American, African, European, and Asian—were fused together by contact, colonialism, and capitalism. Learning how to think and live in this new world along with its various inhabitants constituted (and continues to constitute) a great religious project for every people in this world. This project of religious deconstruction and reconstruction found one of its earliest and most original expressions in Native American prophetic movements. In these sacred revolts,

Native Americans rejected colonial power relations and engaged new prophecies, dances, and stories to find and forge new religious identities suited for the transforming realities of colonial and modern contact.

Notes

Preface

1. Michel Foucault, "Inutile de se soulever?" *Le Monde*, 11 May 1979, p. 2 (translated as "Is It Useless to Revolt?" by James Bernauer in *Philosophy and Social Criticism* 8 [1981]: 6).

Introduction

1. The name "Redsticks" also referred to the bundles of small cane sticks that *mikos* (chiefs) used to time communal gatherings, including gatherings of warriors. Mikos prepared packages containing "as many [sticks] as there are days intervening previous to the one appointed for the gathering. . . . Runners are sent with these [to affiliated villages]. One [stick] is flung aside every day by each receiver. Punctually, on the last day, all, with their respective families, are at the well-known rendezvous." In times of war, the sticks were painted red. (John Howard Payne, "The Green-Corn Dance," *Continental Monthly* 1 [1862]: 19.)
2. "Report of Alexander Cornells, interpreter, to Colonel Hawkins," 22 June 1813, in *American State Papers, Class II: Indian Affairs* (hereafter *ASP: IA*), ed. Walter Lowrie and Matthew Clarke (Washington, D.C.: Gales & Seaton, 1832), 1:846. In writing his report, Alexander Cornells, the interpreter, paraphrased the talk of the prophets that he had heard circulating among the people.
3. Benjamin Hawkins, *Letters, Journals and Writings*, ed. C. L. Grant (Savannah, Ga.: Beehive, 1980), 2:685.

4. James Merrell, "Some Thoughts on Colonial Historians and American Indians," *William and Mary Quarterly* 3d ser., 46 (1989): 95, 96; John H. Peterson, Jr., "The Indian in the Old South," in *Red, White, and Black: Symposium on Indians in the Old South* (Southern Anthropological Society Proceedings no. 5), ed. Charles M. Hudson (Athens, Ga., 1970), 116–33, esp. 118.

5. A tremendous amount of work remains to be done, but a much richer historiography is beginning to emerge. See J. Leitch Wright, Jr., *Creeks and Seminoles: The Destruction and Regeneration of the Muscogulge People* (Lincoln: University of Nebraska Press, 1986); James H. Merrell, *The Indians' New World: Catawbas and Their Neighbors from European Contact through the Era of Removal* (Chapel Hill: University of North Carolina Press, 1989); Peter H. Wood, Gregory A. Waselkov, and M. Thomas Hatley, eds., *Powhatan's Mantle: Indians in the Colonial Southeast* (Lincoln: University of Nebraska Press, 1989).

6. The phrase "subjects of their own history" may draw fire from readers influenced by the poststructuralist critique of humanism. The phrase seems to imply the project of recovering a self-contained will-driven consciousness. This kind of originary consciousness is the very "thing" that poststructuralists such as Michel Foucault and Roland Barthes critically expose as a metaphysical construct. Their critique is powerful and often salutary when applied to European contexts. However, it can be crippling, especially when historians turn to consider the history of imperialism and attempt to recover the experiences of non-European peoples such as the Muskogees. Such a recovery is off-limits, according to the poststructuralists, and we must confine ourselves to deconstructing European discourses about Native Americans. The relevant issues are explicated by Gayatri Spivak, "Subaltern Studies: Deconstructing Historiography," in *In Other Worlds: Essays in Cultural Politics* (New York: Methuen, 1987), 197–221.

7. A more technical name for comparative religion, *Religionswissenschaft*, may be translated as "the general science of religions," but, in practice, English-speaking scholars have adopted the term "history of religions" to refer to the systematic cross-cultural study of religions. On the names, divisions, and history of the discipline, see Joseph M. Kitagawa, "The History of Religions in America," in *The History of Religions: Essays in Methodology*, ed. Mircea Eliade and Joseph M. Kitagawa (Chicago: University of Chicago Press, 1959), 1–30; Eric Sharpe, *Comparative Religion: A History*, 2d ed. (La Salle, Ill.: Open Court, 1986); Frank Whaling, ed., *Contemporary Approaches to the Study of Religion*, 2 vols. (Berlin: Mouton, 1984, 1985); Jacques Waardenburg, *Classical Approaches to the Study of Religion: Aims, Methods and Theories of Research* (The Hague: Mouton, 1973); Jonathan Z. Smith, *Map Is Not Territory: Studies in the History of Religions* (Leiden: Brill, 1978); William E.

Paden, *Religious Worlds: The Comparative Study of Religion* (Boston: Beacon, 1988).

8. See Frank Lawrence Owsley, Jr., *The Struggle for the Gulf Borderlands: The Creek War and the Battle of New Orleans, 1812–1815* (Gainesville: University Presses of Florida, 1981). Owsley's work is a very valuable and well-executed narrative of the war, but it gives scant attention to the rebels' religion. A more recent work by Benjamin W. Griffith, Jr., *McIntosh and Weatherford, Creek Indian Leaders* (Tuscaloosa: University of Alabama Press, 1988), also fails to grasp the rebels' motivations. See Joel Martin, review of *McIntosh and Weatherford*, by Benjamin W. Griffith, Jr., *Gulf Coast Historical Review* 4 (Spring 1989): 80–82. One of the best revisionist articles on intercultural economic exchange barely mentions the role of religion in the Muskogee revolt of 1813. See Daniel Usner, Jr., "American Indians on the Cotton Frontier: Changing Economic Relations with Citizens and Slaves in the Mississippi Territory," *Journal of American History* 72 (1985): 314.

9. Verner W. Crane, "The Origin of the Name of the Creek Indians," *Mississippi Valley Historical Review* 5 (1918): 339–42; William C. Sturtevant, "Creek into Seminole," in *North American Indians in Historical Perspective*, ed. Eleanor Burke Leacock and Nancy Oestreich Lurie (New York: Random House, 1971), 97–98; Charles Hudson, "The Genesis of Georgia's Indians," in *Forty Years of Diversity: Essays on Colonial Georgia*, ed. Harvey H. Jackson and Phinizy Spalding (Athens: University of Georgia Press, 1984), 39.

10. Wright, *Creeks and Seminoles*, 3.

11. By the same token, throughout the eighteenth century, the "Creeks" themselves synecdochically termed all Anglo-Americans "Virginians" because the first English they had any serious knowledge of came from Virginia.

12. "The Hallowing King of the Cowetas and the Fat King of the Cusetas," 14 June 1787, Papers of the Continental Congress, 1774–1789, U.S. National Archives, microcopy M247, roll 87, frames 349–50.

13. "To the Fat King and other head men of the Lower Creeks," 7 August 1787, ibid., frames 361–62.

14. An innocent town was struck in early April 1818. Leaving the old men, women, and children behind, the warriors of Chehaw, a village on Aumuckoalee Creek (near Americus, Ga.), had joined General Andrew Jackson on a campaign against the Seminoles in Florida. On 2 April, Captain Wright, of the Georgia Militia, approached Chehaw with 230 men. Though advised by another officer that the residents of Chehaw were allies, Wright attacked the village. "An advance was ordered, the cavalry rushed forward and commenced to massacre." An elderly chief, Major Howard, "came out of his house with a white flag." In the melee that followed, the chief was gunned down along with six other men, a

woman, and two children. (Thomas Glasscock to General Jackson, Fort Early, 30 April 1818, quoted in J. E. D. Shipp, "The Last Night of a Nation," in *Creek Indian History,* ed. W. B. Hodgson [Americus, Ga.: Americus Book Co., 1938], app., 5.)

15. The Muskogee Confederacy held an annual regional conference to deal with matters of wide-scale concern. See William Bartram, *Travels Through North and South Carolina, Georgia, East and West Florida, The Cherokee Country, The Extensive Territories of the Muscogulges, or Creek Confederacy, and The Country of the Chactaws* (1791; reprint, New York: Penguin, 1988), 181; Louis LeClerc de Milfort, *Memoir or A Cursory Glance at My Different Travels and My Sojourn in the Creek Nation,* trans. Geraldine De Courcy, ed. John Francis McDermott (1802; reprint, Chicago: Donnelley, 1956), 146–49; John Swanton, *The Indians of the Southeastern United States* (1946; reprint, Washington, D.C.: Smithsonian, 1984), 92, 138; Ross Hassig, "Internal Conflict in the Creek War of 1813–1814," *Ethnohistory* 3 (1974): 254.

16. In an important attempt to deal with this difficult problem, the late J. Leitch Wright, Jr., also avoided using "Creeks," opting instead for "Muscogulge" (*Creeks and Seminoles,* xiv, 1). The name "Muscogulge" means people living in a wet land and is probably related to the Algonquian word *muskeg.* See Kathryn E. Holland, "Mutual Convenience, Mutual Dependence: The Creeks, Augusta, and the Deerskin Trade, 1733–1783" (Ph.D. diss., Florida State University, 1986), 24, n. 1.

17. Amelia Bell Walker, "Tribal Towns, Stomp Grounds, and Land: Oklahoma Creeks after Removal," *Native American Land* 14 (1981): 63, n. 1; Swanton, *Indians of the Southeastern United States,* 10; Wright, *Creeks and Seminoles,* xiv.

18. Benjamin Hawkins, "A Sketch of the Creek Country in the Years 1798 and 1799," in *Collections of the Georgia Historical Society,* vol. 3, pt. 1 (1848), reprinted in Hodgson, ed., *Creek Indian History,* 12. Governor Glen to Governor Clinton, 24 May 1751, in *Documents Relating to Indian Affairs, May 21, 1750–August 7, 1754,* ed. William McDowell (Columbia: South Carolina Archives Dept., 1958), 85.

1. Encountering the Sacred

1. Bartram, *Travels,* 385.
2. James Adair, a former deerskin trader, explained Muskogee behavior in another way. Adair thought that the order of Muskogee society did not rest in nature but rather derived from history. According to Adair, the Muskogees were the descendants of the Jewish people; they were "the copper colour American Hebrews," and their government owed much

to Mosaic precedents. If they practiced reciprocity, it was because they had learned the ethic from their biblical ancestors. See James Adair, *Adair's History of the American Indians,* ed. Samuel Cole Williams (London, 1775; reprint, Johnson City, Tenn.: Watauga, 1930), 101. Several other authors advanced the "lost tribe" thesis, including many who wrote after Adair. See ibid., introduction, xxix.

3. The best study of southeastern mythology, ritual practices, and beliefs is Charles Hudson's *The Southeastern Indians* (Knoxville: University of Tennessee Press, 1976), 120–83. In the following discussion, I draw on Hudson's work; George Lankford's *Native American Legends* (Little Rock, Ark.: August House, 1987); John Swanton's *Indians of the Southeastern United States* and *Myths and Tales of the Southeastern Indians,* Bulletin no. 88 (Washington, D.C.: Bureau of American Ethnology, 1929); and James Adair's *History of the American Indians.* Historians of religion consider sacred acts, sacred words, and sacred places to be the three primary forms of religious expression found in any culture (Kees Bolle, "Myth: An Overview," in *The Encyclopedia of Religion* [New York: Macmillan, 1987], 10:261–73).

4. Adair, *History of the American Indians,* 164–67; Albert J. Pickett, *History of Alabama, and Incidentally of Georgia and Mississippi for the Earliest Period* (Charleston, S.C., 1851), 60–64; Swanton, *Indians of the Southeastern United States,* 686–701; Albert S. Gatschet, *Tchikilli's Kasi'hta Legend in the Creek and Hitchiti Languages with a Critical Commentary and Full Glossaries to Both Texts* (St. Louis: R. P. Studley, 1888), 51–52.

5. "Journal of Thomas Bosomworth, July 6, 1752–Jan. 24, 1753," in McDowell, ed., *Documents Relating to Indian Affairs, May 21, 1750–August 7, 1754,* 272.

6. Kristian Hvidt, ed., *Von Reck's Voyage: Drawings and Journal of Philip Georg Friedrich von Reck* (Savannah: Beehive, 1980), 49.

7. Jacque Le Moyne, *Narrative of Le Moyne* (Boston, 1875), 1–12; Bartram, *Travels,* 164, 397–99; Swanton, *Indians of the Southeastern United States,* 534; Caleb Swan, "Position and State of Manners and Arts in the Creek Nation, in 1791," in *Information Respecting the History, Condition and Prospects of the Indian Tribes of the United States,* comp. Henry Rowe Schoolcraft (Philadelphia, 1855), 5:275, 280.

8. John R. Swanton, "Creek Ethnographic and Vocabulary Notes," National Anthropological Archives, Smithsonian Institution, MS, 29.

9. Adair, *History of the American Indians,* 124.

10. Hudson, *The Southeastern Indians,* 274, 340.

11. Swanton, "Creek Ethnographic and Vocabulary Notes," 42–43.

12. James Mooney, *Myths of the Cherokee and Sacred Formulas of the Cherokees* (1900; reprint, Nashville: Cherokee Heritage, 1982), 250–52. Contrary to Calvin Martin's theories, commercial hunting did not arise

from a decline in traditional religion, nor did the deerskin trade contradict religious practices. If anything, the incentive to produce deerskins placed a high premium on those particular practices, including spiritual ones, that enhanced a hunter's chances. See Charles Hudson, Jr., "Why Southeastern Indians Slaughtered Deer," in *Indians, Animals and the Fur Trade: A Critique of Keepers of the Game,* ed. Shepard Krech III (Athens: University of Georgia Press, 1981), 155–76. Compare Calvin Martin, *Keepers of the Game: Indian-Animal Relationships and the Fur Trade* (Berkeley: University of California Press, 1978).

13. Lyda Averill Taylor, "Alabama Field Notes," National Anthropological Archives, Smithsonian Institution, MS, 1, 4.

14. Charles Hudson advances a functionalist interpretation of this practice(see *The Southeastern Indians,* 320). For a discussion of discourses and practices concerning menstruation among contemporary Muskogees, see Amelia Rector Bell, "Separate People: Speaking of Creek Men and Women," *American Anthropologist* 92 (1990): 332–45.

15. "The Creation of the Earth," in *Shem, Ham and Japheth: The Papers of W. O. Tuggle Comprising His Indian Diary, Sketches & Observations, Myths & Washington Journal in the Territory and at the Capital, 1879–1882,* ed. Eugene Current-Garcia with Dorothy B. Hatfield (Athens: University of Georgia Press, 1973), 173. This Yuchi creation myth was recorded by W. O. Tuggle in Oklahoma in 1881. See ibid., 24. The identification of the sun as a female power reveals the Yuchi origins of the myth. Most groups in Muskogee generally identified Upper World beings such as the Sun, the Maker of Breath, or Eagle as male powers. In the Muskogee version of the story, Crawfish retrieves some dirt, and Eagle transforms it into an island that progressively expands to become the land. The Earth-diver myth was told throughout the eastern woodlands and the northern plains across to the Northwest (Lankford, *Native American Legends,* 109).

16. Lankford, *Native American Legends,* 113–16.

17. Hawkins, *Letters, Journals and Writings,* 2:665; Theron Nunez, "Creek Nativism and the Creek War of 1813–1814," *Ethnohistory* 6 (1958): 151; Swan, "Position and State of Manners," 269.

18. Hvidt, ed., *Von Reck's Voyage,* 43.

19. F. L. Cherry, "History of Opelika," *Alabama Historical Quarterly* 15, no. 2 (1953): 184; see also Charles Hudson, "Uktena: A Cherokee Anomalous Monster," *Journal of Cherokee Studies* 3, no. 2 (Spring 1978): 62–75; Raymond D. Fogelson, "Windigo Goes South: Stone-clad among the Cherokees," in *Manlike Monsters on Trial: Early Records and Modern Evidence,* ed. Marjorie M. Halpin and Michael M. Ames (Vancouver: University of British Columbia Press, 1980), 132–51.

20. Swanton, *Myths and Tales of the Southeastern Indians,* 33.

21. Adair, *History of the American Indians,* 158.
22. William Turnbaugh, "Wide-Area Connections in Native North America," *American Indian Culture and Research Journal* 1 (1976): 27.
23. On the theory of the gift, see Maurice Bloch, *Marxism and Anthropology: The History of a Relationship* (Oxford: Clarendon, 1983), 86–87.
24. *Mississippi Provincial Archives: French Dominion, 1729–1748* (hereafter *MPA: FD*), vols. 1–3 edited by Dunbar Rowland and Albert Sanders (Jackson: Mississippi Department of Archives and History, 1929–32), vol. 4 edited by Dunbar Rowland, A. G. Sanders, and Patricia Kay Galloway (Baton Rouge: Louisiana State University Press, 1984), 4:146–47.
25. Edmond Atkin, *Indians of the Southern Colonial Frontier: The Edmond Atkin Report and Plan of 1755,* ed. Wilbur Jacobs (Columbia, S.C., 1954), 28.
26. Hvidt, ed., *Von Reck's Voyage,* 42.
27. Bartram, *Travels,* 318.
28. Hawkins gives the fullest description of the rotunda's construction: "They fix 8 posts forming an octagon of 30 feet diameter in the ground, 12 feet high and large enough to support the roof. They then raise on top of these, 5 or 6 logs on each side, drawing them in as they rise. They then get long poles or rafters to suit the height of the building and lay them on the logs, the upper ends forming a point and the lower ends resting on posts 5 feet high fixed round 6 feet from the Octagon. On these posts they fix plates to which the rafters are tied with splints. . . . These are covered with clay and the whole thing with pine bark. . . . The [interior] space between the Octagon and the wall is one entire sopha where the visitors lie or sit at pleasure. It is covered with reed, or cane, or splint mats. In the center of the house on a small rise the fire is made, of dry cane or dry old pine slabs, split fine, and laid in a spiral circle." (Hawkins, *Letters, Journals and Writings,* 1:319–20; see also Bartram, *Travels,* 357–59; Swan, "Position and State of Manners," 264–65.)
29. Bartram, *Travels,* 360; Swan, "Position and State of Manners," 266–67.
30. Hawkins, *Letters, Journals and Writings,* 1:318–19.
31. Bartram, *Travels,* 360–61.
32. Swan, "Position and State of Manners," 265. Sculpture, an art form that had flourished during the Mississippian period, was rare during the contact period, but it did persist in the important square ground at Tuckabatchee. See Vernon J. Knight, "The Institutional Organization of Mississippian Religion," *American Antiquity* 51 (1986): 679, 683–84.
33. Swan, "Position and State of Manners," 266.

34. Bartram described the *acee* and calumet ceremonies he witnessed in the rotunda of Autossee (*Travels,* 358–59), and Swan described the square ground version of the *acee* rite he saw in Little Tallassee ("Position and State of Manners," 266–67).
35. Swan, "Position and State of Manners," 265.
36. Hawkins, *Letters, Journals and Writings,* 1:324–25.
37. Hudson, *The Southeastern Indians,* 374–75.
38. Hawkins, *Letters, Journals and Writings,* 1:322.
39. The Muskogees employed horticultural practices that did not rapidly exhaust the soil. By planting beans with corn, they offset the latter's great consumption of nitrogen. Hoeing rarely, they carefully avoided eroding the land. Additionally, since the Muskogees cultivated mainly floodplains, annual floods rejuvenated the soils. See Caleb Swan, "State of Arts and Manufactures, with the Creek Indians, in 1791," in *Information Respecting the History, Condition and Prospects of the Indian Tribes of the United States,* 5:693; Richard White, *The Roots of Dependency: Subsistence, Environment, and Social Change among the Choctaws, Pawnees, and Navajos* (Lincoln: University of Nebraska Press, 1983), 20ff.
40. Bartram, *Travels,* 399; Swan, "Position and State of Manners," 276–77; Hudson, *The Southeastern Indians,* 365.
41. Lankford, *Native American Legends,* 147, 155–56.
42. Payne, "The Green-Corn Dance," 19.
43. Bartram, *Travels,* 399; Swan, "Position and State of Manners," 268.
44. Swan, "Position and State of Manners," 267; Hawkins, *Letters, Journals and Writings,* 1:322; Bartram, *Travels,* 399; Adair, *History of the American Indians,* 116.
45. Swan, "Position and State of Manners," 267.
46. On the meaning of sacrifice in religion, see Georges Bataille, *Theory of Religion,* trans. Robert Hurley (New York: Zone, 1989), 50–54.
47. Swan, "Position and State of Manners," 267.
48. Hawkins, *Letters, Journals and Writings,* 1:324.
49. Swan, "Position and State of Manners," 268.
50. Ibid.
51. Payne, "The Green-Corn Dance," 24.
52. Thomas E. Emerson, "Water, Serpents, and the Underworld: An Exploration into Cahokian Symbolism," in Patricia Galloway, ed., *The Southeastern Ceremonial Complex: Artifacts and Analysis* (Lincoln: University of Nebraska Press, 1989), 58–62; Knight, "The Institutional Organization of Mississippian Religion," 677; Theodore Stern, "The Southeast," in *The Native Americans,* ed. Robert F. Spence and J. D. Jennings (New York: Harper & Row), 442; Bartram, *Travels,* 217–20.
53. Bartram, *Travels,* 396–97; Hawkins, *Letters, Journals and Writings,* 2:651; Swanton, "Creek Ethnographic and Vocabulary Notes," 29;

Lankford, *Native American Legends,* 229–42.

54. Hvidt, ed., *Von Reck's Voyage,* 42; Bartram, *Travels,* 390; Jean-Bernard Bossu, *Travels in the Interior of North America, 1751–1762,* trans. and ed. Seymour Feiler (Norman: University of Oklahoma Press, 1962), 149; Swan, "Position and State of Manners," 270–71; Swanton, *The Indians of the Southeastern United States,* 477–79, 774–75.

55. Hvidt, ed., *Von Reck's Voyage,* 42; Bossu, *Travels,* 149; James Adair, *History,* 90; Swan, "Position and State of Manners," 271.

56. My "performance" interpretation of Muskogee culture draws on Ellen Basso, *A Musical View of the Universe: Kalapalo Myth and Ritual Performances* (Philadelphia: University of Pennsylvania Press, 1985), 1–10; and Lawrence E. Sullivan, "Sound and Senses: Toward a Hermeneutics of Performance," *History of Religions* 26 (1986): 1–33.

2. Muskogee and the English Trade in Slaves and Skins

1. White, *The Roots of Dependency,* has shown economic dependency theory to be extremely useful in interpreting the ways in which eighteenth-century Choctaws became dependent on trade, trapped in debt, and vulnerable to colonizers' exploitation. Careful use of dependency theory might provide a useful framework for showing how other southeastern Native Americans participated in the world system, and it might account for why the English prevailed over the Spanish in the region. The portrayal of contact that would emerge, however, would shed little direct light on the experience of groups who never traded extensively with the French or English, groups such as the Apalachees of Florida. Even more important, the portrayal would leave far too undeveloped the ways generations of southeastern Native Americans resisted, undermined, and countered the forces, trends, and practices that produce economic dependency. For classic formulations of the theory, see Andre Gunder Frank, *Capitalism and Underdevelopment in Latin America* (New York: Monthly Review, 1969); and Immanuel Wallerstein, *The Modern World System: Capitalist Agriculture and the Origin of the European World Economy in the Sixteenth Century* (New York: Academic, 1974). For critical appraisals of the theory, see Daniel Garst, "Wallerstein and His Critics," *Theory and Society* 14 (1985): 469–95; and esp. June Nash, "Ethnographic Aspects of the World Capitalistic System," *Annual Review in Anthropology* 10 (1981): 393–423. See also Gary C. Anders, "Theories of Underdevelopment and the American Indian," *Journal of Economic Issues* 14 (1980): 681–701.

2. The intensity of the overlap in New England leads ethnohistorian Neal Salisbury to consider diseases and trade as components of the first phase of contact. This was followed by a second phase, settlement

(*Manitou and Providence: Indians, Europeans, and the Making of New England, 1500–1643* [New York: Oxford University Press, 1982, 12). Compare James Merrell, "The Indians' New World: The Catawba Experience," *William and Mary Quarterly*, 3d ser., 41 (1984): 539. On the basis of his study of the Catawbas, Merrell argues that disease, trade, and settlement constituted "three distinct yet overlapping stages." He also alludes to "a fourth stage, missionaries"; however, it is clear that he has in mind eighteenth-century Protestants. Merrell's model downplays the fact that, in some well-populated regions of the Southeast, numerous Catholic missionaries arrived in the sixteenth and seventeenth centuries.

3. Gregory A. Waselkov, "Seventeenth-Century Trade in the Colonial Southeast," *Southeastern Archaeology* 8 (1989): 117–33.

4. Marvin Smith, *Archaeology of Aboriginal Culture Change* (Gainesville: University of Florida Press, 1987), 27, 119–22; Merrell, "Indians' New World," 549. See Christopher L. Miller and George R. Hamell, "A New Perspective on Indian-White Contact: Cultural Symbols and Colonial Trade," *Journal of American History* 73 (1986): 311–28; James W. Bradley, *Evolution of the Onondaga Iroquois: Accommodating Change, 1500–1655* (Syracuse, N.Y.: Syracuse University Press, 1987). Compare Arthur J. Ray, "Indians as Consumers in the Eighteenth Century," in *Old Trails and New Directions: Papers of the Third North American Fur Trade Conference*, ed. Carol M. Judd and Arthur J. Ray (Toronto: University of Toronto Press, 1980), 255–71. For exemplary theoretical studies of cultural contact outside North America, see Marshall Sahlins, *Islands of History* (Chicago: University of Chicago Press, 1985); and esp. Rena Lederman, "Changing Times in Mendi: Notes towards Writing Highland New Guinea History," *Ethnohistory* 33 (1986): 1–30.

5. Bartram, *Travels*, 368; Adair, *History of the American Indians*, 285; Marvin T. Smith, "Aboriginal Population Movements in the Early Historic Period Interior Southeast," in *Powhatan's Mantle: Indians in the Colonial Southeast*, ed. Peter H. Wood, Gregory A. Waselkov, and Thomas M. Hatley (Lincoln: University of Nebraska Press, 1989), 21–34; Chester B. DePratter, "Late Prehistoric and Early Historic Chiefdoms in the Southeastern United States" (Ph.D. diss., University of Georgia, 1983); Hudson, "The Genesis of Georgia's Indians," 37.

6. Swan, "Position and State of Manners," 260; Bartram, *Travels*, 182; Swanton, *Indians of the Southeastern United States*, 89–91, 158–61, 184–86, 208–11, 212–15; Wright, *Creeks and Seminoles*, 3–13.

7. Michael D. Green, "Alexander McGillivray," in *American Indian Leaders: Studies in Diversity*, ed. R. David Edmunds (Lincoln: University of Nebraska Press, 1980), 41. See Wright, *Creeks and Seminoles*, 17, 19.

8. Knight, "The Institutional Organization of Mississippian Religion," 683.
9. Peter H. Wood, "The Changing Population of the Colonial South: An Overview by Race and Region, 1685–1790," in Wood et al., eds., *Powhatan's Mantle,* 35–103; John R. Swanton, *Early History of the Creek Indians,* Bureau of American Ethnology Bulletin no. 73 (Washington, D.C.: U.S. Government Printing Office, 1922), 434–43. Southern historians wildly disagree in their estimates of Native American populations in the Southeast. For example, J. Leitch Wright claims that "a minimum of 40,000 seems an appropriate, and indeed very conservative, estimate" for Muskogees at the end of the eighteenth century (*Creeks and Seminoles,* 127). In contrast, Daniel Usner estimates that the Muskogees numbered 15,160 ("American Indians on the Cotton Frontier," 298).
10. On the southeastern communication network and the traders' use of existing trails, see William E. Meyer, "Indian Trails of the Southeast," in *Forty-second Annual Report of the Bureau of American Ethnology for 1924–1925* (Washington, D.C.: U.S. Government Printing Office, 1928); Sharon Iowa Goad, "Exchange Networks in the Prehistoric Southeastern United States" (Ph.D. diss., University of Georgia, 1978); Helen Hornbeck Tanner, "The Land and Water Communication Systems of the Southeastern Indians," in Wood et al., eds., *Powhatan's Mantle,* 6–20; Gary Goodwin, *The Cherokees in Transition: A Study of Changing Culture and Environment prior to 1775* (Chicago: University of Chicago Press, 1977), 88; Turnbaugh, "Wide-Area Connections in Native North America," 22–28.
11. Marquette made this observation near Chickasaw Bluffs (John Gilmary, *Discovery and Exploration of the Mississippi Valley* [New York, 1852], 44). On southeastern Native Americans as middlemen, see Charles Hudson, *The Catawba Nation* (Athens, Ga.: University of Georgia Press, 1970), 29–51; James Merrell, " 'Our Bond of Peace': Patterns of Intercultural Exchange in the Carolina Piedmont, 1650–1750," in Wood et al., eds., *Powhatan's Mantle,* 198–204; Goodwin, *Cherokees in Transition,* 94.
12. Merrell, *Indians' New World;* Hudson, *Catawba Nation,* 38. The Spanish also had to rely on native middlemen. During the latter half of the seventeenth century, the Apalachees acted as middlemen between the Spanish and the Apalachicolas (Waselkov, "Seventeenth-Century Trade in the Colonial Southeast," 118–19).
13. J. Frederick Fausz, "Patterns of Anglo-Indian Aggression and Accommodation along the Mid-Atlantic Coast, 1584–1634," in *Cultures in Contact,* ed. William Fitzhugh (Washington, D.C.: Smithsonian, 1985), 225–70; J. Leitch Wright, Jr., *The Only Land They Knew: The*

Tragic Story of the American Indians in the Old South (New York: Free Press, 1981), 95–96, 106–9.

14. Wright, *The Only Land They Knew,* 109–10.

15. Fausz, "Patterns of Anglo-Indian Aggression," 227; see also his "Fighting 'Fire' with Firearms: The Anglo-Powhatan Arms Race in Early Virginia," *American Indian Culture and Research Journal* 3 (1979): 33–50, and "The Powhatan Uprising of 1622: A Historical Study of Ethnocentrism and Cultural Conflict" (Ph.D. diss., College of William and Mary, 1977).

16. The phrase "bonds of peace" was coined by John Banister (John Banister to Dr. Robert Morison, 6 April 1679, in *John Banister and His Natural History of Virginia, 1678–1692,* ed. Joseph Ewan and Nesta Ewan [Urbana: University of Illinois Press, 1970], 42).

17. See Fausz, "Patterns of Anglo-Indian Aggression," 225–26, 247–53.

18. James H. Merrell explores the changing meaning of the "bond of peace" for Catawbas in " 'Our Bond of Peace.' " See also Hudson, *Catawba Nation,* chap. 3, who reflects on the dialectical relation between trade and politics.

19. Peter H. Wood, "Indian Servitude in the Southeast," in *Handbook of North American Indians* (Washington, D.C.: U.S. Government Printing Office, 1988), 4:407–9; Merrell, *Indians' New World,* 36. See also Theda Perdue, *Slavery and the Evolution of Cherokee Society, 1540–1866* (Knoxville: University of Tennessee Press, 1979).

20. "The Indians call the English 'blond men' to distinguish them from the French and Spanish" (Bossu, *Travels,* 138). Historians have long debated the origins and identity of the Westoes. See Wright, *The Only Land They Knew,* 105–7; Hudson, *Catawba Nation,* 32–33; Smith, *Archaeology of the Aboriginal Culture Change,* 132–35. Spain's policy banning the sale of firearms to southeastern Native Americans later caused many to flee from Florida. In 1704, e.g., hundreds of Chatots fled Spanish Pensacola and sought refuge in French Mobile. When Commandant Bienville asked them "why they left the Spaniards," the Chatots replied that the Spanish "did not give them any guns, but that the French gave them to all of their allies" (quoted in Swanton, *Early History of the Creek Indians,* 123). See also the legend near Pensacola on the map reproduced in ibid., plate 3. For discussion of the Spanish policy against distributing guns to southeastern Native Americans, see Lewis Larson, "Guale Indians and the Spanish Mission Effort," in *Tacachale: Essays on the Indians of Florida and Southeastern Georgia during the Historic Period,* ed. Jerald Milanich and Samuel Proctor (Gainesville: University of Florida Press, 1978), 135–36; and John J. TePaske, "French, Spanish, and English Indian Policy on the Gulf Coast, 1513–1763: A Comparison," in *Spain and Her Rivals on the Gulf Coast,* ed.

Ernest F. Dibble and Earle W. Newton (Pensacola: University of West Florida Press, 1971), 18–24. Waselkov argues that, despite the official ban, firearms were sold to Florida Native Americans "in quantity" ("Seventeenth-Century Trade in the Colonial Southeast," 120).

21. *The Shaftsbury Papers, and other Records relating to Carolina and the First Settlement on Ashley River Prior to the Year 1676,* in *Collections of the South Carolina Historical Society,* ed. Langdon Cheves (Richmond: W. E. Jones, 1897), 5:165–66; Swanton, *Early History of the Creek Indians,* 66.

22. William James Rivers, *A Sketch of the History of South Carolina to the Close of the Proprietary Government* (Charleston, S.C.: McCarter & Co., 1856), 53–59; Wright, *The Only Land They Knew,* 102–25; Hudson, *Catawba Nation,* 39–51. The best history of this commerce remains Verner Crane's *Southern Frontier* (Durham, N.C.: Duke University Press, 1928), 21–69, 108–85. See also William S. Coker and Thomas Watson, *Indian Traders of the Southeastern Spanish Borderlands: Panton, Leslie and Company, 1783–1847* (Pensacola: University of West Florida Press, 1986); Goodwin, *Cherokees in Transition;* Merrell, "'Our Bond of Peace'"; Wright, *Creeks and Seminoles.*

23. *Journals of the Commons House of Assembly of South Carolina,* ed. Alexander S. Salley (Columbia, S.C., 1907–49), 13, 14 January 1692/3; David H. Cockran, *The Creek Frontier, 1540–1783* (Norman: University of Oklahoma Press, 1967), 50–51. See also Hudson, *Catawba Nation;* Wright, *The Only Land They Knew,* 102–25; Crane, *Southern Frontier,* 119–22.

24. Nathaniel Johnson, "Report of the Governor and Council, 1708," in *The Colonial South Carolina Scene: Contemporary Views, 1697–1774,* ed. H. Roy Merrens (Columbia: University of South Carolina Press, 1977), 33; James Freeman, "An Interview with James Freeman," in ibid., 53; Crane, *Southern Frontier,* 120–23; Wright, *The Only Land They Knew,* 108, 110.

25. Michael V. Gannon, *The Cross in the Sand: The Early Catholic Church in Florida, 1513–1870* (Gainesville: University of Florida Press, 1965); Amy Turner Bushnell, "That Demonic Game: The Campaign to Stop Indian Pelota Playing in Spanish Florida, 1675–1684," *The Americas* 35 (1978): 1–19, and "Ruling 'the Republic of Indians' in Seventeenth-Century Florida," in Wood et al., eds., *Powhatan's Mantle,* 134–50.

26. The contrasts between the Spanish and the English approaches were noted by French officials eager to emulate the English model. In 1730, Philibert Ory, the French comptroller general of Louisiana, urged Périer, the governor of Louisiana, not to imitate the Spaniards but "to follow the example of the English, who apply themselves only to caus-

ing the Indians to find profit in the trading that they carry on with them" (Ory to Périer, *MPA: FD*, 4:48).

27. Johnson, "Report of the Governor and Council," 36. Crane provides a description of the deer population and trade goods in *Southern Frontier*, 111–16; see also Kathryn E. Holland Braund, "Mutual Convenience–Mutual Dependence: The Creeks, Augusta, and the Deerskin Trade, 1733–1783" (Ph.D. diss., Florida State University, 1986), 139–42.

28. Wright, *The Only Land They Knew*, 105–23; Gene Waddell, *Indians of the South Carolina Lowcountry, 1562–1751* (Spartanburg, S.C.: Reprint Co., 1980), 3–12; White, *The Roots of Dependency*, 35; Wood, "Indian Slavery in the Southeast."

29. Approximately thirteen hundred additional Apalachees voluntarily marched to New Windsor on the Savannah River, where they remained until 1715 ("An Account of What the Army Did, under the Command of Col. Moore . . . ," in *Historical Collections of South Carolina*, ed. Batholomew Rivers Carroll [New York: Harper & Row, 1836], 570–76; Swanton, *Early History of the Creek Indians*, 121–22; John H. Hann, *Apalachee: The Land between the Rivers* [Gainesville: University of Florida Press, 1988], 264–83).

30. Johnson, "Report of the Governor and Council," 34.

31. "Documents of 1705," in *North Carolina Colonial Records* (Raleigh, N.C., 1886), 2:904.

32. *Journals of the Commissioners of the Indian Trade, September 20, 1710–August 29, 1718* (hereafter *JCIT*), ed. William L. McDowell, Jr. (Columbia: South Carolina Archives Dept., 1955), 65 (12 April 1715); Swanton, *Early History of the Creek Indians*, 97–101; Wright, *The Only Land They Knew*, 121–25; Crane, *Southern Frontier*, 162–86.

33. Peter H. Wood, *Black Majority: Negroes in Colonial South Carolina from 1670 through the Stono Rebellion* (New York: Knopf, 1974), 37–42, "The Changing Population of the Colonial South," 35–103, and "Indian Servitude in the Southeast," 407–9.

34. Louis R. Smith, Jr., "British-Indian Trade in Alabama, 1670–1756," *Alabama Review* 27 (January 1974): 70; Louis De Vorsey, Jr., "The Colonial Georgia Backcountry," in *Colonial Augusta: "Key of the Indian Country,"* ed. Edward J. Cashin (Macon, Ga.: Mercer University Press), 11.

35. "A State of the Province of Georgia," in *Collections of the Georgia Historical Society* (Savannah, Ga., 1842), 72.

36. Wright, *Creeks and Seminoles*, 59.

37. Peter J. Hamilton, *Colonial Mobile* (New York: Houghton, Mifflin, 1897), 203–4; Bienville and Salmon to Maurepas, 5 April 1734, *MPA: FD*, 3:652. White estimates that in the 1730s annual French gifts were

worth "8,500 to 25,000 deer." French giving remained at high levels until 1763. (White, *The Roots of Dependency*, 67, 63; see also Patricia Galloway, "'The Chief Who Is Your Father': Choctaw and French Views of the Diplomatic Relation," in Wood et al., eds., *Powhatan's Mantle*, 254–78.)

38. Hubert to the Council, 26 October 1717, *MPA: FD*, 2:250–51.

39. Périer to Maurepas, 1 April 1730, ibid., 4:31; Atkin, *Indians of the Southern Colonial Frontier*, 12; from de Bienville, 15 May 1733, *MPA: FD*, 1:193; Périer and Salmon to Maurepas, 5 December 1731, ibid., 4:91; Ory to Périer, 1 November 1730, ibid., 46; Hubert to the Council, 26 October 1717, ibid., 2:249–50.

40. Board of Commissioners to Capt. Charlesworth Glover, 3 June 1718, *JCIT*, 281–82.

41. Crémont to Salmon, 18 August 1732, *MPA: FD*, 4:122; Adair, *History of the American Indians*, 296–97; McDowell, ed., *Documents Relating to Indian Affairs, May 21, 1750–August 7, 1754*, 411; Atkin, *Indians of the Southern Colonial Frontier*, 31.

42. Atkin, *Indians of the Southern Colonial Frontier*, 27, n. 36; McDowell, ed., *Documents Relating to Indian Affairs, May 21, 1750–August 7, 1754*, 401–13. The irrationality of the system troubled the British, but they found no good alternative for distributing presents in Charleston and did not dare abandon the practice. See Atkin, *Indians of the Southern Colonial Frontier*, 27–33.

43. King's Paper, 29 May 1738, *MPA: FD*, 1:368; "Journal of an Indian Trader," in *Documents Relating to Indian Affairs, 1754–1765*, ed. William McDowell (Columbia: University of South Carolina Press, 1970), 57–60.

44. The fear of the French prompted Edmond Atkin to write his plan for regulating the deerskin trade (Atkin, *Indians of the Southern Colonial Frontier*, 4, 7–13).

45. David Taitt, "Journal of David Taitt's Travels from Pensacola, West Florida, to and through the Country of the Upper and Lower Creeks, 1772," in *Travels in the American Colonies*, ed. Newton D. Mereness (New York: Macmillan, 1916), 532. The figure "five pounds" for a buckskin was an exaggeration. In 1718, Carolina officials considered a heavy skin to be any "raw" skin that weighed more than two pounds or any "drest" skin that weighed more than one pound (*JCIT*, 269). Most raw skins probably weighed on average about 2.5 pounds, and that is a generous estimate (White, *The Roots of Dependency*, 67).

46. "I have had five hundred a day during the congress to entertain in this manner, and now that the main body is gone, I must have twenty or thirty that dine every day in the house and must have Indian corn to

carry to their camp for their children" (Farmar to the secretary of war, 24 January 1764, *Mississippi Provincial Archives: 1763–1766, English Dominion,* ed. Dunbar Rowland [Nashville, Tenn., 1911], 1:7–17).

47. Cecil Johnson, *British West Florida, 1763–1783* (New Haven, Conn.: Yale University Press, 1943), 39–43.

48. Ibid., 21, n. 50.

49. Bartram, *Travels,* 258 (see also 350–51); Adair, *History of the American Indians,* 230; "Dannll. Pepper to Governor Lyttleton," 30 March 1757, in McDowell, ed., *Documents Relating to Indian Affairs, 1754–1765,* 354; William S. Willis, Jr., "Anthropology and Negroes on the Southern Colonial Frontier," in *The Black Experience in America: Selected Essays,* ed. James C. Curtis and Lewis L. Gould (Austin: University of Texas Press, 1970), 48–49; Kenneth Wiggins Porter, *The Negro on the American Frontier* (New York: Arno Press and the New York Times, 1971), 47, 50, 58, 61, 172–73; Wright, *Creeks and Seminoles,* 57, 94, and *The Only Land They Knew,* 269, 270; Wood, *Black Majority,* 115; Daniel F. Littlefield, Jr., *Africans and Creeks: From the Colonial Period to the Civil War* (Westport, Conn.: Greenwood, 1979), 40–47.

50. Taitt, "Journal," 505.

51. Adair, *History of the American Indians,* 35.

52. Atkin, *The Indians of the Southern Colonial Frontier,* 35.

53. Bartram, *Travels,* 53–62; Taitt, "Journal," 507, 513, 524–25. The traders gained over one million acres above the Little River for Georgia in the Second Treaty of Augusta, 1773. A map representing this and other cessions is provided in Edward Cashin, "'But Brothers, It Is Our Land We Are Talking About': Winners and Losers in the Georgia Backcountry," in *An Uncivil War: The Southern Backcountry during the American Revolution,* ed. Ronald Hoffman, Thad W. Tate, and Peter J. Albert (Charlottesville: University of Virginia Press, 1985), 243; see also Pickett, *History of Alabama,* 328–29.

54. Taitt, "Journal," 553.

55. Merrell, *Indians' New World,* 137–38; Goodwin, *Cherokees in Transition,* 132–44; Albert E. Cowdrey, *This Land, This South: An Environmental History* (Lexington, Ky., 1983), 56–58.

56. Bartram, *Travels,* 181–82; for descriptions of ample game in Florida, see 165, 170, 172.

57. Governor Johnstone confessed, "The present Rupture is very fortunate for us more specially as it has been effected without giving them the least possibility of thinking we had any share in it. It was undoubtedly our interest to foment the dispute between these Nations. . . . I am of the opinion we should now feed the war" (quoted in White, *The Roots of Dependency,* 77). The Choctaw-Muskogee war probably diverted the Muskogees from waging war on their English neighbors to the east. In

1772, a Muskogee chief "observed that they were already at war with the Choctaws and thought these Sufficient without falling out with the white people." Another chief, Effatiskiniha, told David Taitt that he purposely promoted war with the Choctaws in order to avoid war with the English. Since his town was on the eastern border of Muskogee country and most vulnerable to English attack, Effatiskiniha "made war on purpose to keep his Young people from falling out with the English and as soon as his Nation makes peace with the Chactaws he will Spoil it again as he knows they must be at war with some body" (Taitt, "Journal," 553–54).

58. During times of war, as a Cherokee leader in 1752 complained, it was virtually impossible to "hunt in Safety and get Skins" ("Talk of the Cherokee Emperor and Others," 27 April 1752, in McDowell, ed., *Documents Relating to Indian Affairs, 1750–1754,* 256). Because of hostilities with the Cherokees, the Muskogees at Coweta also lost "their Winter Hunts" ("Second Journal of Thomas Bosomworth," in ibid., 321). See also, White, *The Roots of Dependency,* 77. During the Choctaw-Muskogee war, hunting slowed, but did not cease. In 1774, William Bartram observed a band of forty Muskogee warriors "destined against the Chactaws of West Florida." Though prepared to fight, they claimed that "the principal object of this expedition was hunting on the plentiful borders of the Chactaws" (Bartram, *Travels,* 215–16).

59. Atkin, *Indians of the Southern Colonial Frontier,* 11.

3. Intimate Strangers, Hostile Neighbors

1. Hawkins, *Letters, Journals and Writings,* 1:305.

2. Indeed, George Galphin fathered children with a Yuchi woman named Metawney and another southeastern Native American named Nitshukey. He also fathered children with an African American slave named Mina, the sister of Ketch. See "The Last Will and Testament of George Galphin," in "Creek Indian Letters, Talks, and Treaties, 1705–1839," ed. Mrs. J. E. [Louise Frederick] Hays, Georgia Department of Archives and History, Atlanta, 1939, p. 8.

3. "The Hollowing King of the Cowetas and the Fat King of Cusetas," frame 352. African Americans had long played an important role in frontier commerce. Working as packhorsemen and interpreters in the deerskin trade and as cowboys on the Muskogee-Carolina frontier, a small number of African Americans traveled into Muskogee, meeting the people, learning the languages, striking up affairs, trading a little on the side, exchanging dances and stories, talking politics. Even though such mingling was feared by Anglo-Americans and often forbidden by colonial laws, this contact could not be stopped; the trade

required the skills of African Americans. See *JCIT,* 252 (28 January 1717/18); Littlefield, *Africans and Creeks,* 9, 14, 15, 28; Adair, *History of the American Indians,* 121; Thomas Cooper and David J. McCord, eds., *The Statutes at Large of South Carolina,* 10 vols. (Columbia: A. S. Johnson, 1836–41), 2:693; "Instructions for the Government of South Carolina," *South Carolina Public Records,* (5 June 1682); John Donald Duncan, "Servitude and Slavery in Colonial South Carolina, 1670–1776" (Ph.D. diss., Emory University, 1972), 33, 604–29; Wright, *The Only Land They Knew,* 272; William S. Willis, "Divide and Rule: Red, White, and Black in the Southeast," in Hudson, ed., *Red White, and Black,* 99–115; J. H. Johnston, "Documentary Evidence of the Relations of Negroes and Indians," *Journal of Negro History* 14 (1929): 21–43; Wood, *Black Majority,* 116.

4. Thomas Woodward, *Woodward's Reminiscences of the Creek, or Muscogee Indians, Contained in Letters to Friends in Georgia and Alabama* (1859; reprint, Tuscaloosa: Alabama Book Store, 1939), 105–6. Woodward is vague on precisely how long Ketch remained among the Muskogees. Ketch lived to be "near a hundred years old."

5. Duncan, "Servitude and Slavery," 40. For a discussion of slave resistance, see Eugene Genovese, *Roll, Jordan, Roll: The World the Slaves Made* (New York: Vintage, 1976), 587–660. Beginning in 1682, the Carolina Proprietors paid allied Native Americans to pursue runaway African American slaves. Later, Carolina used African Americans as soldiers against Native American opponents. Throughout the colonial period, Carolina officials banned African Americans from Muskogee because they believed that "the carrying of Negroes among the Indians . . . [is] detrimental, as an Intimacy between them ought to be avoided" (Daniel Pepper to William Henry Lyttleton, 30 March 1757, in McDowell, ed., *Documents Relating to Indian Affairs, 1754–1765,* 357). See also Merrell, *Indians' New World,* 99, 316, n. 16; Duncan, "Servitude and Slavery," 604–13; Willis, "Divide and Rule"; Littlefield, *Africans and Creeks,* 14–19.

6. James Wright to the earl of Hillsborough, 4 July 1768, in *Colonial Records of the State of Georgia,* ed. Allen D. Candler and Lucien Lamar Knight (Atlanta: [state printers], 1904–16), 27:330. Of course, not all runaways found refuge in Muskogee. Some were ransomed by Muskogees for the reward offered by colonial officials. See Duncan, "Slavery and Servitude," 630–32. As Peter H. Wood notes, running away was "a more frequent, more complicated and more politically significant act than was once imagined [by scholars]" (Peter H. Wood, "'I Did the Best I Could for My Day': The Study of Early Black History during the Second Reconstruction, 1960 to 1976," *William and Mary Quarterly,* 3d ser., 35, no. 2 [April 1978]: 217). Pertinent studies of run-

aways include John J. TePaske, "The Fugitive Slave: Intercolonial Rivalry and Spanish Slave Policy, 1686–1764," in Procter, ed., *Eighteenth-Century Florida and Its Borderlands*, 1–12; Daniel D. Meaders, "South Carolina Fugitives as Viewed through Local Colonial Newspapers with Emphasis on Runaway Notices, 1732–1801," *Journal of Negro History* 60 (1975): 288–319; Lathan A. Windley, "A Profile of Runaway Slaves in Virginia and South Carolina from 1730 through 1787" (Ph.D. diss., University of Iowa, 1974).

7. Swan, "Position and State of Manners," 277, and "State of Arts and Manufactures," 692.

8. A war chief named Tustennuggee Emathla ("Jim Boy") had "negro blood" ("From the Notebook of Michael Johnstone Kenan," Swanton Papers, National Anthropological Archives, Smithsonian Institution, 4). Abraham, a runaway from Pensacola, became a very prominent leader among the Seminoles (Porter, *The Negro on the American Frontier*, 61). William Willis notes that, "since most Negroes in the Indian country were males, these intermarriages mainly united Black males with Indian women. As the clans were matrilineal in descent, the mixed offspring became bona fide Creek citizens" (Willis, "Anthropology and Negroes on the Southern Colonial Frontier," 48–49). See also Porter, *The Negro on the American Frontier*, 47, 50, 58, 61, 172–73; Wright, *The Only Land They Knew*, 269, 270, and *Creeks and Seminoles*, 94; Wood, *Black Majority*, 115; Littlefield, *Africans and Creeks*, 40–47.

9. Current-Garcia, ed., *Shem, Ham and Japheth*, 37.

10. William G. McLoughlin, with Walter H. Conser, Jr., and Virginia Duffy McLoughlin, *The Cherokee Ghost Dance: Essays on the Southeastern Indians, 1789–1861* (Macon, Ga.: Mercer University Press, 1984), 263; Porter, *The Negro on the American Frontier*, 47.

11. Albert J. Raboteau, *Slave Religion: The "Invisible Institution" in the Antebellum South* (New York: Oxford, 1980); Genovese, *Roll, Jordan, Roll*, 209–84; Gayraud S. Wilmore, *Black Religion and Black Radicalism: An Interpretation of the Religious History of Afro-American People* (Maryknoll, N.Y.: Orbis, 1983), 1–28. While dealing with an entirely different context, Vicente Rafael's *Contracting Colonialism: Transition and Christian Conversion in Tagalog Society under Early Spanish Rule* (Ithaca, N.Y.: Cornell University Press, 1988) provides a stimulating discussion of religious exchange under colonialism.

12. Francis Le Jau to John Chamberlayne, St. James, Goose Creek, S.C., 1 February 1709/10, quoted in Frank Klingberg, *An Appraisal of the Negro in Colonial South Carolina: A Study in Americanization* (Washington, D.C.: Associated Publishers, 1947), 16.

13. The Carolina planters' need for labor led them to raid interior villages and bring Native American women and children back as slaves. Because

most of the enslaved Africans were men, the slave quarters became the locus of fusion of African and Native American cultural heritages. This fact led J. Leitch Wright to claim that African Americans gained much of their material culture and folklore from southeastern Native Americans (see *The Only Land They Knew*, 248–78).

14. Walter H. Brooks, "The Priority of the Silver Bluff Church and Its Promoters," *Journal of Negro History* 7 (1922): 172–96; Raboteau, *Slave Religion*, 139.

15. Wright, *Creeks and Seminoles*, 81; Brooks, "The Priority of the Silver Bluff Church," 187–88.

16. Littlefield, *Africans and Creeks*, 28; Willis, "Anthropology and Negroes on the Southern Colonial Frontier," 46.

17. Milfort, *Memoir*, 11; Hawkins, *Letters, Journals and Writings*, 1:5, 13.

18. Carl Mauelshagen and Gerald H. Davis, trans., *Partners in the Lord's Work: The Diary of Two Moravian Missionaries in the Creek Indian Country*, Research Paper no. 21 (Atlanta: Georgia State College, 1969), 73, 58.

19. Hawkins, *Letters, Journals and Writings*, 1:18; Lud. Grant to Governor Glen, 3 May 1752, in *Documents Relating to Indian Affairs, May 21, 1750—August 7, 1754*, 263; Atkin, *Indians of the Southern Colonial Frontier*, 8, 22; Adair, *History of the American Indians*, 242.

20. Bartram, *Travels*, 170; Swan, "Position and State of Manners," 268.

21. Bartram, *Travels*, 215; Swan, "Position and State of Manners," 254.

22. Hawkins, "Sketch of the Creek Country," 69.

23. Adair, *History of the American Indians*, 147.

24. Bartram, *Travels*, 402.

25. Bossu, *Travels*, 153; Swan, "Position and State of Manners," 269; Hawkins, "Sketch of the Creek Country," 70; Hawkins, *Letters, Journals and Writings*, 1:301; Adair, *History of the American Indians*, 394.

26. Taitt, "Journal," 525; John A. Pope, *A Tour Through the Southern and Western Territories of the United States of North America; The Spanish Dominion on the River Mississippi and the Floridas; The Countries of the Creek Nation and Many Uninhabited Parts* (1791; reprint, New York: Charles L. Woodward, 1888), 57; Swan, "Position and State of Manners," 255, n. 1, 256, 260, 261. Taitt's use of the term "half-breed" antedates the examples noted in the *Oxford English Dictionary*. See Jennifer S. H. Brown, "Linguistic Solitudes and Changing Social Categories," in Judd and Ray, eds., *Old Trails and New Directions*, 147–59.

27. The best introduction to the métis people of the Great Lakes region is Jacqueline Louise Peterson's "The People in Between: Indian-White Marriage and the Genesis of a Métis Society and Culture in the Great Lakes Region, 1680–1830" (Ph.D. diss., University of Illinois at Chicago Circle, 1981). For a general overview of pertinent scholarship, see

Jacqueline Peterson and John Anfinson, "The Indian and the Fur Trade," in *Scholars and the Indian Experience: Critical Reviews of Recent Writing in the Social Sciences,* ed. W. R. Swagerty (Bloomington: Indiana University Press, 1984), 223–58.

28. Taitt, "Journal," 525, 547, 549.
29. Hawkins, *Letters, Journals and Writings,* 1:17 (14 December 1796).
30. Bartram, *Travels,* 58, 71, 165, 172, 185.
31. Hawkins, *Letters, Journals and Writings,* 1:21, 28.
32. John Walton Caughey, *McGillivray of the Creeks* (Norman: University of Oklahoma Press, 1938); Green, "Alexander McGillivray."
33. Spanish Governor Zespedes complained of the Muskogees' "insatiable greed" for presents (James F. Doster, *The Creek Indians and Their Florida Lands, 1740–1823* [New York: Garland, 1974], 1:61); see also Coker and Watson, *Indian Traders,* 63, 65.
34. Elizabeth H. Yamaguchi, "Macon County, Alabama: Its Land and Its People from Pre-history to 1870" (M.A. thesis, Auburn University, 1981), 1–31.
35. Green, "Alexander McGillivray," 51.
36. Swan, "Position and State of Manners," 279.
37. Milfort, *Memoir,* 32.
38. Swan, "Position and State of Manners," 281–82. See also Coker and Watson, *Indian Traders,* 55–58, 68, 69; Green, "Alexander McGillivray," 50–52; Doster, *Creek Indians,* 1:41–42, 57–58, 66. McGillivray also directed attacks against Anglo-American settlers on the eastern and northern frontiers of Muskogee. In 1786, his warriors destroyed a small settlement at the Muscle Shoals.
39. "To the Tame King of the Cowetas and the Fat King of the Cusetas," 7 August 1787, Papers of the Continental Congress, U.S. National Archives, microcopy M247, roll 87, frames 361–62; Doster, *Creek Indians,* 1:72–73.

4. The Gaze of Development

1. Hawkins, "Sketch of the Creek Country," 22, 20, 39.
2. Green, "Alexander McGillivray," 41–42; Mary Young, "Tribal Reorganization in the Southeast, 1800–1840," in *The Struggle for Political Autonomy,* Occasional Papers in Curriculum Series no. 11 (Chicago: Newberry Library, 1989), 62, 66–67, 74, n. 15.
3. Hawkins, "Sketch of the Creek Country," 29, 33, 45, 47, 40, 53.
4. Swan, "Position and State of Manners," 257, 258.
5. Bartram, *Travels,* 46, 57, 60, 134, 199.
6. Bartram himself had failed as an indigo planter in East Florida in the 1760s. His father, John, a famous botanist, espoused a much harsher

attitude toward Native Americans, viewing them as savage obstacles to progress. See Wayne Franklin, *Discoverers, Explorers, Settlers: The Diligent Writers of Early America* (Chicago: University of Chicago Press, 1982), 49–68.

7. Swan, "State of Arts and Manufactures," 692, and "Position and State of Manners," 255, n. 2.

8. Swan, "Position and State of Manners," 258.

9. Wright, *Creeks and Seminoles*, 130–53.

10. On Tennessee's early history, see J. G. M. Ramsey, *The Annals of Tennessee to the Eighteenth Century* (Chattanooga, Tenn.: Kingsport, 1926).

11. J. F. H. Claiborne, *Mississippi as a Province, Territory and State* (Jackson, Miss.: Power & Barksdale, 1880), 113–16; Usner, "American Indians on the Cotton Frontier," 298.

12. Pickett, *History of Alabama*, 416–19. The name "Tensaw" was taken from the small community of Taensa people who had lived in the region from 1744 to 1763. See Swanton, *Indians of the Southeastern United States*, 188.

13. Judge Campbell to Governor Caswell, 30 November 1786, in Ramsey, *Annals of Tennessee*, 350.

14. Pickett, *History of Alabama*, 442, 446–48. It was partly as a result of this scandal that Hawkins first became involved in Muskogee affairs. During the fall of 1795, he served on the president's commission charged with settling boundary disputes and other manners of concern to Georgia, the Muskogees, and the United States. At a conference in Georgia, Hawkins helped formulate the Treaty of Colerain. C. L. Grant, introduction to Hawkins, *Letters, Journals and Writings*, 1:xv.

15. As early as 1786, frontiersmen believed that "the continent of America one day [is] to become one consolidated government of United States" (Judge Campbell to Governor Caswell, 30 November 1786, in Ramsey, *Annals of Tennessee*, 350).

16. Big Ten University, *Liberty's Legacy: Our Celebration of the Northwest Ordinance and the United States Constitution* (Columbus: Ohio Historical Society, 1987), 28 (map of the eastern half of the United States, 1784), 34; see also Peter S. Onuf, *Statehood and Union: A History of the Northwest Ordinance* (Bloomington: Indiana University Press, 1987).

17. Such an approach owes much to the historical phenomenology of the late Michel Foucault. For a useful and accessible introduction to Foucault's methods, see Hubert L. Dreyfus and Paul Rabinow, *Michel Foucault: Beyond Structuralism and Hermeneutics* (Chicago: University of Chicago Press, 1982), For a discussion of the category "gaze," see Dana Polan, "Powers of Vision, Visions of Power," *Camera Obscura* 18 (1988): 112–13.

18. This practical way of viewing land was constructed in, communicated through, and reinforced by a distinctive kind of rhetoric. Three varieties of this rhetoric, the narrative of discovery, the narrative of exploration, and the narrative of settlement, have been analyzed thoroughly by Wayne Franklin. Of the three varieties, the narrative of exploration was the one that emphasized most strongly the land's abject need for Europeans and their processing systems of discipline and culture. By the end of the eighteenth century, the narrative of exploration dominated travelers' accounts of Muskogee. See Franklin, *Discoverers, Explorers, Settlers,* 17, 71.

19. Hawkins, "Sketch of the Creek Country," 54–55.

20. Pickett, *History of Alabama,* 449.

21. In 1791, George Washington had urged that "rational experiments should be made for imparting to [American Indians] the blessings of civilization" (Third Annual Message, 25 October 1791, in *State of the Union Messages of the Presidents, 1790–1966,* ed. Fred L. Israel [New York: Chelsea House–Robert Hector, 1966], 1:9). According to a Georgia newspaper, Washington used the word "experiment" in describing Hawkins's mission (*Republican and Savannah Evening Ledger,* 15 September 1812, quoted in Grant, introduction to Hawkins, *Letters, Journals and Writings,* 1:xvii).

22. Hawkins was born in 1754, the son of a planter family in Warren County, North Carolina. He was educated at Princeton, served in the Continental Congress, and during the 1780s and 1790s represented the federal government in several treaty talks with southeastern Native Americans. For Hawkins's biography, see Florette Henri, *The Southern Indians and Benjamin Hawkins, 1796–1816* (Norman: University of Oklahoma Press, 1986).

23. Nunez, "Creek Nativism and the Creek War of 1813–1814," 132.

24. Hawkins, *Letters, Journals and Writings,* 1:226, 229, "A Sketch of the Creek Country," 53, and *Letters, Journals, and Writings,* 1:199. On the location of Coweta Tallahassee, see Hawkins, *Letters, Writings and Journals,* 309; and Merritt B. Pound, *Benjamin Hawkins—Indian Agent* (Athens: University of Georgia Press, 1951), 143, and frontispiece.

25. Hawkins, "A Sketch of the Creek Country," 30; Yamaguchi, "Macon County, Alabama," 25–28.

26. H. Warren Button and Eugene F. Provenzo, *History of Education and Culture in America* (Englewood Cliffs, N.J.: Prentice-Hall, 1983), 63–66; Howard A. Ozmon and Samuel M. Craver, *Philosophical Foundations of Education* (Columbus, Ohio: Merrill, 1986), 51. Hawkins's efforts antedated those of Robert Owen (b. 1771) in New Lanark, Scotland, and New Harmony, Indiana.

27. Hawkins, *Letters, Journals and Writings,* 1:209, and "Sketch of the Creek Country," 53.
28. Hawkins, "Sketch of the Creek Country," 54. Mauelshagen and Davis, trans., *Partners in the Lord's Work,* 6; *ASP: IA,* 1:598–99; Pound, *Benjamin Hawkins,* 91, 140.
29. Hawkins, *Letters, Journals and Writings,* 2:551–52. Hawkins had provided Muskogee women with cards for cleaning cotton and producing thread. For a sketch of the agency, which clearly shows six slave cabins, see the plan of the Creek Agency made by F. H. Schumann in 1810, reproduced as the centerpiece of Mauelshagen and Davis, trans., *Partners in the Lord's Work.* By 1816, Hawkins's property included seventy-five slaves. Ibid., 52, n. 38.
30. Hawkins, *Letters, Journals and Writings,* 2:552.
31. Hawkins, "Sketch of the Creek Country," 58; Hawkins, *Letters, Journals and Writings,* 2:520, 552; Elizabeth Yamaguchi, "Macon County, Alabama," 189, n. 2. After 1797, these lessons were reinforced at the federal store at Fort Wilkinson on the Oconee River. Established by Congress in 1796, this store was intended to compete with trading firms in Spanish Florida and provide Muskogees with a closely regulated commerce.
32. Hawkins, "Sketch of the Creek Country," 30. The dynamic of "settling out" was evident in many of the villages visited by the agent (ibid., 44, 46).
33. See the analysis of Charles Post, "Primitive Accumulation, Class Struggle and the Capitalist State: Political Crisis and the Origins of U.S. Capitalism" (Ph.D. diss., State University of New York at Binghamton, 1984).
34. McLoughlin, *The Cherokee Ghost Dance,* 14, 24, 261–68, 271; George D. Harmon, *Sixty Years of Indian Affairs, 1789–1850* (Chapel Hill: University of North Carolina, 1941); Usner, "American Indians on the Cotton Frontier," 297–317.
35. Thomas Jefferson to Horatio Gates, 11 July 1803, quoted in Winthrop Hudson, *White over Black* (Chapel Hill: University of North Carolina Press, 1968), 480.
36. Hawkins, *Letters, Journals and Writings,* 1:47–48.
37. Ibid., 163–64.
38. Hawkins's Muskogee writings, in their published form, fill nearly eight hundred pages. This does not include the many papers lost when his house burned in 1816. Hawkins's library was enormous, numbering nearly two hundred books. The subject areas included practical arts, government, law, biography, philosophy, travel accounts, literature, geographies, and atlases. See Henri, *The Southern Indians and Benjamin Hawkins,* 34–35.

39. Milfort, *Memoir,* 51–52.
40. Hawkins, "Sketch of the Creek Country," 63.
41. Hawkins, *Letters, Journals and Writings,* 1:29 and "Sketch of the Creek Country," 36.
42. Pickett, *History of Alabama,* 325–26.
43. Woodward, *Reminiscences,* 129, 105; Swan, "Position and State of Manners," 252; H. S. Halbert and T. H. Ball, *The Creek War of 1813 and 1814* (Montgomery, Ala.: White, Woodruff, & Fowler, 1895), 157–66.
44. Johnson, *British West Florida,* 7, 9.
45. Pickett, *History of Alabama,* 417, 326.
46. The Muskogees received thousands of dollars in annuities each year as a result of the Treaty of New York (1790), the Treaty of Fort Wilkinson (1802), and the Treaty of Washington (1805). For a synopsis, see Yamaguchi, "Macon County, Alabama," 193.
47. See J. Anthony Paredes, "Back from Disappearance: The Alabama Creek Indian Community," in *Southeastern Indians since the Removal Era,* ed. Walter L. Williams (Athens: University of Georgia Press, 1979).
48. Hawkins, "Sketch of the Creek Country," 29.
49. Hawkins, "Sketch of the Creek Country," 29, 38 and *Letters, Journals and Writings,* 1:29.
50. See Carol Mason, "Eighteenth Century Culture Change among the Lower Creeks," *Florida Anthropologist* 16 (1963): 65–81. The challenge of achieving economic strength without desecrating the land and culture remains a vital issue for almost all Native American groups in the United States. See D'Arcy McNickle Center for the Study of the American Indian, *Overcoming Economic Dependency,* Occasional Papers in Curriculum Series, no. 9 (Chicago: Newberry Library, 1988).
51. Richard Bailey, the son of an English trader and a Muskogee woman, "was educated in Philadelphia . . . and he . . . brought with him into the nation so much contempt for the Indian mode of life, that he . . . got himself into discredit with them" (Hawkins, "Sketch of the Creek Country," 31). On the métis rejection of the ceremonial cycle, see Yamaguchi, "Macon County, Alabama," 28–29.
52. Swan, "Position and State of Manners," 270.
53. Doster, *Creek Indians,* 1:142–43.
54. Halbert and Ball, *The Creek War of 1813 and 1814,* 113, 168; Mauelshagen and Davis, trans., *Partners in the Lord's Work,* 10, 63.
55. On the relations between Quakers and Native Americans, see Sydney V. James, *A People among Peoples: Quaker Benevolences in Eighteenth Century America* (Cambridge, Mass.: Harvard University Press, 1963), 298–315.

56. Nehemiah Curnock, ed., *Journal of John Wesley*, Standard Edition (London: Robert Culley, 1910), 1:160, 205.

57. Charles C. Jones, *Historical Sketch of Tomo-chi-chi, Mico of the Yamacraws* (Albany, N.Y.: Joel Munsell, 1868), 103.

58. Mauelshagen and Davis, trans., *Partners in the Lord's Work*, 22; see also 30, 72.

59. For a similar interaction between missionaries and Native Americans in the Northeast, see James Axtell, *The European and the Indian: Essays in the Ethnohistory of Colonial North America* (New York: Oxford University Press, 1981), 44–79. Compare Rafael's *Contracting Colonialism*.

60. Hawkins, "Sketch of the Creek Country," 38, 30. Mauelshagen and Davis, trans. *Partners in the Lord's Work*, 59.

61. Clifford Geertz, "Religion as a Cultural System," in *The Interpretation of Cultures* (New York: Basic, 1973), 93–94.

62. Yamaguchi, "Macon County, Alabama," 193; Doster, *Creek Indians*, 2:14.

5. The Resounding Land

1. Halbert and Ball, *The Creek War of 1813 and 1814*, 71. Geologists refer to this event as the New Madrid earthquake and estimate that it would have measured 8.2 on the Richter scale, thus making it the largest such event to have occurred in North America in the last several centuries.

2. Moravian Mission diary entry, Springplace, Ga., 10 February 1811, Moravian Archives, Winston-Salem, N.C., quoted in McLoughlin, *The Cherokee Ghost Dance*, app. E, 142.

3. Francis Howard to Dr. Porter, Jefferson, Ga., 14 February 1812, in Hays, ed., "Creek Indian Letters, Talks and Treaties, 1705–1839"; Mauelshagen and Davis, trans., *Partners in the Lord's Work*, 68; Moravian Mission diary entry, 17 December 1811, quoted in McLoughlin, *The Cherokee Ghost Dance*, app. E, p. 143; R. A. Eppley, *Earthquake History of the United States, Part I* (Washington, D.C.: U.S. Government Printing Office, 1965), 67–68; Yamaguchi, "Macon County, Alabama," 197; *Niles Weekly Register*, 4 January 1812.

4. Homi Bhabha theorizes the problematic of the Book in the colonial context in his "Signs Taken for Wonders: Questions of Ambivalence and Authority under a Tree Outside Delhi, May 1817," *Critical Inquiry* 12 (1985): 144–65, and "Of Mimicry and Man: The Ambivalence of Colonial Discourse," *October* 28 (1984): 125–33; see also Peter Worsley, *The Trumpet Shall Sound* (New York: Schocken, 1974), 241.

5. Mauelshagen and Davis, trans., *Partners in the Lord's Work*, 53. In some Native American millenarian movements, prophets constructed "Books." For a description of the Lenape prophet Neolin and the "In-

dian Bible," see John G. Heckewelder, *History, Manners and Customs of the Indian Nations Who Once Inhabited Pennsylvania* (Philadelphia: Historical Society of Pennsylvania, 1876), 291–93.

6. As many students of colonialism have noted, rumormongering plays a critical role in political/religious movements of the oppressed. See Kenelm Burridge, *New Heaven, New Earth: A Study of Millenarian Activities* (New York: Schocken, 1969), 106, 107; Shahid Amin, "Gandhi as Mahatma: Gorakhpur District, Eastern UP, 1921–22," in *Subaltern Studies: Writings on South Asian History and Society, III,* ed. Ranajit Guha (Oxford: Oxford University Press, 1984), 1–61.

7. Nunez, "Creek Nativism and the Creek War of 1813–1814," 146.

8. The Shawnees had begun their southern tour among the Chickasaws and Choctaws, but these peoples were indifferent or even hostile to Tecumseh's plan. See Halbert and Ball, *The Creek War of 1813 and 1814,* 40–84.

9. Swanton, *Indians of the Southeastern United States,* 184–86; R. David Edmunds, *Tecumseh and the Quest for American Indian Leadership* (Boston: Little, 1984), 19; Wright, *Creeks and Seminoles,* 168; Henri, *The Southern Indians and Benjamin Hawkins,* 71.

10. For these developments among the Shawnee, see Edmunds, *Tecumseh,* 17, 62–65, 89.

11. Halbert and Ball, *The Creek War of 1813 and 1814,* 71; Owsley, *Struggle for the Gulf Borderlands,* 13.

12. "Decree of the Creek Council of Muscogee," 25 October 1791, quoted in Doster, *Creek Indians,* 1:116. On Bowles's career, see ibid., 80–88, 112–21; J. Leitch Wright, Jr., *William Augustus Bowles: Director General of the Creek Nation* (Athens: University of Georgia Press, 1967); Hawkins, *Letters, Journals and Writings,* 1:263; 267–70, 344, 347–79; 2:427, 442, 453–58.

13. Swan, "Position and State of Manners," 275.

14. Nunez, "Creek Nativism and the Creek War of 1813–1814," 137, 142.

15. Edmunds, *Tecumseh,* 109.

16. Hawkins, *Letters, Journals and Writings,* 2:453, 562; Doster, *Creek Indians,* 1:235, 254, 2:5–6.

17. Sec. of War Dearborn to Hawkins, 24 May 1803, quoted in Doster, *Creek Indians,* 1:235.

18. Hoboheilthlee Micco [Hopoithle Miko] to the president of the United States, Letters Received by the Office of the Secretary of War on Indian Affairs, 1800–1823, microcopy M271, roll 1, frame 554, U.S. National Archives, Washington, D.C. See also Hawkins, *Letters, Journals and Writings,* 2:541; Doster, *Creek Indians,* 2:6; Usner, "American Indians on the Cotton Frontier," 303.

19. Edmunds, *Tecumseh,* 223; see also 109, 110, 126–28.

20. Doster, *Creek Indians*, 2:36–37; Hawkins, *Letters, Journals and Writings*, 2:591; Claiborne, *Mississippi*, 316; Owsley, *Struggle for the Gulf Borderlands*, 12; Gregory A. Waselkov and Brian M. Wood, "The Creek War of 1813–1814: Effects on Creek Society and Settlement Pattern," *Journal of Alabama Archaeology* 32, no. 1 (1986): 2.

21. Hoboheilthlee Micco [Hopoithle Miko] to the president of the United States, 15 May 1811, Letters Received by the Office of the Secretary of War on Indian Affairs, 1800–1823, microcopy M271, roll 1, frame 554, U.S. National Archives, Washington, D.C.

22. Hawkins, *Letters, Journals and Writings*, 2:594. See James Madison to the chiefs of the Creek Nation, 14 January 1811, Records of the Secretary of War, Letters Sent Relating to Indian Affairs, 1800–1824, microcopy M15, roll 3, frame 57; William Eustis to Col. Hawkins, 15 January, 27 June, 20 July 1811, ibid., frames 58, 85, 90.

23. Halbert and Ball, *The Creek War of 1813 and 1814*, 73. No copy of Tecumseh's speech to the Muskogees exists, although Halbert and Ball include J. F. H. Claiborne's stirring reconstruction of the speech. Claiborne's version is historically dubious, and I have avoided using it. Compare Owsley, *Struggle for the Gulf Borderlands*, 12–13.

24. "Journal of an Indian Trader," 11 January 1755, in McDowell, ed., *Documents Relating to Indian Affairs, 1754–1765*, 67; Hallowing King to Governor Matthews, 18 September 1794, quoted in Doster, *Creek Indians*, 1:174; Green, "Alexander McGillivray," 52–53; minutes of the treaty at Colerain, 18, 19 June 1796, in *ASP: IA*, 1:598; Hawkins, *Letters, Journals and Writings*, 1:184–85, 2:460; William Hill to David Emanuel, Fort Wilkinson, 2 July 1801, in Hays, ed., "Creek Indian Letters, Talks and Treaties, 1705–1839."

25. Hawkins, *Letters, Journals and Writings*, 2:562; Doster, *Creek Indians*, 2:16. President Jefferson responded by urging the Muskogees to adopt civilization. "Fence in your lands, plow as much land as you can, raise corn and hogs and cattle. Learn your young women to spin, and let those who are older learn to weave. You will then have food and clothing and live comfortably. . . . You can shoot some turkeys and kill some deer; but it is better for you to plow the land and raise corn and cattle" (ibid., 17).

26. Hawkins, *Letters, Journals and Writings*, 2:525, 555.

27. Ibid., 1:162.

28. Halbert and Ball, *The Creek War of 1813 and 1814*, 73.

29. The following discussion of shamans is based on Bartram, *Travels*, 390; Bossu, *Travels*, 149; Adair, *History of the American Indians*, 90; Swanton, "Creek Ethnographic and Vocabulary Notes," and *The Indians of the Southeastern United States*, 774; Wright, *Creeks and Seminoles*, 157–59; and Waselkov and Wood, "The Creek War of 1813–1814," 4.

30. Bartram, *Travels*, 390.

31. Bossu, *Travels,* 149. This particular ceremony bears a weak resemblance to the sweat lodge ceremony performed throughout North America and a very strong resemblance to the "shaking-tent" ceremonies practiced by shamans among northern groups such as the Anishinaabeg.
32. Nunez, "Creek Nativism and the Creek War of 1813–1814," 149. Nunez's article includes a reprint of the Stiggins narrative. Stiggins was born in Muskogee in 1788, the son of a Nauchee (Natchez) woman and an Anglo-American man. Although he wrote his account between 1831 and 1842, many of its chronological and biographical details are independently confirmed. Captain Isaacs, e.g., is identified as a rebel leader in contemporary documents. What makes the Stiggins account invaluable is that it provides a good glimpse into the way the Muskogees interpreted their history.
33. Isaacs had visited Tecumseh in the northwest. According to Woodward, Isaacs was a Muskogee from the town of "Coowersortda [Coosaudee]" (*Reminiscences,* 36–37).
34. Hawkins, *Letters, Journals and Writings,* 2:612, 615–16; Hassig, "Internal Conflict in the Creek War of 1813–1814," 256; Waselkov and Wood, "The Creek War of 1813–1814," 7.
35. Hawkins, *Letters, Journals and Writings,* 2:631–32, 632–34; Owsley, *Struggle for the Gulf Borderlands,* 15–16.
36. Nunez, "Creek Nativism and the Creek War of 1813–1814," 297. Woodward (*Reminiscences,* 97) confused Cussetaw Haujo (High-Headed Jim) with another Redstick named Jim Boy, a Tallassee war chief. Jim Boy, "it was said, had some *negro* blood" ("From the Notebook of Michael Johnstone Kenan").
37. On Paddy Walch's linguistic abilities, see Nunez, "Creek Nativism and the Creek War of 1813–1814," 299. On other prophets, see ibid., 8, 9, 12, 145, 151, 299; Woodward, *Reminiscences,* 97; Halbert and Ball, *The Creek War of 1813 and 1814,* 89, 91, 92; Wright, *Creeks and Seminoles,* 168.
38. Rebel war chiefs included Peter McQueen (from Tallassee on the Lower Tallapoosa River), Tuskegee Hopie Tustanugga (Far-Off Warrior), Red Eagle (William Weatherford), and Menawa, leader at the Battle of Tohepeka. Peter McQueen, a war chief of the Tallassees, was the son of a Scottish trader and a Muskogee woman. In 1799, Hawkins wrote that McQueen had "a valuable property in negroes and stock"(*Letters, Journals and Writings,* 1:290). William Weatherford (b. 1781) was the son of a Scottish trader and a métis mother named Sehoy. Weatherford was the nephew of Alexander McGillivray. For Weatherford's biography, see Griffith, *McIntosh and Weatherford,* 1–172.
39. Theron Nunez, "Creek Nativism, and the Creek War of 1813–1814," 152. See also Hudson, *The Southeastern Indians,* 175. Though most of the facts concerning Isaacs's life are confirmed in multiple sources, the

Stiggins narrative is the only primary source that asserts that Captain Isaacs was a shaman, that he had a vision, and that he consorted with the serpent. Thus, it is possible that we are dealing with a much more complicated process than the fairly straightforward one I have suggested. The actual chronological sequence might have run something like this: (1) Isaacs was no shaman; (2) the prophets determined that he was a traitor; (3) they identified him as a malicious conjuror; (4) retrospectively, the prophets and/or the people determined that Isaacs must have consorted with aquatic spirits and been a shaman; and (5) Stiggins, writing in 1831–44, passed on the people's conclusions as if they were the original "true" facts. In short, Isaacs, as we know him in the Stiggins manuscript, may bear little relation to the "real" man of 1813; the folk had already completed "the metamorphosis of a historical figure into a mythical hero" (Mircea Eliade, *The Myth of the Eternal Return, or Cosmos and History,* trans. Willard R. Trask [Princeton, N.J.: Princeton University Press, 1974], 42; see also 37–48). If this is the case, it in no way reduces, but actually dramatizes, how the Muskogees insisted on interpreting their history as the result of interactions with spirits. Interestingly enough, during the same period (1835–56), white Americans were busy mythicizing the biography of Davy Crockett, transforming him from a frontier settler and soldier into a violent superhero mastering the spirit of the wilderness (Catherine Albanese, "King Crockett: Nature and Civility on the American Frontier," *Proceedings of the American Antiquarian Society* 88 [1979]: 225–50).

40. Hawkins, *Letters, Journals and Writings,* 2:665; Nunez, "Creek Nativism and the Creek War of 1813–1814," 151; Swan, "Position and State of Manners," 269.
41. Hvidt, ed., *Von Reck's Voyage,* 43.
42. Owsley, *Struggle for the Gulf Borderlands,* 17.
43. "Report of Alexander Cornells," 1:845–46; Hawkins, *Letters, Journals and Writings,* 2:641; Owsley, *Struggle for the Gulf Borderlands,* 17; Hassig, "Internal Conflict in the Creek War," 266; "The Deposition of Samuel Manac, of lawful age, a Warrior of the Creek Nation," 2 August 1813, quoted in Halbert and Ball, *The Creek War of 1813 and 1814,* 93.
44. Hawkins, *Letters, Journals and Writings,* 2:651–52.
45. Affidavit of James Moore, Jones County, Ga., 13 July 1813, Telamon Cuyler Collection, Hargrett Rare Book and Manuscript Library, University of Georgia Library, Athens. "Report of Alexander Cornells," 1:845. Hawkins, *Letters, Journals and Writings,* 2:649.
46. Hawkins, *Letters, Journals and Writings,* 2:644, 651–52; Nunez, "Creek Nativism and the Creek War of 1813–1814," 155.
47. Hawkins, *Letters, Journals and Writings,* 2:642.

48. Writing in June and July 1813, Hawkins termed the movement "a scene of embarrassment" and a "sudden explosion of fanaticism" (ibid., 642, 644).

49. Affidavit of James Moore, 13 July 1814, and Major General Adams to David B. Mitchell, Jasper County, Ga., 14 July 1813, Telamon Cuyler Collection.

50. Hawkins, *Letters, Journals and Writings,* 2:647, 642, 649.

51. Ibid., 648.

52. "Report of Alexander Cornells," 1:846. In writing his report, Cornells, the interpreter, paraphrased the prophetic talks that he heard circulating among the people.

53. Hawkins, *Letters, Journals and Writings,* 2:648.

6. Muskogee Millenarian Initiation

1. Hoboheilthlee Micco to the president of the United States, 15 May 1811, Letters Received by the Office of the Secretary of War on Indian Affairs, 1800–1823, U.S. National Archives, microcopy M271, roll 1, frame 554.

2. Hawkins, *Letters, Journals and Writings,* 1:296, 2:643; Angie Debo, *A History of the Indians of the United States* (Norman: University of Oklahoma Press, 1970), 81.

3. *ASP: IA,* 1:839–55; Hawkins, *Letters, Journals and Writings,* 1:285–307; 2:612, 636, 652; Wright, *Creeks and Seminoles,* 172; Waselkov and Wood, "The Creek War of 1813–1814," 12–14; Hassig, "Internal Conflict in the Creek War of 1813–1814," 261–62; Henri, *The Southern Indians and Benjamin Hawkins,* 301–2.

4. Woodward, *Reminiscences,* 37, 95; see also, 94, 118. Thomas Woodward received his information from Sam Moniac, a métis who knew many of the Muskogees' leaders and was related to one of the rebel leaders (William Weatherford). Woodward states that Tustunnuggee Thlucco's son, Tuskenea, had visited the Shawnees before Tecumseh's southern tour. See also Hassig, "Internal Conflict in the Creek War of 1813–1814," 268.

5. Hawkins, *Letters, Journals and Writings,* 1:301, 2:652–53, 656, 669, 681.

6. Ibid., 1:313, 2:650, 655, 664, 666, 672.

7. Ibid., 2:612, 636, 646, 648, 651, 654, 656–57; Griffith, *McIntosh and Weatherford,* 79, 83, 86–87.

8. "To the Fat King and other head men of the Lower Creeks," 7 August 1787, Papers of the Continental Congress, U.S. National Archives M247, roll 87, frames 361–62.

9. Hawkins, *Letters, Journals and Writings,* 2:646.

10. Lyda Averill Taylor, "Alabama Field Notes," National Anthropological Archives, Smithsonian Institution, MS, 1, 4.

11. Hans Peter Duerr advances this philosophical understanding of initiation in his *Dreamtime: Concerning the Boundary between the Wilderness and Civilization,* trans. Felicitas Goodman (Oxford: Basil Blackwell, 1985), 61–92.

12. Hawkins, *Letters, Journals and Writings,* 1:324.

13. Kenelm Burridge writes eloquently on the complex moral awareness brought about by transition rites (see *New Heaven, New Earth,* 166).

14. See Anthony F. C. Wallace, "Revitalization Movements," *American Anthropologist* 58 (1956): 264–81.

15. Hawkins, *Letters, Journals and Writings,* 2:666.

16. Ibid., 666, 669; Nunez, "Creek Nativism and the Creek War of 1813–1814," 145; Waselkov and Wood, "The Creek War of 1813–1814," 5–6; Hassig, "Internal Conflict in the Creek War of 1813–1814," 257, 259; Return J. Meigs, 19 March 1812, quoted in McLoughlin, *The Cherokee Ghost Dance,* 146.

17. Hawkins (17 August 1813), *Letters, Writings and Journals,* 2:652, 656.

18. Religious acts of renunciation have played a political role in other colonial contexts, e.g., the Gandhian Non-Co-operation Movement in Bengal. See Sumit Sarkar, "The Conditions and Nature of Subaltern Militancy: Bengal from Swadeshi to Non-Co-operation, c. 1905–1922," in Guha, ed., *Subaltern Studies,* esp. 314–16.

19. Bartram, *Travels,* 399; Swan, "Position and State of Manners," 268; Waselkov and Wood, "The Creek War of 1813–1814," 4–5.

20. This is a pattern that occurs in other colonial millenarian movements. Burridge provides a moral interpretation for these acts of destruction. They serve as a kind of "hinge" between two social orders. "Destruction of crops, livestock and other means of gaining a livelihood, through which men and women express and discharge their obligations to each other, represent or symbolize the millenium. No rules are expressed in the lack of means for incurring obligations. No rules and new rules meet in the prophet who initiates the one whilst advocating the other" (*New Heaven, New Earth,* 165–66).

21. Taylor, "Alabama Field Notes," 42–43, and "Folklore and Religion," "Lifecycle," "Birth," and "Menstruation," in "Alabama Ethnographic Material," National Anthropological Archives, Smithsonian Institution, and "Comparative Southeast Ethnographic Material," 70, National Anthropological Archives.

22. Hallowing King to Governor Mathews, 18 September 1794, quoted in Doster, *Creek Indians,* 1:174.

23. Nunez, "Creek Nativism and the Creek War of 1813–1814," 168. See Waselkov and Wood, "The Creek War of 1813–1814," 8–10. Many

Muskogees displaced by war gathered in the temporary camps of Hoithlewaulee, a settlement near the mouth of Line Creek on the Tallapoosa River.

24. Bartram, *Travels*, 396.
25. These included the horse dance, chicken dance, buffalo dance, duck dance, small frog dance, screech owl dance, horned owl dance, beaver dance, quail dance, crane dance, bean dance, and buzzard dance (Swanton, "Creek Ethnographic and Vocabulary Notes," 37).
26. Loretta Czernis, "Elder: Artaud after Telsat," *Canadian Journal of Political and Social Theory* 10 (1986): 271. Dance played a key role in millenarian movements not only in North America but also in South America. See Lawrence E. Sullivan, *Icanchu's Drum: An Orientation to Meaning in South American Religions* (New York: Macmillan, 1988), 187.
27. Vernon Kinietz and Erminie W. Voegelin, eds., *Shawnee Traditions: C. C. Trowbridge's Account* (Ann Arbor: University of Michigan Press, 1939), 18.
28. Ebenezer Denny, *Military Journal of Major Ebenezer Denny* (Philadelphia: J. B. Lippincott, 1859), 275–76.
29. J. F. H. Claiborne, *Life and Times of General Sam Dale, the Mississippi Partisan* (New York: Harper & Bros., 1860), 61–62.
30. "The Deposition of Samuel Manac," 2 August 1813, quoted in Halbert and Ball, *The Creek War of 1813 and 1814*, 91.
31. On the originary power of dance, see Burridge, *New Heaven, New Earth*, 82–83, 112.
32. Edmnd Shackelford to Miss Ann or Francis Shackelford, 3 December 1813, Typescript, National Anthropological Archives, Smithsonian Institution.
33. The road was completed in December 1811 and was soon "'filled from one end to the other' with parties of white families bound for the river and the western settlements" (Halbert and Ball, *The Creek War of 1813 and 1814*, 36). By May 1812, more than thirty-five hundred settlers and 233 vehicles had traversed it (Yamaguchi, "Macon County, Alabama," 198).

7. The Invasion of Muskogee

1. "Deposition of Samuel Manac," 2 August 1813, quoted in Halbert and Ball, *The Creek War of 1813 and 1814*, 92; Owsley, *Struggle for the Gulf Borderlands*, 26. Hawkins heard thirdhand that McQueen's party "had received ten horse loads of ammunition from the Spaniards" (*Letters, Journals and Writings*, 2:653; see also 648).

2. Halbert and Ball, *The Creek War of 1813 and 1814,* 134; Owsley, *Struggle for the Gulf Borderlands,* 30–32; Nunez, "Creek Nativism and the Creek War of 1813–1814," 156–58.
3. Woodward, *Reminiscences,* 24, 98; Nunez, "Creek Nativism and the Creek War of 1813–1814," 157.
4. Woodward, *Reminiscences,* 97; Nunez, "Creek Nativism, and the Creek War of 1813–1814," 158.
5. Hawkins, *Letters, Journals and Writings,* 2:643. See also "Deposition of Samuel Manac," quoted in Halbert and Ball, *The Creek War of 1813 and 1814,* 91–92. A traveler on the Federal Road, Arthur Lott, had been killed 23 May 1812, but the "sole motive was to plunder the wagon" (Mauelshagen and Davis, trans., *Partners in the Lord's Work,* 73).
6. Mauelshagen and Davis, trans., *Partners in the Lord's Work,* 76; Hawkins, *Letters, Journals and Writings,* 2:656.
7. "Report of Alexander Cornells," 22 June 1813, *ASP: IA,* 1:845–46. Although some individuals claimed that the Redsticks intended to attack Anglo-Americans, these reports were not completely reliable. For example, an affluent métis named Samuel Manac swore that the Redsticks intended "to make a general attack on the American Settlements" ("Deposition of Samuel Manac," 2 August 1813, in Halbert and Ball, *The Creek War of 1813 and 1814,* 92). Manac's claim must be taken with a grain of salt. He had great incentive to persuade Anglo-Americans to intercede and harm the Redsticks. The rebels had destroyed a large quantity of his cattle and burned houses on his river plantation (ibid., 93, 89).
8. Hawkins, *Letters, Journals and Writings,* 2:655.
9. Affidavit of James Moore, 13 July 1814, Jones County, Ga., and Major General Adams to David B. Mitchell, Jasper County, Ga., 14 July 1813, Telamon Cuyler Collection, University of Georgia Library, Athens.
10. Halbert and Ball, *The Creek War of 1813 and 1814,* 140, 141–42.
11. Hawkins, *Letters, Journals and Writings,* 2:636; see also 637, 657. The United States gained control over Mobile in April 1813 in an attack on the Spanish territory (Owsley, *Struggle for the Gulf Borderlands,* 23).
12. Quoted in Michael Paul Rogin, *Fathers and Children: Andrew Jackson and the Subjugation of the American Indian* (New York: Knopf, 1975), 147.
13. Ibid., 147. Jackson had long sought vengeance and in 1808 had unsuccessfully argued for an Indian war; see ibid., 131, 132, 139.
14. Ibid., 147. For a summary of Blount's schemes to obtain Muskogee lands, see Henri, *The Southern Indians and Benjamin Hawkins,* 190–207.
15. Hawkins, *Letters, Journals and Writings,* 2:615, 617, 618; Wright, *Creeks and Seminoles,* 163–66; Doster, *Creek Indians,* 1:62–63. After

the conflict erupted between the United States and the Redsticks, the Redsticks and the Seminoles unsuccessfully attempted to coordinate their actions. In October 1813, they intended to converge their forces on Coweta. See Hawkins, *Letters, Journals and Writings,* 2:671, 672.

16. Hawkins, *Letters, Journals and Writings,* 2:668.

17. Pickett, *History of Alabama,* 419. See also Doster, *Creek Indians,* 1:90–91; Swan, "Position and State of Manners," 252. For even earlier examples of tension, see Taitt, "Journal," 536–37, 546.

18. Halbert and Ball, *The Creek War of 1813 and 1814,* 31–32, 109–10.

19. Ibid., 107. In 1810, the residents of the Bigbe settlement had bitterly complained that the Muskogees were not paying the duty. They thought it unfair that "the Savages pass on *our waters* every day to Mobille, reaping every advantage therefrom, trading with a foreign Nation, and paying the U.S. no duties" (Richard Sparks to the secretary of war, 12 July 1810, in *Territory of Mississippi, 1798–1817,* ed. Clarence Edwin Carter, vol. 5 of *The Territorial Papers of the United States* [Washington, D.C.: U.S. Government Printing Office, 1937], 80); Hawkins, *Letters, Journals and Writings,* 2:588. Stiggins cited this conflict as a cause of the Redstick attack on Fort Mims. Nunez, "Creek Nativism and the Creek War of 1813–14," 159.

20. Judge Toulmin to John Graham, 10 March 1812, in Carter, ed., *Territory of Mississippi,* 283. Toulmin himself suspected that "the dangers are greatly magnified . . . false." He deemed "it very probable that a troublesome chief called Capn Isaacs may be brewing mischief,—and if supported by the Creek nation would endeavour to exterminate this settlement" (ibid.). When William Lott was killed in the Creek Nation in May 1812, the settlers in the Forks grew even more anxious. See Governor Holmes to the secretary of war, 29 June 1812, in ibid., 297.

21. Nunez, "Creek Nativism and the Creek War of 1813–1814," 159. Hawkins, *Letters, Journals and Writings,* 2:668.

22. Halbert and Ball (*The Creek War of 1813 and 1814,* 105–17, 149) describe twenty forts in the region, many small and makeshift, and provide a sketch of Fort Mims.

23. The prophetic shaman Paddy Walch selected four men to "make invulnerable and proof against a white mans bullet." While other warriors took control of the fort's portholes, the four were "to enter the fort and fight inside as long as they thought fit, their safe retreat out of the Fort again, was to be an omen that they were to take the place." Three of the four died (Nunez, "Creek Nativism and the Creek War of 1813–1814," 164).

24. Ibid., 163.

25. "Extract of a Communication from the Chiefs of Coweta to Benjamin Hawkins," in Hawkins, *Letters, Journals and Writings,* 2:664.

26. Hawkins, *Letters, Journals and Writings*, 2:665. The source of this information was an African American survivor whose testimony Hawkins considered "substantially true."

27. Ibid., 1:165; Owsley, *Struggle for the Gulf Borderlands*, 38–39. Owsley argues that there may have been more than a hundred slaves in the fort. In a conversation with the author (16 October 1985, Auburn, Ala.), Owsley indicated that he was convinced that many of the "whites" were actually métis.

28. Nunez, "Creek Nativism and the Creek War of 1813–1814," 167. According to Hawkins's sources, the Redsticks lost forty or fifty men (*Letters, Journals and Writings*, 2:664).

29. Hawkins, *Letters, Journals and Writings*, 2:672, 1:167.

30. Owsley, *Struggle for the Gulf Borderlands*, 39–40.

31. Rogin, *Fathers and Children*, 148; James Caller to Governor David Holmes, 11 June 1812, and Governor William Blount to General Thomas Flournoy, 15 October 1813, both quoted in Doster, *Creek Indians*, 2:67, 84.

32. Halbert and Ball, *The Creek War of 1813 and 1814*, 271–73; Henri, *The Southern Indians and Benjamin Hawkins*, 290–91; Virginia Pounds Brown and Helen Morgan Akens, *Alabama Heritage* (Huntsville, Ala.: Strode, 1967), 50; David Crockett, *A Narrative of the Life of David Crockett of Tennessee* (1834; reprint, Knoxville: University of Tennessee Press, 1987), 83–100. For a detailed account of the battles, see Griffith, *McIntosh and Weatherford*, 79–155.

33. Owsley, *Struggle for the Gulf Borderlands*, 47; Nunez, "Creek Nativism and the Creek War of 1813–1814," 168.

34. Nunez, "Creek Nativism and the Creek War of 1813–1814," 151.

35. Ibid., 168–70.

36. Ibid., 170.

37. Owsley, *Struggle for the Gulf Borderlands*, 54–59, 79.

38. James Moore and James Taylor to Major General David Adams, Ocmulgee, Jasper County, Ga., 20 May 1814, Telamon Cuyler Collection, Hargrett Rare Book and Manuscript Library, University of Georgia Library, Athens.

39. Owsley, *Struggle for the Gulf Borderlands*, 79–82. An uncertain number, perhaps as many as two hundred, escaped after nightfall.

40. James Moore and James Taylor to Major General David Adams, 20 May 1814; Sturtevant, "Creek into Seminole," 106. The First Seminole War took place in 1817–18, and the Second Seminole War, a much more serious conflict, lasted from 1835 to 1842.

41. Hawkins, *Letters, Journals and Writings*, 2:688, 680–81. On 12 August 1815, Benjamin Hawkins wrote Andrew Jackson, providing him with intelligence concerning "the negro force at Apalachicola . . . under the

command of a negro Cyrus from Pensacola who can read and write. . . . They expect 100 blacks, men, women and children from East Florida." (Was this "Cyrus" the same "Siras" who cut down the pickets at Fort Mims?) On 9 February 1816, Hawkins's assistant Timothy Barnard reported that a total of twenty-four "runaway negroes . . . have left Georgia and gone to the negro fort" (ibid., 774; Timothy Barnard, March 1816, quoted in Doster, *Creek Indians*, 2:165).

42. *ASP: IA*, 1:827, Waselkov and Wood, "The Creek War of 1813–1814," 12–14.

43. *Georgia Journal*, 11 May 1814; Hawkins, *Letters, Journals and Writings*, 2:687.

44. Hawkins, *Letters, Journals and Writings*, 2:683; Waselkov and Wood, "The Creek War of 1813–1814," 10.

45. Thomas Pinckney to Benjamin Hawkins, 23 April 1814, in *ASP: IA*, 6:341.

46. Ibid.

47. Hawkins, *Letters, Journals and Writings*, 2:744. Andrew Jackson to the secretary of war, 10 August 1814, quoted in Doster, *Creek Indians*, 2:118. Hawkins, *Letters, Journals and Writings*, 2:744.

48. Doster, *Creek Indians*, 2:107.

49. Owsley, *Struggle for the Gulf Borderlands*, 91.

50. Knowing full well how harsh his demands were going to be, Jackson had anticipated more trouble from the friendly Indians than from the hostiles. He had desired to draw the lines of cession with the militia present. See Doster, *Creek Indians*, 2:109–10.

51. Hawkins, *Letters, Journals and Writings*, 2:745, 1:114, 2:745; Return J. Meigs to Benjamin Hawkins, 17 September 1815, U.S. National Archives microcopy M271, roll 1, frame 1235.

52. "We the natives of the Creek Nation," 29 May 1815, U.S. National Archives microcopy M271, roll 1, frame 838.

53. Usner, "American Indians on the Cotton Frontier," 316–17.

54. John Read to Edward Tiffin, 18 November 1814, in Carter, ed., *Territory of Mississippi*, 405. See also Rogin, *Fathers and Children*, 175.

55. William Crawford to Benjamin Hawkins, 16 October 1815, U.S. National Archives microcopy M15, roll 3, frame 275.

56. Yamaguchi, "Macon County, Alabama," 42–69, 205–10; Mary Elizabeth Young, *Redskins, Ruffleshirts, and Rednecks: Indian Allotments in Alabama and Mississippi, 1830–1860* (Norman: University of Oklahoma Press, 1961), and "Tribal Reorganization in the Southeast, 1800–1842," 59–82; Marvin L. Ellis III, "The Indian Fires Go Out: Removing the Creeks from Georgia and Alabama, 1825–1837" (M.A. thesis, Auburn University, 1982).

57. Pickett, *History of Alabama*, 86–87.

58. When W. O. Tuggle visited the Indian Territory in 1879, he learned that the town of Tookafabotcha still possessed the plates, which were "kept as sacred." He was warned that if "an unholy man should see the sacred vessels he would die ere he reached home, that the vessels were kept buried and only taken out at 'Busk' and in the meantime no one could be permitted to see them" (Current-Garcia, *Shem, Ham and Japheth*, 42, 92).

8. Religious Renewal in the New World

1. Waselkov and Wood, "The Creek War of 1813–1814," 6.
2. This interpretation concords with Kenelm Burridge's evaluation of millenarian activities: "The issue is not a pole, or a flag, a load of canned meat or whether a ritual will make bullets actually turn into water, but a satisfactory measure of the nature of [the human]. In this sense all millenarian activities succeed" (*New Heaven, New Earth,* 112).
3. See Peterson, "The Indian in the Old South," 116–33, esp. 118.
4. Usner, "American Indians on the Cotton Frontier"; Merrell, *Indians' New World.*
5. Among non-Muskogee groups, the Cherokees came closest to joining the movement. However, having lost so much fighting Anglo-Americans in 1760 and again in 1776, the great majority of them refused and ultimately cast their lot with the "friendly" side. The struggle of the Cherokees to survive development and transform their culture as well as their response to the earthquakes of 1811–12 are carefully related in McLoughlin's *The Cherokee Ghost Dance.*
6. Report of Alexander Cornells," 1:845–46; Hawkins, *Letters, Journals and Writings,* 2:651.
7. On this dynamic, see Hassig, "Internal Conflict in the Creek War," 265, 268.
8. Arnold Van Gennep, *The Rites of Passage,* trans. Monika B. Vizedom and Gabrielle L. Caffee (Chicago: University of Chicago Press, 1960), 65–115.
9. Victor W. Turner, "A Few Definitions," in *The Encyclopedia of Religion,* 12:386.
10. Victor W. Turner, *The Ritual Process: Structure and Anti-structure* (Chicago: Aldine, 1969), 94–112.
11. This line of interpretation has been implied by students of other millenarian movements. In his discussion of Native American "new religions," Sam Gill noted that these movements enabled groups from many different backgrounds to recognize a common identity (*Native American Traditions: Sources and Interpretations* [Belmont, Calif.: Wadsworth, 1983], 144–45). Outside the American context, Peter Worsley found

something similar in his important study of Melanesian "cargo" cults. Worsley found that these movements "weld previously hostile and separate groups together in a new unity" (*The Trumpet Shall Sound,* 228). What needs to be emphasized in the case of Native American movements is that this "welding" of previously separate groups came about as a result of a process that very much resembled an initiation ceremony.

12. Gordon Brotherston, *Image of the New World: The American Continent Portrayed in Native Texts* (London: Thames & Hudson, 1979), 48.

13. Milo Milton Quaife, *The John Askin Papers* (Detroit: Detroit Public Library, 1931), 15.

14. David F. Aberle, *The Peyote Religion among the Navaho* (Chicago: Aldine, 1966), 323; see also Weston LaBarre, *The Ghost Dance: Origins of Religion* (New York: Doubleday, 1970).

15. While literacy appeared as a theme in the prophetic discourse of the Redstick prophets, the concern with the Book and its absence is exemplified most clearly in the Delaware prophetic movement with its pictographic chart of heaven and hell. See Charles E. Hunter, "The Delaware Nativist Revival of the Mid-Eighteenth Century," *Ethnohistory* 18 (1971): 39–49.

16. For an example of how these themes were united, see Pontiac's charge (Richard Ford, *Journal of Pontiac's Conspiracy, 1763* [Detroit: Speaker-Hines, 1912], 30–32).

17. Compare Melburn Delano Thurman, "The Delaware Indians: A Study in Ethnohistory" (Ph.D. diss., University of California, Santa Barbara, 1973), 163–65.

18. Edward P. Thompson, "Eighteenth-Century English Society: Class Struggle without Class," *Social History* 3 (1978): 149.

19. The Ottawa prophet urged Native Americans "to cultivate peace between your different tribes, that they may become one great people." Tecumseh, the Shawnee chief, argued that "all the lands in the western country was the common property of all the tribes." His brother, the prophet, affirmed that "no sale was good unless made by all the tribes." (Gregory Evans Dowd, "Paths of Resistance: American Indian Religion and the Quest for Unity, 1745–1815" [Ph.D. diss., Princeton University, 1986], 635, 628.)

20. Ibid., 709–10, 631; Kinietz and Voegelin, eds., *Shawnese Traditions,* 3. See also McLoughlin, *The Cherokee Ghost Dance,* 253–61; Lankford, *Native American Legends,* 140–41.

21. Merrell, "Indians' New World," 538; see also his *Indians' New World.*

22. The weakness of Merrell's argument is that it neither provides an integrative perspective nor advances a theoretical framework capable of articulating the historical forces bringing various Atlantic societies into

Index

Abekas, 7, 9, 144. *See also* Muskogees
Accohannocs, 53
Accomacs, 53
Acee (white-drink) ceremony, 33, 40
Adair, James, 63, 66, 76, 78
Adams, David, 130
Adultery, 27, 40, 78
African American Christianity, 71, 73–76
African Americans, 65, 167, 173, 185; as cultural influence on Muskogees, 5, 42, 43, 71–76, 79, 80, 102, 103, 141; free, 91; Muskogees intermarried with, 73; Redstick rebellion and, 155, 156–57, 160, 161, 163. *See also* African American slaves
African American slaves, 60, 91, 111, 112; of métis people, 79, 80, 94, 103; of the Muskogees, 72–73, 75–76, 105. *See also* Runaway slaves; Slaves
Agriculture, 141, 142; clan system and, 97–98, 106; land policies and, 88, 90, 97–98, 102, 103, 106–7, 112
Alabamas, 9, 51; gift exchange and, 28, 29, 61, 62; male initiation among, 140–41; Redstick rebellion and, 133, 134, 138, 139, 155, 174. *See also* Muskogees

Alcohol, 41; trade practices and, 44, 66–67, 180–81, 184; violence and, 67
Apalachees, 44, 177; trade practices and, 47, 49, 56, 58–59
Apalachicolas, 59
Apocalypticism, 74–75, 76
Architecture, 30–33
Assimilationist plan, 97–102
Atkin, Edmond, 66
Ayekace ceremony, 144

Bacon, Nathaniel, 51
Bailey, Dixon, 153
Bailey, Richard, 102
Barnard, Timothy, 102
Bartram, William, 17, 67, 89, 92, 123, 145
Battle of Burnt Corn, 151–53, 154, 155, 156, 163
Battle of Fort Mims, 156–57, 158
Battle of Tohopeka, 1–3, 10, 161–63
Benton, Thomas Hart, 154
Bigbe, 91, 103–4, 106, 112, 152–53, 155
Black-drink. *See Acee*
Blount, William, 154, 155
Bossu, Jean-Bernard, 123
Bowles, William Augustus, 117